Visual Reference

Microsoft
Internet Explorer 5
At a Glance

Microsoft Press

PUBLISHED by **Microsoft Press**
A Division of Microsoft Corporation
One Microsoft Way
Redmond, Washington 98052-6399

Library of Congress Cataloging-in-Publication Data
Microsoft Internet Explorer 5 At a Glance. Perspection.
      p.   cm.
    Includes index.
    ISBN 1-57231-964-X
    1. Microsoft Internet Explorer.   2. Internet (Computer network).   I. Microsoft Press.
TK5105.883.M53M5355   1999
005.7'3769—dc21   98-31457
                                    CIP

Printed and bound in the United States of America.

3 4 5 6 7 8 9   WCWC   4 3 2 1 0

Distributed in Canada Penguin Canada limited.

A CIP catalog record for this book is available from the British Library.

Microsoft Press books are available through booksellers and distributors worldwide. For further information about international editions, contact your local Microsoft Corporation office. Or contact Microsoft Press International directly at fax (425) 936-7329. Visit our Web site at mspress.microsoft.com.

For Perspection, Inc.
Writer: Douglas W. Allen
Managing Editor: Steven M. Johnson
Series Editor: Jane E. Pedicini
Production Editor: David W. Beskeen
Developmental Editor: Jane E. Pedicini
Technical Editors: Gary Bellig; Nicholas Chu

For Microsoft Press
Acquisitions Editors: Kim Fryer; Susanne Forderer
Project Editor: Jenny Moss Benson

Contents

about

Learn about Internet
Explorer 5.
See page 6

Connect to the Internet.
See page 8

*"How do I add a
favorite?"*

See page 34

1 **About This Book** 1
    No Computerese! 1
    What's New .... 2 **New**
    Useful Tasks 2
    And the Easiest Way to Do Them 2
    A Quick Overview 2
    A Final Word (or Two) 4

2 **Browsing the Web with Internet Explorer** 5
    Getting Started with the Internet Explorer Suite 6
    Connecting to the Internet 8
    Starting Internet Explorer 10
    Viewing the Internet Explorer Window 11
    Browsing the Web .... 12 **New**
    Browsing Your Local Hard Disk .... 14 **New**
    Navigating Basics 16
    Using the Standard Toolbar 18
    Working with Dialog Boxes 20
    Viewing an Internet-Enabled Active Desktop 21
    Using the Active Desktop 22
    Customizing the Active Desktop 24
    Getting Help and Training .... 26 **New**
    Quitting Internet Explorer 28

3 **Finding Information with Internet Explorer** 29
    Understanding Search Sites, Favorites, and Channels 30
    Finding Information on a Web Page 31
    Searching for Information on the Internet .... 32 **New**
    Creating and Organizing Your Favorites List .... 34 **New**
    Viewing and Adding to Your Favorites List 36
    Viewing and Maintaining a History List 38
    Viewing Your Favorites Offline .... 40 **New**
    Adding a Channel 42

Managing Offline Pages .... 44 **New**

Importing Favorites and Bookmarks .... 46 **New**

Obtaining Information from Microsoft .... 47 **New**

Getting Software from Microsoft .... 48 **New**

4 **Handling Information with Internet Explorer 49**

Understanding Common Error Messages 50

Avoiding Viruses 51

Downloading Files from a Web Site 52

Downloading Files from an FTP Site 54

Copying and Saving Graphics 56

Copying and Saving Background Graphics 58

Copying and Pasting Text from a Web Page 60

Getting Media Clips from the Web 61

Creating and Using Style Sheets 62

 Editing and Updating an Office Web Page .... 64 **New**

Printing a Web Page 66

Saving a Web Page .... 68 **New**

5 **Personalizing Internet Explorer 69**

 Customizing the Microsoft Home Page 70

Adding the Address and Links Bars to Your Taskbar 71

Modifying the Links Bar 72

Modifying the Internet Explorer Window 74

Understanding Security on the Internet 76

Creating Security Zones 78

Setting Ratings Using the Content Advisor 80

Storing Personal Information 81

Shopping on the Internet .... 82 **New**

Adding a Language 84

Changing Colors and Font Settings 86

Improving Performance 88

Changing Advanced Options 90

Choosing Programs to Use with Internet Explorer 91

Download files from
a Web site.
See page 52

Learn how to use
security zones.
See page 78

Use the Content Advisor
to set ratings.
See page 80

*"How do I use
ActiveX controls?"*

See page 102

Play sounds and video.
See page 106

Compose and send an
e-mail message.
See page 122

6 **Expanding Functionality with Internet Explorer** **93**

Understanding Add-Ons, Plug-Ins, and Viewers 94

Finding Add-Ons, Plug-Ins, and Viewers on the Web 95

Installing Add-Ons and Viewers 96

Using Add-Ons and Viewers 98

Understanding Java and ActiveX 100

Using ActiveX Controls 102

Running Java Applets 103

Controlling ActiveX and Java Content 104

Playing Sounds and Videos .... 106 **New**

Changing Sound and Video Properties 108

Broadcasting Audio and Video with NetShow 110

Playing a VRML Animation 112

Playing an Internet Game 113

7 **Exchanging E-Mail Using Outlook Express** **115**

Starting Outlook Express... 116

Setting Up Your Account... 117 **New**

Viewing the Outlook Express Start Page .... 118 **New**

Viewing the Outlook Express Window .... 119 **New**

Adding Contacts to the Address Book 120

Composing and Sending E-Mail 122

Reading and Replying to E-Mail 124

Attaching a File to E-Mail 126

Deleting Your E-Mail 127

Managing Your E-Mail... 128

Creating E-Mail Stationery .... 130 **New**

Diverting Incoming E-Mail to Folders .... 132 **New**

Working with Multiple Accounts .... 134 **New**

Finding People on the Web 136

Importing and Exporting E-Mail Settings 137

Printing in Outlook Express 138

Learn how to subscribe
to a newsgroup.
See page 145

8 **Exploring Outlook Express News** **139**

Starting Outlook Express News 140

Viewing the News Window .... 142 **New**

Understanding Newsgroups 143

Configuring the News Reader .... 144 **New**

Subscribing to a Newsgroup 145

Reading the News 146

Finding a Particular Newsgroup or Message .... 148 **New**

Posting Messages 150

Reading Messages Offline .... 152 **New**

Customizing the Outlook Express Window .... 154 **New**

Changing Outlook Express Message Options .... 156 **New**

Getting a Personal Certificate 158

9 **Using NetMeeting to Communicate** **159**

Understanding Internet User Location Service 160

Starting NetMeeting 162

Viewing the NetMeeting Window 164

Making and Receiving a Call 166

Conferencing with People 168

Using SpeedDial Shortcuts 169

Communicating with Audio and Video 170

Exchanging Chat Messages 172

Using the Whiteboard 174

Sharing Applications 176

Sending and Receiving Files 178

Changing NetMeeting Settings 180

Chatting for Fun 182

Changing Your Chat Character 184

10 **Creating a Web Page with FrontPage Express** **185**

Starting FrontPage Express 186

Viewing the FrontPage Express Window 187

Use NetMeeting to
communicate.
See page 159

Viewing the FrontPage Express Toolbars 188
Creating a Web Page Using Templates or Wizards 190
Inserting and Modifying Text 192
Inserting and Modifying an Image 194
Moving and Copying Text and Images 196
Creating and Editing Hyperlinks 198
Creating a Bookmark 200
Setting Up Your Web Page for Printing 201
Printing Your Web Page 202
Saving Your Web Page 204
Opening Your Web Page 206
Viewing Your Web Page in Internet Explorer 208

11 Enhancing Web Pages with FrontPage Express 209
Formatting Text 210
Formatting Paragraphs 212
Changing Paragraph Styles 213
Working with Paragraph Lists 214
Inserting Web Page Elements 216
Inserting a Video Clip 217
Changing a Background 218
Creating a Marquee 220
Creating Tables 222
Modifying Tables 224
Using WebBots 226
Using Interactive WebBots 228
Creating Forms Using Templates or Wizards 230
Working with Forms 232
Inserting ActiveX Controls 234
Inserting Java Applets 236
Inserting Plug-Ins 237

"How do I create my own Web page?"

See page 190

Work with paragraph lists.
See page 214

Learn to use WebBots.
See page 226

Set up a Microsoft
Personal Web Server.
See page 246

Customize Internet Explorer.
See page 256

12 **Working with Internet Explorer Tools** **239**

Getting Support and Tools for Web Page Developers 240

Getting Online Support 242

Using the Internet Explorer Logo in Your Web Page 243

Publishing Your Web Page 244

Setting Up a Personal Web Server .... 246 **New**

Understanding Office Server Extensions .... 248 **New**

Understanding Web Discussions .... 249 **New**

Having a Web Discussion .... 250 **New**

Joining a Web Discussion .... 252 **New**

Installing Internet Explorer from the Web 254

Administering to Internet Explorer Users 256

Uninstalling Internet Explorer 257

Getting Updates to Internet Explorer 258

Index **259**

Acknowledgments

The task of creating any book requires the talents of many hardworking people pulling together to meet almost impossible demands. For their effort and commitment we'd like to thank the outstanding team responsible for making this book possible: the writer, Doug Allen; the developmental editor, Jane Pedicini; the technical editors, Gary Bellig and Nicholas Chu; the production team, Gary Bellig and Tracy Teyler; and the indexer, Michael Brackney.

At Microsoft Press, we'd like to thank Kim Fryer and Susanne Forderer for the opportunity to undertake this project, and Jenny Benson for project editing and overall help when needed most.

Perspection

Perspection

Perspection, Inc., is a software training company committed to providing information to help people communicate, make decisions, and solve problems. Perspection writes and produces software training books, and develops interactive multimedia applications for Windows-based and Macintosh personal computers.

Microsoft Internet Explorer 5 At a Glance incorporates Perspection's training expertise to ensure that you'll receive the maximum return on your time. With this straightforward, easy-to-read reference tool, you'll get the information you need when you need it. You'll focus on the skills that increase productivity while working at your own pace and convenience.

We invite you to visit the Perspection World Wide Web site. You can visit us at:

http://www.perspection.com

You'll find descriptions of all of our books, additional content for our books, information about Perspection, and much more.

About This Book

IN THIS SECTION

No Computerese!

New **What's New**

Useful Tasks...

**...And the Easiest Way
to Do Them**

A Quick Overview

A Final Word (or Two)

Microsoft Internet Explorer 5 At a Glance is for anyone who wants to get the most from the Internet with the least amount of time and effort. We think you'll find this book to be a straightforward, easy-to-read, and easy-to-use reference tool. With the premise that your computer should work for you, not you for it, this book's purpose is to help you get your work done quickly and efficiently so that you take advantage of the Internet while using your computer and its software to the max.

No Computerese!

Let's face it—when there's a task you don't know how to do but you need to get it done in a hurry, or when you're stuck in the middle of a task and can't figure out what to do next, there's nothing more frustrating than having to read page after page of technical background material. You want the information you need—nothing more, nothing less—and you want it now! And the information should be easy to find and understand.

That's what this book is all about. It's written in plain English—no technical jargon and no computerese. There's no single task in the book that takes more than two pages. Just look up the task in the index or the table of contents, turn to the page, and there it is. Each task introduction gives you information that is essential to performing the task, suggesting situations in which you can use the task or providing examples of the benefit you gain from completing the procedure. The task itself is laid out step by step and accompanied by a graphic that adds visual clarity. Just read the introduction, follow the steps, look at the illustrations, and get your work done with a minimum of hassle.

You may want to turn to another task if the one you're working on has a "See Also" in the left column. Because there's a lot of overlap among tasks, we didn't want to keep repeating ourselves; you might find more elementary or more advanced tasks laid out on the pages referenced. We wanted to bring you through the tasks in such a way that they would make sense to you. We've also added some useful tips here and there and offered a "Try This" once in a while to give you a context in which to use the task. But, by and large, we've tried to remain true to the heart and soul of the book, which is that information you need should be available to you *at a glance*.

What's New

If you're looking for what's new in Microsoft Internet Explorer 5, just look for our new icon: **New**. We've inserted it throughout this book. You will find the new icon in the table of contents so you can quickly and easily identify new or improved features in Internet Explorer. You will also find the new icon on the first page of each section. There it will serve as a handy reminder of the latest improvements in Internet Explorer as you move from one task to another.

Useful Tasks...

Whether you use Internet Explorer for work, play, or some of each, we've tried to pack this book with procedures for everything we could think of that you might want to do, from the simplest tasks to some of the more esoteric ones.

...And the Easiest Way to Do Them

Another thing we've tried to do in *Microsoft Internet Explorer 5 At a Glance* is to find and show the easiest way to accomplish a task. Internet Explorer often provides many ways to accomplish a single result, which can be daunting or delightful, depending on the way you like to work. If you like to stick with one favorite and familiar approach, we think the methods described in this book are the way to go. If you prefer to try out alternative techniques, go ahead! The intuitiveness of Internet Explorer invites exploration, and you're likely to discover ways of doing things that you think are easier or that you like better. If you do, that's great! It's exactly what the creators of Internet Explorer had in mind when they provided so many alternatives.

A Quick Overview

You don't have to read this book in any particular order. The book is designed so that you can jump in, get the information you need, and then close the book, keeping it near your computer until the next time you need it. But that doesn't mean we scattered the information about with wild abandon. If you were to read the book from front to back, you'd find a logical progression from the simple tasks to the more complex ones. Here's a quick overview.

First, we assume that Internet Explorer is already installed on your computer. If it's not, the setup wizard makes installation so simple that you won't need our help anyway. So, unlike most computer books, this one doesn't start out with installation instructions and a list of system requirements. You've already got that under control.

Section 2 of the book covers the basics: introducing the Internet Explorer suite of programs; starting Internet Explorer; connecting to the Internet; using the Active Desktop and customizing it to your way of working; browsing the Web or your local hard disk; moving around in Internet Explorer; and getting online Help and training for Internet Explorer.

Section 3 explores how to find and update information: searching for information on the Internet using different service providers; creating a list of favorite Web sites; maintaining a list of sites you have recently visited and for which you may have forgotten the addresses; viewing Web sites offline; adding a channel so you can have the most up-to-date information; and obtaining information directly from Microsoft.

Section 4 describes tasks that allow you to save information: downloading files from the Web; copying and saving text and graphics; using style sheets to change the look of a Web page; editing and updating an Office Web page; printing a Web page you may need; and saving a Web page that you like. This section also provides information about error messages and computer viruses.

Section 5 examines tasks for personalizing Internet Explorer: personalizing your home page; changing the appearance of the Internet Explorer window; creating security zones and setting ratings for your family or your work environment; shopping on the Internet; improving the performance of your computer by turning off options that might slow down your system and by increasing the storage for temporary files; changing the colors, fonts, and languages used by the Web sites you visit; and setting other advanced options.

Section 6 describes tasks for expanding the functionality of Internet Explorer: understanding and installing specialized programs called add-ons, plug-ins, and viewers; finding and using these specialized programs; receiving broadcasts over the Internet of audio and video with Microsoft's built-in NetShow; playing sounds and videos you find on the Internet; using ActiveX and Java programs; and controlling ActiveX and Java content so you don't have to deal with inappropriate or unsafe content.

Sections 7 and 8 examine tasks for working with e-mail and newsgroups using Outlook Express: creating and sending mail messages; adding contacts to the Address Book; adding attachments to mail messages; reading and replying to mail messages; working with multiple e-mail accounts; configuring the newsreader; reading news online; finding and subscribing to a newsgroup so you can communicate with people around the world on topics that interest you; and posting your own messages, opening up even further the lines of international communication on subjects you value.

Section 9 describes tasks for communicating using NetMeeting, another tool that will make you life easier and simpler: making and receiving a call; starting an online conference; using NetMeeting Chat; sending and receiving files even during a conference; chatting for fun; and changing your chat character.

Sections 10 and 11 describe tasks for creating Web pages using FrontPage Express: creating a Web page using wizards; adding and modifying Web pages; inserting and modifying images; creating and editing hyperlinks; creating a bookmark so you aren't limited to using one Web browser; printing Web pages that you create; creating and formatting tables to be used on your Web page; using WebBots, easy-to-use Web-enhancement tools; working with forms; and inserting ActiveX controls, Java applets, and plug-ins, which expand the capabilities of your Web page.

Section 12 describes tasks for working with Internet Explorer tools: getting online support; publishing a Web page; setting up a personal Web server; downloading, installing, and removing the Internet Explorer program; getting updates to Internet Explorer; and administering to Internet Explorer users.

A Final Word (or Two)

We had three goals in writing this book. We want our book to help you:

- ◆ Do all the things you want to do with Internet Explorer 5.

- ◆ Discover how to do things you didn't know you wanted to do with Internet Explorer 5.

- ◆ Enjoy doing your work with Internet Explorer 5.

Our "thank you" for buying this book is the achievement of those goals. We hope you'll have as much fun using *Microsoft Internet Explorer 5 At a Glance* as we've had writing it. The best way to learn is by doing, and that's what we hope you'll get from this book.

Jump right in!

Browsing the Web with Internet Explorer

IN THIS SECTION

Getting Started with the Internet Explorer Suite

Connecting to the Internet

Starting Internet Explorer

Viewing the Internet Explorer Window

New Browsing the Web and Your Local Hard Disk

Navigating Basics

Using the Standard Toolbar

Working with Dialog Boxes

Viewing an Internet-Enabled Active Desktop

Using the Active Desktop

Customizing the Active Desktop

New Getting Help and Training

Quitting Internet Explorer

Microsoft Internet Explorer 5 is more than a traditional Web browser program. It is a flexible tool you can use to navigate your computer, network, or company intranet, as well the Internet. By integrating Internet Explorer with the Office 2000 suite of programs, Microsoft has opened new windows to the Internet from which you can:

◆ Easily set up your connection to the Internet

◆ Jump directly to your favorite Web sites from your desktop

◆ View Web pages as wallpaper—even have the content updated automatically

◆ Use the same "Explorer" to view Web pages, folders on your hard disk, or your Office documents

Learn One Method to Work Efficiently

With Internet Explorer, you can browse your hard disk with the same ease that you browse the Internet. And most content is only a click away—whether you're opening a Word document or a site on the Web.

Getting Started with the Internet Explorer Suite

The Internet Explorer Suite is a variety of programs that work together to provide you the simplest and most efficient way to create and view content, as well as to communicate with others on the Internet. Each program serves a distinct purpose, but their features all function similarly, so learning the entire suite is easy. The suite includes:

Connection Wizard—A program that enables you to get connected to the Internet. The Connection Wizard walks you through setting up a new or existing Internet account.

Internet Explorer—A browsing program for exploring content on the World Wide Web, a network or intranet, or your computer's hard drives. With Internet Explorer, you can view Web content online or offline, and protect yourself and your computer with features such Microsoft Wallet and the Content Advisor.

Outlook Express—A messaging program for sending or reading e-mail or newsgroup messages. Outlook Express accesses and manages multiple e-mail and newsgroup accounts, provides offline reading and composing capabilities, and offers security options.

Address Book—A program that enables you to keep track of names, street and e-mail addresses, personal and business Web sites, and other related information. Address Book is also used by other programs, such as Outlook Express.

NetMeeting—A program that allows you and your multimedia PC to communicate and collaborate with people around the world through voice (with speakers and a microphone) or video conferencing (with a connected video camera), and through data conferencing using a shared whiteboard and chat features.

NetShow—A program that enables you to receive multimedia shows from the Internet or a local intranet. NetShow content might come from a video or audio program or a slide show with a soundtrack. Like other programs in the Internet Explorer Suite, NetShow allows you to listen to or view this content online or offline.

FrontPage Express—A WYSIWYG HTML editor based on the Web authoring and management tools in Microsoft FrontPage. FrontPage Express walks you through creating new Web pages and editing existing HTML documents. When you use the Web Publishing Wizard, your Web pages are easily transferred to a server on the Internet.

Personal Web Server—A network file and application server that enables you to publish Web pages. You can use a Personal Web Server to publish your Web pages on the Internet or over a local area network (LAN) on an intranet and to transmit or receive files using an FTP (File Transfer Protocol) service.

Windows Media Player—A program that enables you to receive audio, video, and mixed-media files in most popular formats—including streaming media. You can use Media Player to listen to or view live news updates or broadcasts of your favorite sports teams, music videos or concerts, and movies on the Web.

Active Channels—A feature that turns your desktop into a virtual television for Web sites. For those upgrading from Internet Explorer 4 or installing on Windows 98, the channels feature specializes in content developed especially for Internet Explorer that you can display as wallpaper on your desktop, as Web pages, or as a screen saver. When you add an active channel, Internet Explorer downloads new content to you as it's made available from the channel provider.

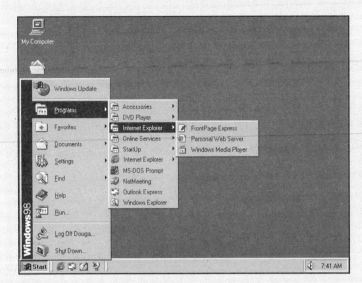

Connecting to the Internet

Sometimes connecting your computer to the Internet can be the most difficult part of getting started. Internet Explorer's Connection Wizard simplifies the process, whether you want to set up a new connection using an existing account, or you want to select an Internet service provider (ISP) and set up a new account. You may need to obtain connection information from your ISP or your system administrator. If you are on a corporate intranet, you may need to use a *proxy server*, which provides a secure barrier between your intranet and the Internet and prevents other people from seeing confidential information on your intranet. You can also configure Internet Explorer with a settings file supplied by your corporate system administrator.

Get Connected Using the Internet Explorer Connection Wizard

1. Double-click the Connect To The Internet icon on the desktop.

   Or click the Start button on the taskbar, point to Programs, point to Accessories, point to Communications, and then click Connection Wizard.

2. Click the option button for the setup you want to use. Click Next to continue.

3. Read the information in each wizard dialog box, and then enter the required information. Click Next to move from one wizard dialog box to another.

4. In the final wizard dialog box, click Finish.

TIP

Connect first. *Before you can configure your computer to use a proxy server or automatically configure Internet Explorer on a corporate system, your computer must be connected to a local area network (LAN).*

TIP

Set up proxy settings for different servers. *You can set up multiple connections on different networks. Internet Explorer allows you to set up multiple connections, each with different proxy servers.*

SEE ALSO

See "Administering to Internet Explorer Users" on page 256 for information on getting the Internet Explorer Administration Kit (IEAK).

Configure to Use a Proxy Server

1 Start Internet Explorer, click the Tools menu, and then click Internet Options.

2 Click the Connections tab.

3 Click LAN Settings.

4 Click to select the Use A Proxy Server check box.

5 Enter the proxy information.

6 Click OK.

7 Click OK.

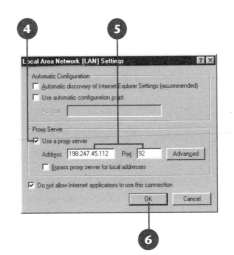

Configure Internet Explorer on a Corporate Network

1 Start Internet Explorer, click the Tools menu, and then click Internet Options.

2 Click the Connections tab.

3 Click LAN Settings.

4 Click to select the Use Automatic Configuration Script check box.

5 Type the address or the file and its location supplied by your administrator.

6 Click OK.

7 Click OK.

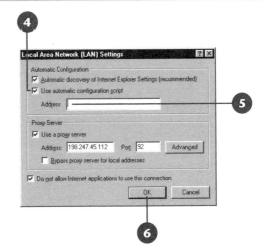

Starting Internet Explorer

Internet Explorer is one of the default icons installed on the desktop and on the Quick Launch toolbar. You can double-click the desktop icon or single-click the Quick Launch icon to start Internet Explorer. If you have removed either or both icons, you can always use the Start menu to start Internet Explorer.

TIP

Password required. *If you have an account with an ISP, you may need to type your user name and password before Internet Explorer will connect to the Internet. When you start Internet Explorer, you will be prompted to connect to your ISP.*

TIP

First time welcome screen. *The first time you start Internet Explorer, a welcome screen appears, asking you to take a tour or go to your home page.*

Start Internet Explorer from the Quick Launch Toolbar

1. Click the Launch Internet Explorer Browser button on the Quick Launch toolbar.

2. If necessary, click Connect to dial your ISP.

   The Internet Explorer window is displayed.

Start Internet Explorer from the Start Menu

1. Click the Start button on the taskbar.

2. Point to Programs.

3. Click Internet Explorer.

4. If necessary, click Connect to dial your ISP.

   The Internet Explorer window is displayed.

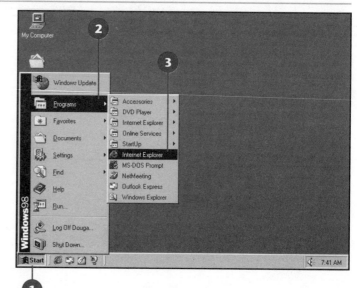

Viewing the Internet Explorer Window

Menu bar
Contains all the commands you need to access and move around Web pages, customize Internet Explorer, and get Help

Title bar
Displays the name of the Web page you are viewing

Standard toolbar
Provides buttons to locate and move around Web pages, as well as work in Internet Explorer

Address bar
Displays the address of the current Web page or document you are viewing or trying to access

Links bar
Contains buttons for quick access of favorite Web sites

Browser pane
Displays the current Web page, document, or folder contents

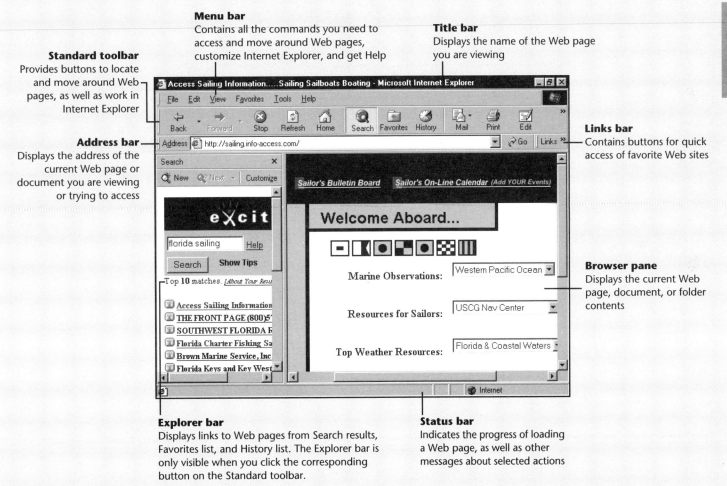

Explorer bar
Displays links to Web pages from Search results, Favorites list, and History list. The Explorer bar is only visible when you click the corresponding button on the Standard toolbar.

Status bar
Indicates the progress of loading a Web page, as well as other messages about selected actions

Browsing the Web

With Internet Explorer, you can browse sites on the Web with ease by entering a Web address or by clicking a link. Each method is better at different times. For example, you might type an address in the Address bar to start your session. Then you might click a link on that Web page to access a new site. With Internet Explorer, you can find Internet addresses faster with *AutoComplete*. When you type an Internet address in the Address bar, Internet Explorer tries to find a recently visited page that matches what you've typed so far. If Internet Explorer finds a match, it automatically fills in the rest of the address. You can also use AutoComplete to fill out forms on the Web, including single-line edits, and user names and passwords.

View a Web Page

Use any of the following methods to display a Web page:

◆ In the Address bar, type the Web page address, and click Go or press Enter.

◆ Click the Address bar drop-down arrow, and select a Web page address you've opened in the current session.

◆ Click the File menu, click Open, type the Web page address, and then click OK.

To open a folder located on a Web server, click to select the Open As Web Folder check box.

◆ Click any link, such as a 3-D image, a picture, or colored, underlined text on a Web page.

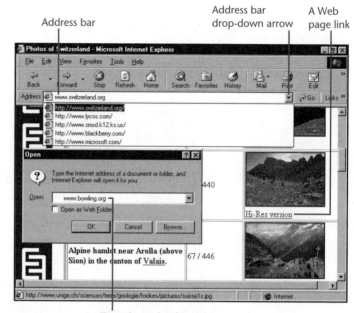

Address bar

Address bar drop-down arrow

A Web page link

Type the Web address here.

AutoCorrect common misspellings in URLs.
Internet Explorer automatically corrects common misspellings in URLs, such as http://, www, and .com.

Open a Web page in a new window. *Click the File menu, point to New, click Window, and then type a Web address in the Address bar of the new Internet Explorer window.*

Web addresses and URLs.
Every Web page has a Uniform Resource Locator (URL), *a Web address in a form your browser program can decipher. Like a postal address, each URL contains specific parts that identify where a Web page is located. For example, the URL for Microsoft's Web page is* **http://www.microsoft.com/**, *where "http://" indicates the address is on the Web and "www.microsoft.com" indicates the computer that stores the Web page. As you browse various pages, the URL might also include folders and filenames.*

Enter an Address Using AutoComplete

1. Begin to type an address that you have recently entered.

   AutoComplete remembers previously entered addresses and tries to complete the address for you. The suggested match is highlighted.

   If you want, continue to type until the address you want appears in the Address list.

2. Click the correct address in the Address list.

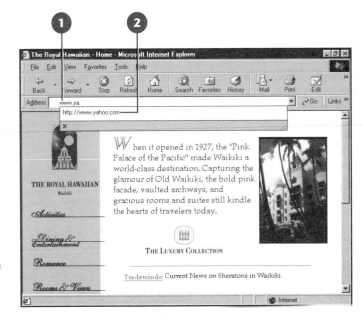

Turn Off AutoComplete Options

1. Click the Tools menu, and then click Internet Options.

2. Click the Content tab.

3. Click AutoComplete.

4. Click to clear the check boxes with the Auto-Complete options you want to turn off.

5. Click OK.

6. Click OK.

Browsing Your Local Hard Disk

Internet Explorer isn't only for viewing Web pages. You can also use it to browse folders on your local hard disk and run programs in the same way that you browse Web pages on the Internet—from the Address bar. You'll see an Address bar and the Links bar when you browse folders because Windows Explorer and Internet Explorer share many of the same functions. Because of this shared functionality, you have the option of changing the way your folders are displayed. You can have your folders and your computer act like the Web or work in the classic Windows mode, or you can choose your own settings.

Browse Folders and Open Files from the Address Bar

1. Type the location of the hard disk you want to open in the Address bar. For example, "C:" or "C:\My Documents\"

2. Click Go on the Address bar or press Enter.

   The menus and toolbar change to the ones used in Windows Explorer.

3. If you want, click the Views button drop-down arrow on the Standard toolbar, and then select the view option you want to use.

4. Double-click any icon to open that drive, folder, or program.

5. Click the Go menu, and then click Home Page to return to Internet Explorer.

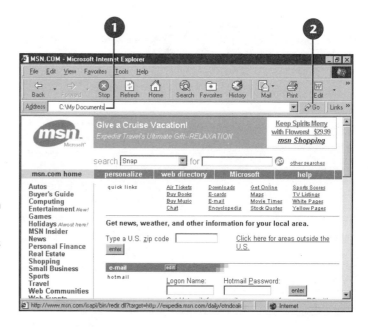

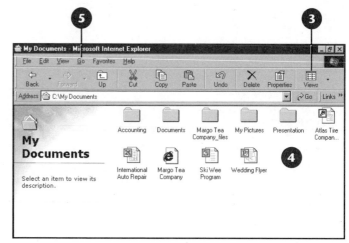

TIP

Mind your slashes. *To open a file on your computer, type "\folder\filename." To open a Web page, type "/Web site." Internet Explorer knows the difference between \ and /.*

TRY THIS

Sort drive or folder lists alphabetically. *When you view your hard disk or folders by the List or Details option, click the Name column header to sort the list alphabetically.*

TRY THIS

Customize a folder. *Open the folder you want to customize, click the View menu, click Customize This Folder, click the Customize option you want, and then follow the Customize This Folder Wizard instructions to complete the task.*

SEE ALSO

See "Using the Active Desktop" on page 22 for information about changing double-clicking options to single-clicking them.

Change the Folder Display

1. Type the drive or folder location in the Address bar, and then press Enter.

2. Click the View menu, and then click Folder Options.

3. Click the General tab.

4. Click one of the Windows Desktop Update option buttons.

   ◆ Web Style

   ◆ Classic Style

   ◆ Custom

5. Click OK.

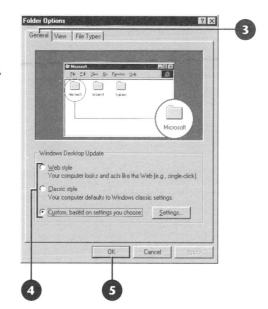

Change the Folder Display Settings

1. Type the drive or folder location in the Address bar, and then press Enter.

2. Click the View menu, and then click Folder Options.

3. Click the View tab.

4. Click any of the Advanced Settings option buttons you want to turn on or turn off.

5. Click OK.

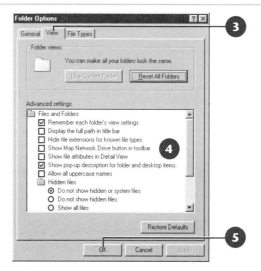

Navigating Basics

As you browse the Web or your local hard disk, you may want to retrace your steps and return to a Web page, document, or hard disk you've recently visited. You can move backward or forward one location at a time, or you can jump directly to any location from the Back list or Forward list, which shows locations you've previously visited in this session.

After you start to load a Web page, you can stop if the page opens too slowly or if you decide not to access it. If a Web page loads incorrectly or you want to update the information it contains, you can reload, or *refresh*, the page.

If you get lost on the Web, you can start over with a single click of the Home button. You can also resize your toolbars so you can see more of the Web address or Links bar.

Move Back or Forward

◆ To move back or forward one Web page or document at a time, click the Back button or Forward button on the Standard toolbar.

◆ To move back or forward to a specific Web page or document, click the Back or Forward drop-down arrow on the Standard toolbar, and then select the Web page or document you want to visit.

Back button
Forward button

Back button drop-down arrow

Forward button drop-down arrow

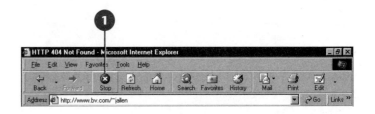

Stop an Unwanted Load

1. Click the Stop button on the Standard toolbar.

TIP

Change your home page.
Click the Tools menu, and then click Internet Options. Click the General tab. In the Address box, type the URL of the Web page you want for your home page.

TIP

Keyboard shortcuts. *Here are the keyboard shortcuts for navigating a Web page:*
Back	*Alt+left arrow*
Front	*Alt+right arrow*
Stop	*Esc*
Refresh	*F5*

TIP

Do I click here or not?
You'll know that you can click something because the mouse pointer changes from an arrow to a hand with a pointed finger whenever you hover over a clickable link.

TIP

Tab from link to link. *While viewing a Web page, you can move from link to link quickly by pressing the Tab key.*

SEE ALSO

See "Modifying the Links Bar" on page 72 for information on how to add your own favorite Web pages to the Links bar.

Refresh a Web Page, Document, or Drive

1. Click the Refresh button on the Standard toolbar.

Go Home and Start Over

1. Click the Home button on the Standard toolbar.

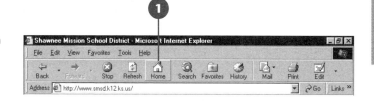

Resize the Links Bar

1. Position the mouse pointer over the handle on the far left of the Links bar.

2. Drag the handle to the left to reveal more of the links.

3. Click the double angle-bracket button at the far right to see the rest of the links.

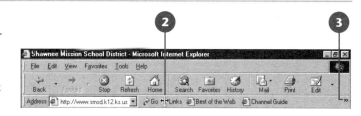

Make Room for All the Toolbars

1. Position the mouse pointer over the lowest toolbar.

2. Drag the toolbar downward to make room for both the Address and Links bars.

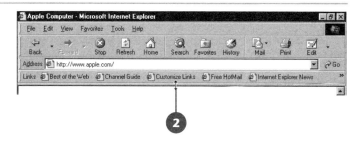

Using the Standard Toolbar

All Office applications have a Standard toolbar, which provides shortcut methods for accessing the most frequently used commands. Internet Explorer's Standard toolbar provides even more. As you open files and documents and move from one Web site to another, Internet Explorer's Standard toolbar recognizes the difference between folder paths and Web addresses, and it displays only the buttons related to the type of file currently open. Web buttons appear on the Standard toolbar when a Web page is displayed, while document buttons appear on the Standard toolbar when a document, hard disk, or folder is displayed.

Navigate with Web Buttons

Clicking a toolbar button will do one of the following things.

◆ Immediately perform an action.

◆ Open a menu containing more options.

◆ Display or hide the Explorer bar.

◆ Change the contents of the Explorer bar.

◆ Open a dialog box.

WEB BUTTONS	
Button	**Action**
Back	Moves you to the previous page. Click the drop-down arrow to select a page from a list of current back pages.
Forward	Moves you to the next page. Click the drop-down arrow to select a page from a list of current forward pages.
Stop	Stops loading the current page.
Refresh	Reloads the current page.
Home	Jumps you to your home page.
Search	Opens the Explorer bar so you can enter a keyword with which to search the Web.
Favorites	Opens the Explorer bar so you have access to your personal collection of favorite pages.
History	Opens the Explorer bar to display a list of previously accessed pages.
Mail	Starts Outlook Express or your default mail client program.
Print	Prints the current page or active frame.
Edit	Starts a Web page editor and opens the current Web page for editing. Click the drop-down arrow to select an edit program.
Discuss	Starts a Web discussion with the current Web page.

TIP

Display or hide toolbars.
Right-click any blank area on a toolbar, and then click the toolbar you want to display or hide, or click Customize to change other toolbar options.

SEE ALSO

See "Modifying the Internet Explorer Window" on page 74 for information on displaying and hiding the Internet Explorer toolbars.

TRY THIS

Watch the Standard toolbar change. *In the Internet Explorer Address bar, type "C:" and then press Enter. Click the My Documents folder, and then click any document. Use the Back and Forward buttons to move between the open programs and files. Watch the toolbar change!*

SEE ALSO

See "Navigating Basics" on page 16 for information about browsing the Web or your local hard disk.

Navigate with Document Buttons

Clicking a toolbar button will do one of the following things.

◆ Immediately perform an action.

◆ Open a menu containing more options.

◆ Open a dialog box.

DOCUMENT BUTTONS	
Button	**Action**
Back	Moves you to a previous folder or document. Click the drop-down arrow to select a folder from the list of current back folders.
Forward	Moves you to the next folder or document. Click the drop-down arrow to select a folder from the list of current forward folders.
Up	Displays the next higher folder or drive.
Cut	Removes the selected material and places it on the Clipboard.
Copy	Places a copy of the selected material on the Clipboard.
Paste	Copies selected material from the Clipboard to the insertion point location.
Delete	Moves selected files or folders to the Recycle Bin.
Properties	Opens a dialog box with file type and creation information.
Views	Switches the view to large or small icons, or a simple or detailed list. Click the drop-down arrow to select from a list of views.

2

Working with Dialog Boxes

A dialog box appears after you select a menu command that is followed by an ellipsis, click its corresponding toolbar button, or press its assigned keyboard shortcut. A *dialog box* is a special window that provides additional options and settings associated with a command. Related options within a dialog box are often grouped together on *tabs*. To make your choices, you may need to type text, select items from drop-down lists, or click option buttons or check boxes.

Select Dialog Box Options

A dialog box can contain one or more of the following components.

◆ Tabs

◆ Text boxes

◆ Drop-down lists

◆ Spin boxes

◆ Sliders

◆ Check boxes

◆ Option buttons

A dialog box usually contains an OK button and a Cancel button. Some dialog boxes also contain an Apply button.

◆ Click OK to apply your selections and close the dialog box.

◆ Click Cancel to close the dialog box without applying your selections.

◆ Click Apply to display the results of your current selections without closing the dialog box, enabling you to modify your choices as needed.

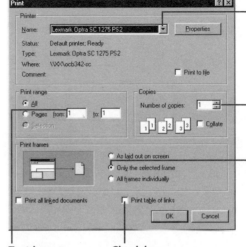

Drop-down list
Click the drop-down arrow and select an option from the list.

Spin box
Click the up or down arrow to increase or decrease the value.

Option button
Click the option you want to select. Only one option can be selected at a time. To deselect an option, you must choose another.

Text box
Click in the box and type the value or text you want.

Check box
Click one or more check boxes to select the options you want. Click a selected check box to remove the x.

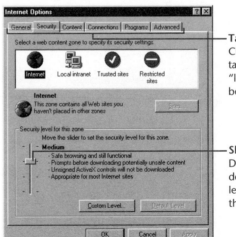

Tabs
Click the appropriate tab to select a different "layer" of the dialog box.

Slider
Drag the slider up or down (and sometimes left or right) to select the appropriate level.

Viewing an Internet-Enabled Active Desktop

If you use the Internet a lot, you'll love how integrate Internet Explorer with Windows 98's Active Desktop. When you turn on, or "enable," the various Internet options, you can quickly jump to your favorite Web sites, enter Web addresses from the taskbar, and even view channel content right from the desktop! Learning how to Internet-enable your Active Desktop will make your computer and Internet experience easy and productive.

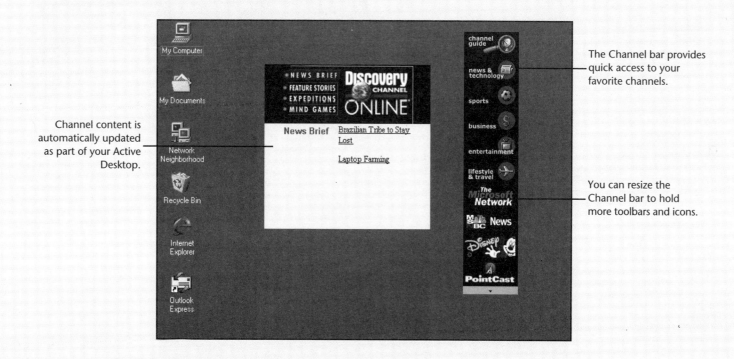

Channel content is automatically updated as part of your Active Desktop.

The Channel bar provides quick access to your favorite channels.

You can resize the Channel bar to hold more toolbars and icons.

Using the Active Desktop

If you are comfortable browsing the Web, then the Active Desktop is for you. The Active Desktop looks and functions like a personalized Web page. In addition to changing your desktop icons from the classic Windows style of double-clicking to the Web style of single-clicking, you can invoke standard Internet Explorer functions right from the Start menu. And it's easy to turn Web items on or off as well as quickly reset the Active Desktop back to the old inactive desktop.

TIP

Show the desktop quickly.
To see the desktop without closing or minimizing windows, click the Show Desktop button on the Quick Launch toolbar.

Show or Hide the Active Desktop

1 Right-click the desktop.

2 Point to Active Desktop.

3 Click View As Web Page.

A check mark next to the menu item indicates the Active Desktop is shown; no check mark indicates the Active Desktop is hidden.

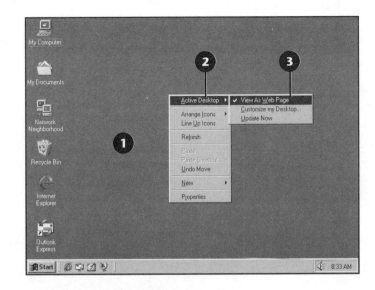

Show or Hide Web Items on the Active Desktop

1 Right-click the desktop, point to Active Desktop, and then click Customize My Desktop.

2 Click the check box for the Web element you want to show or hide. A check mark indicates the option is shown; no check mark indicates the option is hidden.

3 Click OK.

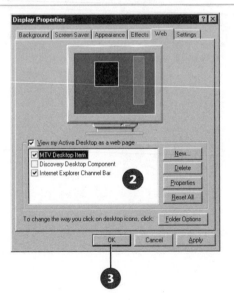

TIP

Move Start menu items. *To change the location of files on your Start menu, drag them to a new location in any folder on the menu.*

TIP

Drag files to the Start menu. *To add files and programs to your Start menu, drag them to the Start button on the taskbar.*

TIP

Set up single-clicking without putting underlines under everything. *Click the Start menu, point to Settings, and click Folder Options. On the General tab, make sure the Custom option button is selected. Click the Settings button. In the Click Items As Follows section, click the Single-Click option button, and then click the Underline Icons Title Only When I Point At Them option button.*

SEE ALSO

See "Customizing the Active Desktop" on page 24 for information about adding Web items to the desktop.

Access a Web Site from the Start Menu

1. Click the Start button on the taskbar.

   ◆ Point to Favorites, and then click a favorite to start Internet Explorer and display your favorite Web site.

   ◆ Point to Find, and then click On The Internet to start Internet Explorer and search for a Web site.

   ◆ Click Run, and then enter a URL to start Internet Explorer and display the Web site.

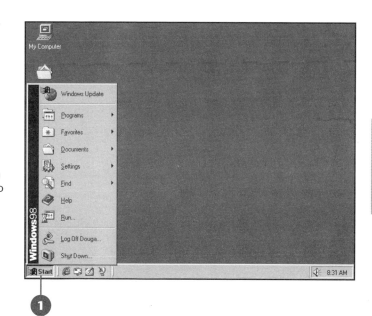

Change Your Desktop to the Single-Click Web Style

1. Click the Start menu on the taskbar, point to Settings, and click Folder Options.

2. On the General tab, click the Web Style option button.

3. Click OK.

4. If asked to confirm the single-click icons option, click OK.

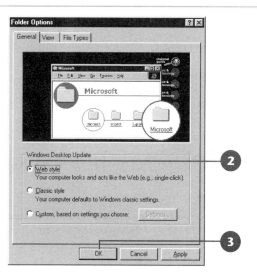

Customizing the Active Desktop

With Internet Explorer, you can bring live Web content to your Active Desktop. You can place pieces of Web pages or HTML-based code directly on your desktop. For example, you can add Web content to continuously display weather information on your desktop. To use Web items, you must be running Internet Explorer with the Active Desktop turned on.

You can check out the cool Web items in Microsoft's Windows Media Showcase. You can also activate a Web screen saver that cycles through a series of Web pages. The Web screen saver is created with a screen saver channel. The screen saver uses the full screen view of Internet Explorer.

Add Web Items to Your Active Desktop

1. Right-click the desktop, point to Active Desktop, and then click Customize My Desktop.

2. Click New.

3. Click the categories you want to search, and enter any keywords you may want to use for your search.

4. Click Search.

5. Choose a channel from the results on the left side of the page.

   The channel's preview page appears on the right side of the page.

6. Click Add To Active Desktop. If necessary, scroll to display the command button.

7. Click Yes when asked if you want to add this item to your Active Desktop.

8. Click OK to make the channel available offline.

9. Click the Show Desktop button on the Quick Launch toolbar to see the Web item you chose.

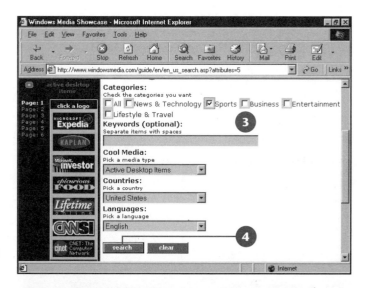

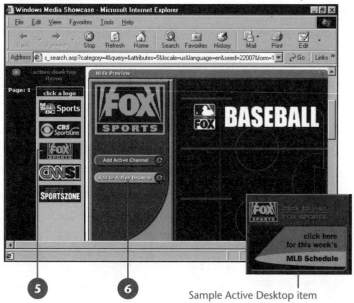

Sample Active Desktop item

TRY THIS

Select a channel screen saver and display time. *Right-click the desktop, and then click Properties on the shortcut menu. Click the Screen Saver tab, click Settings, select the channels you want to use, set the display time, and then click OK.*

SEE ALSO

See "Viewing an Internet-Enabled Active Desktop" on page 21 for information about available Web items for your desktop.

SEE ALSO

See "Saving a Web Page" on page 68 for information about saving a page that you can then use as a background on your desktop.

TRY THIS

Click the links on your Web page background. *If the Web page you chose for a desktop background has links on it, then you can click those links from the background image. Internet Explorer will launch and load the page.*

Create a Channel Screen Saver

1. Right-click the desktop, point to Active Desktop, and then click Customize My Desktop.

2. Click the Screen Saver tab.

3. Click the Screen Saver drop-down arrow, and then select Channel Screen Saver.

4. If you want, click Preview. Press any key to return.

5. Click OK.

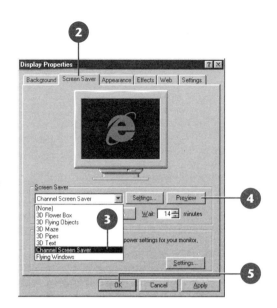

Add a Web Background

1. Right-click the desktop, point to Active Desktop, and then click Customize My Desktop.

2. Click the Background tab.

3. Select the Internet document (HTML file) you want to use as a background or click Browse to help you find the file.

4. Click Apply. The background is applied to the desktop.

5. Click OK.

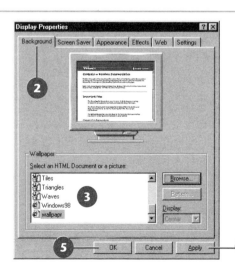

Getting Help and Training

If you want to know what a particular feature is or how it works, that information is easily accessible from the Help screens. You can browse by category from the Contents tab or search by keyword from the Index. The Help topics are conveniently hyperlinked so that one click displays a related Help screen. More extensive help is available on the Microsoft Web site which you can quickly access from the Help menu. If you are new to Internet Explorer, take the Internet Explorer tour, which walks you through the basics of online browsing.

TIP

Print your Help topic.
Click the Options button, and then click Print to print a Help screen.

SEE ALSO

See "Obtaining Information from Microsoft" on page 47 for more information on getting help and training.

Get Help Using Help Contents

1. Click the Help menu, and then click Contents And Index. If necessary, click the Show button on the toolbar.

2. Click the Contents tab.

3. Click a category.

4. Click any topic to open it.

5. Read the Help information provided.

6. If you want, click a related topic listed at the end of the Help information.

7. When you're done, click the Close button.

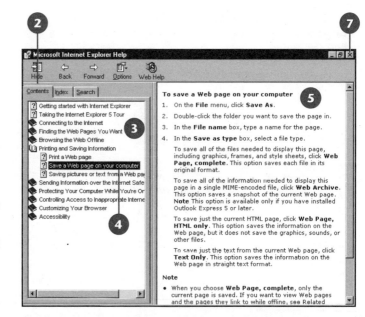

Search the Help Index

1. Click the Help menu, and then click Contents And Index. If necessary, click the Show button on the toolbar.

2. Click the Index tab.

3. Type the topic about which you want more information. Notice that the index list scrolls as you type each character.

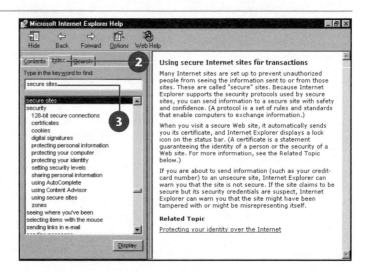

TIP

Get Help in a dialog box.
Click the Help button in the upper-right corner of a dialog box (if available). The mouse pointer changes to the Help pointer. Then click the element for which you want help. A brief description appears and remains displayed until you click the dialog box again.

TRY THIS

Search the entire Help file.
When the Help window is open, click the Search tab, and then type a keyword. Click List Topics to see the Help topics that contain your keyword.

TIP

Help for Netscape users.
Click the Help menu, and then click For Netscape Users.

TIP

Get a quick tip. *Click the Help menu, and then click Tip Of The Day. A pane with a tip appears at the bottom of the screen. Click Next Tip to see another tip. When you're done, click the tip pane Close button.*

④ When the topic you want appears in the list, double-click the topic, or click the topic and then click Display.

Some topics display a dialog box with additional related topics.

⑤ Read the Help information provided.

⑥ If you want, click a related topic listed at the end of the Help information.

⑦ When you're done, click the Close button.

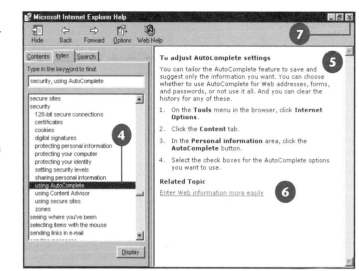

Take the Internet Explorer Tour

① Click the Help menu, and then click Tour.

② Click a link and read more about that topic.

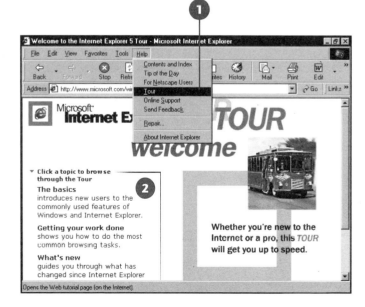

Quitting Internet Explorer

When you have finished browsing the Web, reading news, searching for information, and so forth, you need to quit Internet Explorer. When you quit Internet Explorer, it disconnects you from the Internet (unless you connected before starting Internet Explorer).

Quit Internet Explorer Using the File Menu

1. Click the File menu.

2. Click Close.

3. If necessary, disconnect from the Internet.

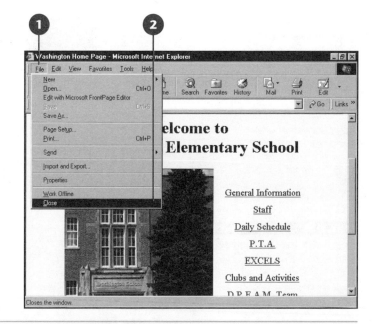

Quit Internet Explorer Using the Close Button

1. Click the Close button in the upper-right corner of the Internet Explorer window.

2. If necessary, disconnect from the Internet.

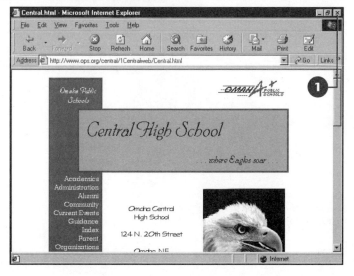

Finding Information with Internet Explorer

IN THIS SECTION

Understanding Search Sites, Favorites, and Channels

Finding Information on a Web Page

New **Searching for Information on the Internet**

New **Creating and Organizing Your Favorites List**

Viewing and Adding to Your Favorites List

Viewing and Maintaining a History List

New **Viewing Your Favorites Offline**

Adding a Channel

New **Managing Offline Pages**

New **Importing Favorites and Bookmarks**

New **Obtaining Information and Software from Microsoft**

Microsoft Internet Explorer 5 allows you to:

◆ Search a list of search engines and directory listings for Web sites that match your criteria

◆ Quickly initiate a search request without going to a search provider

◆ Use the Favorites folder to save and organize links to your favorite Web sites

◆ Download your favorite Web sites so you can browse these sites at high speed without even being connected to the Internet

Finding Information on the Web

Internet Explorer offers some exciting features to find and organize information and to automatically receive information from Web sites on the Internet. Internet Explorer's two search features offer you direct links to the major search engines and Internet indexes. With the Favorites feature, you can return to the Web sites you enjoy or use the most. Through the Channels feature, you can now have information delivered directly to you in the form of a Web page or directly to your desktop from channels you have added.

Understanding Search Sites, Favorites, and Channels

Search engines, such as AltaVista, AOL NetFind, and Lycos, gather their information by using "robots," or special programs, to collect words from Web pages. These words are then stored and indexed in the search engine's databases. The goal of any good search engine is to seek out and find as many Web pages on the Internet as possible and to create a quick reference to their locations. When you specify a word or phrase for a search engine to locate on the Internet, the search engine locates the word or phrase along with the corresponding Web address on which the word appears in the database. The more general your request is, the longer the list of results; the more specific your request, the fewer the number of Web sites in the results.

Internet directories, such as Yahoo, differ from search engines in that a person actually reviews every link placed in the directories' databases. And that person decides under which category, be it sports, news, weather, and so forth, a site should be cataloged. This level of editorial review guarantees a much smaller list of Web sites will be stored (compared to a search engine), but the list will have a much higher guarantee of quality. Only those sites that have been tested are listed in the database—not by the words that appear on the Web page, but by the category under which it falls.

When you search a directory of Web sites, you'll get far fewer choices than if you used a search engine, but those choices will be more in tune with your search request, particularly if you are looking for sites that fall under broad categories. Because Internet directories don't index most sites on the Web, they are not the place to go to locate hard-to-find information such as the name of a particular person. Search engines are a better choice for hard-to-find information because they have indexed words and phrases from millions of Web pages.

Whether searching the Web or just browsing it, you are likely to find a number of sites that you want to return to. You can easily add these pages to your Favorites folder. *Favorites* are links to your favorite Web sites, which you can immediately access at any time from the Favorites menu.

In addition to visiting Web pages for information, you can have the facts come to you through the use of channels. A *channel* is a Web site that delivers information to your computer—sometimes without the need of a browser. When you add a channel to your list of favorites, the content of that site—sports scores, financial information, movie reviews, and so on—can come directly to your computer. Internet Explorer follows the channel's schedule to automatically update the information. In addition to the channel's Web page, the data can be viewed as part of your desktop or in the form of a screen saver. Adding channels isn't the only way to automatically get up-to-date information. You can also have Internet Explorer periodically check some (or all) of your favorites to see if the Web pages have new information. You can then view the Web page offline and even be notified via e-mail when the Web page has changed.

Finding Information on a Web Page

When you need to find information fast, you may not want to scroll through an entire Web page looking for it. Internet Explorer lets you quickly search the page you are currently viewing for the information you want by simply specifying a word or phrase. Search words are automatically highlighted on the page that returns results.

TIP

Use a keystroke shortcut to find information on a Web page. *Press Ctrl+F to display the Find dialog box.*

TIP

Copy and paste into the Find dialog box. *You can copy and paste text in the Find dialog box from other sources. Copy the text and then press Ctrl+V to paste it in the Find dialog box.*

Search a Web Page

1. Open the Web page that contains the text you are looking for.

2. Click the Edit menu, and then click Find (On This Page).

3. Type the word or phrase you want to find.

4. Click to select the Match Whole Word Only check box to avoid selecting words that contain the word you are looking for.

5. If you want to match the word based on uppercase or lowercase spelling, click to select the Match Case check box.

6. Click the Up or Down option button to specify the direction in which to search the page.

7. Click Find Next to move through the page, stopping to highlight the word as it's found.

8. Click OK when the search is complete.

9. Click Cancel to exit the search.

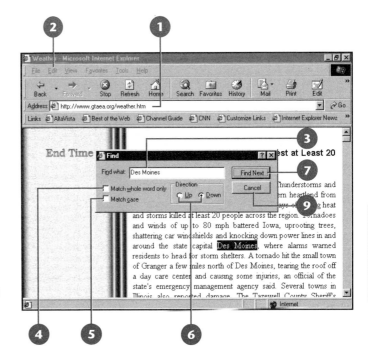

Searching for Information on the Internet

The Web can be overwhelming; there is a great deal of information to plow through. Internet Explorer makes it easy for you to quickly access the most popular search engines and Internet directories with the click of a button. You can also customize your search settings so you work with only the search providers that you prefer. For quick searches, you can use *AutoSearch* to locate the information you want. You can enter a search request directly into Internet Explorer's Address bar. Simply type your keywords into the Address bar and press Enter.

Search the Internet Using the Search Button

1. Click the Search button on the Standard toolbar. Internet Explorer chooses a search engine at random.

2. Click the search category option button you want.

3. Type the information you want to use for the search.

4. Click the Search, Find, or Seek button. (Each search provider labels its search button differently.)

5. If a Security Alert message box appears, click Yes.

6. Click the link for the Web site you want to view.

7. If you don't find the Web site you want, click the Next button to perform the same search with another search engine.

8. To perform a new search, click the New button.

9. Click the Close button or click the Search button on the Standard toolbar to view the entire Web page.

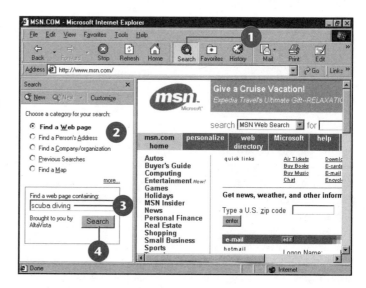

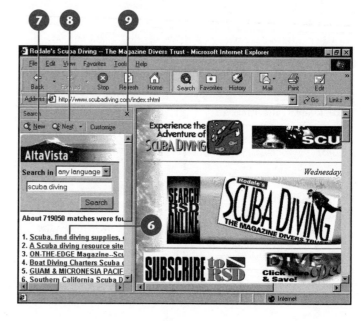

Choose a default search provider. *Click the Search button on the Standard toolbar, click the Customize button, scroll to the bottom of the page, click the Choose A Default Provider link, and then click the link for the search provider you want to use.*

Get ScreenTips when you search. *To get a description of a Web site returned by a search without clicking its link, move the pointer over the link in the Choose Search pane and hold it there. A ScreenTip appears, listing the Internet address, URL, and other relevant information about the Web page—if the search provider supports this feature.*

Other AutoSearch options. *You can also type the word* **go** *or* **find** *or just a question mark before your search request. For example, typing* **? Colorado hiking** *is the same as typing* **Colorado hiking***.*

Customize Your Search Options

1. Click the Search button on the Standard toolbar.

2. Click the Customize button.

3. Click the check box to select or clear search providers.

4. Scroll down and select search providers in each search category.

5. When you're done, click OK.

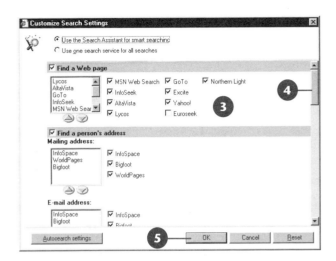

Use AutoSearch to Locate information

1. In the Address bar, type the keywords you want to use for the search. For example, type **scuba diving**

2. Press Enter or click Go.

   Internet Explorer randomly selects a search provider and submits your request. The results are displayed in the main browser window.

3. Click the link for the Web site you want to view.

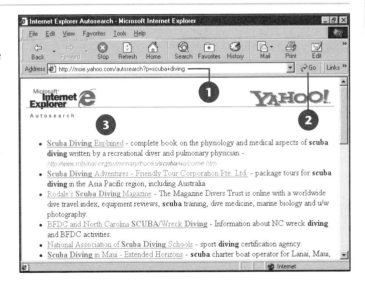

Creating and Organizing Your Favorites List

How about creating a permanent link to your favorite Web site? With a list of favorites you can quickly read top news headlines, check current weather conditions, or track stock prices. As your list of favorites grows, you can organize them into different folders. For example, if your hobby is fishing, you may have a Favorites folder named Fly Fishing Locations and another named, Fly Fishing Equipment. You can also find out the number of times you visited a favorite and the date it was last visited.

TRY THIS

Right-click to add a favorite. *Right-click anywhere in the background of a Web page, click Add To Favorites on the shortcut menu, and then complete the Add Favorite dialog box.*

Create a Favorites List

1 Open the Web site you want to add to your Favorites list.

2 Click the Favorites menu, and then click Add To Favorites.

3 Type the name for the site, or use the default name supplied.

4 If you want, click Create In to add the site to a folder within the Favorites folder.

5 If the currently listed folders don't represent a category for your selected Web site, click New Folder, type a folder name, and then click OK.

6 Click OK.

Favorites list

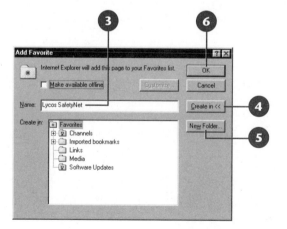

Drag and drop to organize favorites. *You can drag sites into the folders of your choice while the Organize Favorites dialog box is open.*

Delete a favorite. *Click the Favorites menu, click Organize Favorites, click the favorite you want to delete, click Delete, and then click Close.*

Rename a favorite. *Click the Favorites menu, click Organize Favorites, click the favorite you want to rename, click Rename, type the new name, press Enter, and then click Close.*

See "Viewing and Adding to Your Favorites List" on page 36 or "Viewing Your Favorites Offline" on page 40 for more information on viewing your favorites.

Create a Folder in Your Favorites List

1. Click the Favorites menu, and then click Organize Favorites.

2. Click Create Folder.

3. Type the name of the folder, and then press Enter.

4. When you're done, click Close.

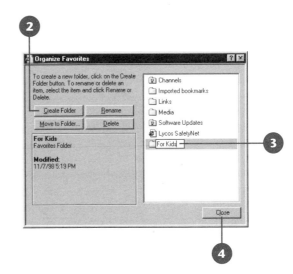

Move a Favorite to a Folder

1. Click the Favorites menu, and then click Organize Favorites.

2. Click the favorite you want to move to another folder.

3. Click Move To Folder.

4. Click the folder where you want to move the favorite.

5. Click OK.

6. When you're done, click Close.

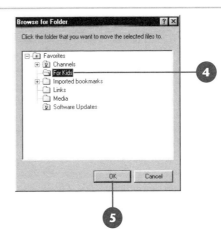

Viewing and Adding to Your Favorites List

To make it easier to view your Favorites list, you can display your favorites in a split window called the *Explorer bar*. The panes in the Explorer bar work the same way as the panes in Windows Explorer work. When you click a favorite listed in the left pane, its content is displayed in the pane on the right. In addition to adding Web pages, you can add drives, folders, and even files that you access frequently to your Favorites list. Adding drives, folders, and files to your Favorites list gives you instant access to your computer to manage and open files quickly right from Internet Explorer.

View Your Favorites List in the Explorer Bar

1. Click the Favorites button on the Standard toolbar.

2. If necessary, click the folder with the favorite you want to view.

   The contents of the folder are displayed. Click the folder again to hide the contents.

3. Click the favorite you want to view.

   Your favorite is displayed in the right pane.

4. When you're done, click the Close button.

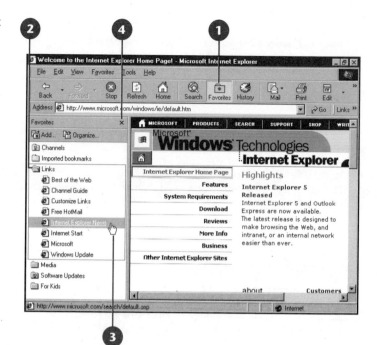

TIP

Scroll the list of favorites.
If your list of favorites is very long, directional arrows appear in the middle of the Favorites pane. To scroll down or up the Favorites list, click the down arrow or up arrow.

TIP

Use drag and drop to add a favorite. *Click the Favorites button on the Standard toolbar and then drag the page icon of the currently displayed page, located in the Address bar, to a folder in the Explorer bar.*

TIP

A favorite is grayed out.
When you're working offline, AutoDetect Offline grays out unavailable favorites. Click the File menu, and then click Work Offline to deselect the option.

SEE ALSO

See "Creating and Organizing Your Favorites List" on page 34 for information on adding and organizing favorites using the Favorites menu.

View Your Hard Disk and Add a Folder to Your List of Favorites

① Display the contents of your hard disk. For example, type **C:** in the Address bar, and then press Enter.

② If necessary, click the View menu, point to Explorer Bar, and then click Favorites to display your Favorites list in the left pane.

③ Drag a folder from the right pane to the Favorites pane.

④ Release your mouse button when the folder icon is positioned correctly within the Favorites list or in an expanded folder.

The folder from the hard disk is added to the Favorites list. You can also add a file to the Favorites list.

⑤ When you're done, click the Close button.

⑥ Click the Go menu, and then click Home Page to return to Internet Explorer.

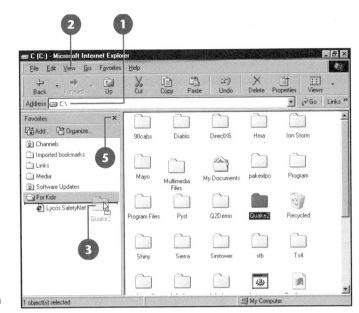

Viewing and Maintaining a History List

Sometimes you run across a great Web site and simply forget to add it to your Favorites list. With Internet Explorer there's no need to try to remember all the sites you've visited. The History feature keeps track of where you've been for days, weeks, or even months at a time. Because the History list can grow to occupy a large amount of space on your hard disk, it's important that you control the length of time visited Web sites are retained in the list. Internet Explorer will delete the History list periodically based on the settings you specify. You can also delete individual listings in the History folder as needed.

View a Web Site from the History List

1. Click the History button on the Standard toolbar.

2. Click a week or day to expand or compress the list of Web sites visited.

3. Click the folder for the Web site you want to view, and then click a page within the Web site.

4. When you're done, click the Close button.

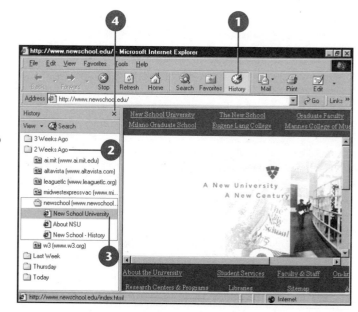

Change the History List View

1. Click the History button on the Standard toolbar.

2. Click the View button, and then click the view option you want.

3. When you're done, click the Close button.

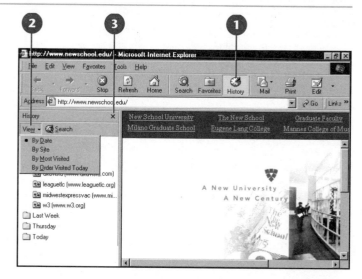

Clear the History List

1. Click the Tools menu, and then click Internet Options.

2. Click the General tab.

3. Click Clear History, and then click Yes.

4. Click OK.

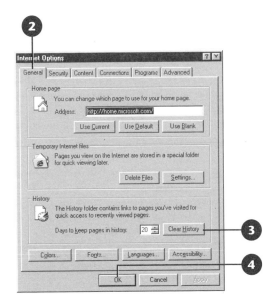

Change the Number of Days Pages Are Saved in Your History Folder

1. Click the Tools menu, and then click Internet Options.

2. Click the General tab.

3. Specify the total number of days you want to keep links listed in the History folder.

4. Click OK.

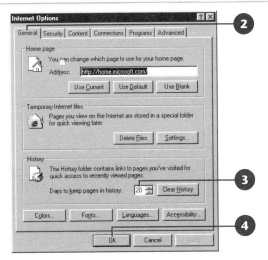

Viewing Your Favorites Offline

When you add a Web site to your list of favorites, you have the option of making that Web site available for viewing offline. Internet Explorer will store a copy of the site on your hard disk and you can view the contents anytime—not just when you are connected to the Internet. Offline viewing is much faster because the Web pages are being loaded from your hard disk instead of across your telephone line or company network. When you *synchronize* your offline pages, Internet Explorer visits each one and brings the most current version of the page back to your hard disk. You can also schedule automatic synchronization (every night, for example) so that each morning you can read your favorite Web sites offline at top speed.

Set Up a Web Site for Offline Viewing

1. Open the Web site you want to add.

2. Click the Favorites menu, and then click Add To Favorites.

3. Click to select the Make Available Offline check box.

4. Click Customize.

5. Click Next to configure your page for offline viewing.

6. Click the Yes option button to allow viewing of the entire Web site, or click the No option button to restrict your offline viewing to the single page. Click Next to continue.

7. Choose the synchronization schedule option you want, and then click Next to continue. If a Web site provides a schedule you may want to choose this option to receive the most up-to-date information.

8. If the Web site requires user authentication, enter your user name and password. Click Finish.

9. Choose the folder, and then click OK.

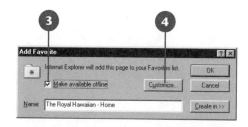

Set up an existing favorite for offline viewing. *Click the Favorites menu, and then click Organize Favorites. Click the name of a favorite you want to view offline, and then click the Make Available Offline check box. To set up your own schedule, click the Properties button, and then click the Schedule tab. Click the Add button to define and name a synchronization schedule. Click the Edit button to change the schedule settings.*

Not every link is available offline. *When Internet Explorer synchronizes a Web page, it can't gather every link on every Web page (eventually you would run out of hard disk space). You can tell that a link will require an online connection because the mouse pointer changes to a circle with a line through it. You can still click those links, but you will have to choose to go online (reconnect to the Internet) to see the content.*

Free Computer Training

Synchronize Your Favorites

1. Click the Tools menu, and then click Synchronize.

2. Select the Web site(s) you want to synchronize.

3. Click Synchronize.

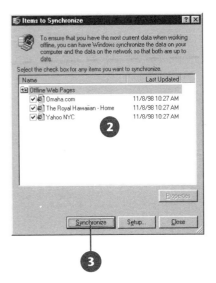

Work Offline

1. Click the File menu, and then click Work Offline.

2. Click the Favorites menu, and then click one of your favorites that has been synchronized.

3. Browse the site at high speed from your hard disk.

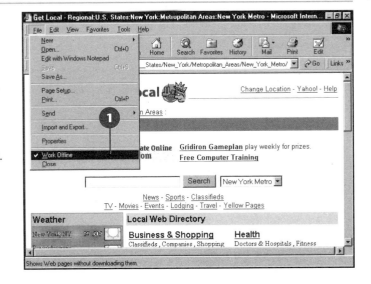

Adding a Channel

The first time you visit a channel from the Favorites menu, you will see the channel's *preview page*—a kind of ad for the channel's content. If the channel looks interesting, you can add the active version to Internet Explorer so that your next visit will reveal the channel's content. You can then have Internet Explorer update this active content whenever new information becomes available from the channel provider. There are hundreds of channel partners ready to deliver content to your computer, including MSNBC, Disney, and CBS SportsLine, to name a few. More are added every day.

TRY THIS

Add a channel quickly.
Click the Favorites button on the Standard toolbar, and then click the Channels folder in the left pane. Right-click the channel you want to add, and then click Make Available Offline on the shortcut menu.

Add a Channel to Your Favorites List

1 Click the Favorites button on the Standard toolbar.

2 Click the Channels folder in the left pane, click a channel topic, and then click the channel you want to add.

The channel's preview page appears in the right pane.

3 Click the Add Active Channel button. A Channel Refresh message box may appear, indicating that the channel is being synchronized. Click Next to continue.

4 Click the Yes option button to link to other pages when offline, or click the No option button to see just the first page. Click Next to continue.

5 Choose the synchronization schedule option you want.

6 Click Finish. If a Channel Screen Saver message box appears, click Yes to use the content of this channel on your desktop, or click No to close the message box.

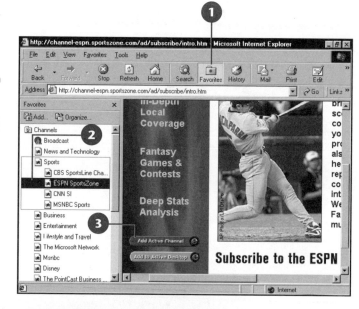

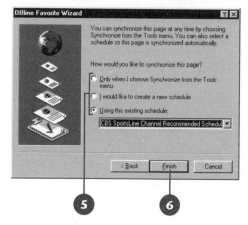

TIP

Add a channel to your desktop. *After viewing a channel's preview page, click the Add To Active Desktop button (not all channels offer this option). You still set up the channel for offline viewing using the channel's update schedule, but the content will now appear on your desktop!*

TRY THIS

Visit the Channel Guide. *The best place to find channels is Microsoft's Channel Guide. On the Links bar, click Channel Guide. From this Web page you can search for and add channels on hundreds of different topics.*

TRY THIS

Add a channel to the Channel bar. *Click the Favorites button on the Standard toolbar, and then click the Channels folder in the left pane. Drag the channel from the left pane to the Channel bar on your desktop (you may need to resize your Explorer window so that you can see both the Channel bar and Internet Explorer).*

View a Favorites Channel

1. Click the Favorites button on the Standard toolbar.

2. Click the Channels folder, click the channel topic you want to select from.

3. Click the channel you want to view.

4. Click the Close button or click the Favorites button on the Standard toolbar.

View the Channel Bar

1. Right-click the desktop, and then click Properties on the shortcut menu.

2. Click the Web tab.

3. Click to select the View My Active Desktop As A Web Page check box.

4. Click to select the Internet Explorer Channel Bar check box.

5. Click OK.

The Channel bar appears on your desktop.

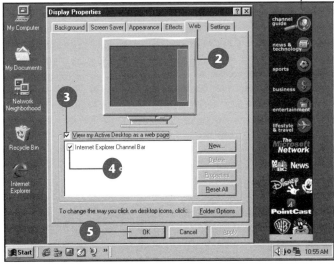

Managing Offline Pages

If you have added several channels or Web pages for offline viewing, you might want to change how often Internet Explorer synchronizes your local copy with the Internet. You may also want to have Internet Explorer send you a mail message letting you know that the content has changed. Maybe you are about to disconnect from the Internet and want to synchronize all your Web pages and channels at once for an extended offline session. Or perhaps a site now requires that you supply a user name and password. By managing your offline pages, you can easily make changes to the way Internet Explorer synchronizes with the Internet.

TIP

Update a page or channel.
Right-click any individual Web page or channel, and then click Synchronize on the shortcut menu to update the content immediately.

Manage an Offline Page

1 Click the Tools menu, and then click Synchronize.

2 Click the Web site or channel you want to modify, and then click Properties.

3 To change properties settings for the selected offline content, click:

◆ The Web Document tab to change the availability of the page or channel for offline viewing.

◆ The Schedule tab to change the frequency of synchronization. You can set it to follow a schedule or to synchronize only when you choose the favorite.

◆ The Download tab to limit the amount of hard disk space the local copy uses, specify user name and password options for sites that require them, or enter an e-mail address where notification of changes should be sent.

4 Click OK.

5 Click Close.

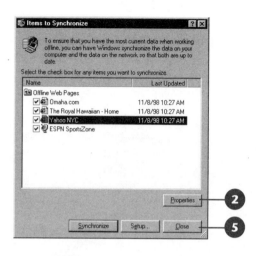

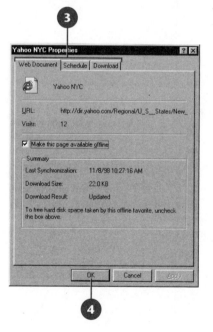

Synchronize on any schedule. *Click the Tools menu, and then click Synchronize. Click the Setup button. Click the Scheduled tab. You can add your own schedule—maybe every three days at 1:40 in the morning.*

Fast LAN connection or slower dial-up? *Click the Tools menu, and then click Synchronize. Click the Setup button. Click the Logon/Logoff tab. You can specify different update options for your different connection speeds to the Internet. Synchronize large Web sites while connected to the corporate LAN, but not when using your dial-up connection.*

Special consideration for laptop users. *Click the Tools menu, and then click Synchronize. Click the Setup button. Click the On Idle tab, and then click the Advanced button. You specify whether or not you want to synchronize while your computer is running on batteries.*

Synchronizing Offline Pages

1 Click the Tools menu, and then click Synchronize.

2 Click Setup.

3 To change synchronization settings for your selected Web pages or channels, click:

◆ The Logon/Logoff tab to decide what content should be updated when you are using different connections to the Internet.

◆ The On Idle tab to only update content when your computer is idle, because synchronizing may slow down your computer.

◆ The Scheduled tab to add new synchronization days or times. You can also change any of the existing schedules.

4 Click OK.

5 Click Synchronization or click Close.

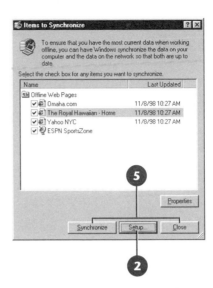

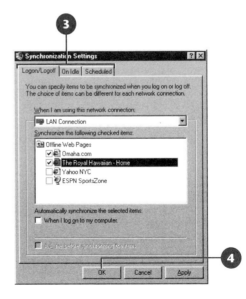

3

Importing Favorites and Bookmarks

If you regularly use another browser along with Internet Explorer, you might have saved favorite Web sites as bookmarks in that other program. When you switch back to Internet Explorer, you may find yourself wishing you had access to those favorite pages you bookmarked in another browser. With Internet Explorer, you can import those bookmark files and add the Web sites to your Favorites list.

TIP

Import regularly. *To avoid duplicate files, Internet Explorer checks to see if bookmarks exist in your Favorites list. Import as often as you want to keep your Favorites list current with other browsers you may use.*

Import a Bookmark File

1. Click the File menu, and then click Import And Export.

2. Click Next to continue.

3. Click Import Favorites. Click Next to continue.

4. Click Browse to locate the file that contains the bookmark(s) you want to import, and then click Save. Click Next to continue.

5. Select a destination folder. Click Next to continue.

6. Click Finish.

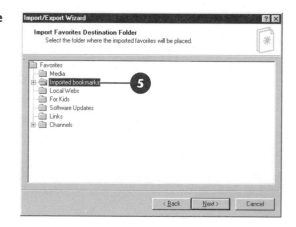

Export Favorites to a Bookmark File

1. Click the File menu, and then click Import And Export.

2. Click Next to continue.

3. Click Export Favorites. Click Next to continue.

4. Select a folder to export. Click Next to continue.

5. Click Browse to choose a destination file, and then click Save. Click Next to continue.

6. Click Finish.

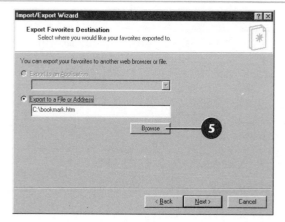

Obtaining Information from Microsoft

Not sure where to look to improve your Internet experience? Internet Explorer offers direct links to Microsoft Web sites offering everything from Internet Explorer repairs to help specifically for Netscape users. Search the support database, read the Tip Of The Day, take the Internet Explorer tour, and even give suggestions to Microsoft on how it could improve its Web site to make your time on the Internet more productive.

Access Microsoft on the Web

◆ Click the Help menu, and then click the Web page or Help menu option you want to view.

Refer to the table for information on Help menu commands.

MICROSOFT ON THE WEB	
Menu Choice	**Description**
Contents And Index	Internet Explorer Help. This is not a Web page, and you can access it at any time.
Tip Of The Day	A quick tip to make your Internet Explorer experience more productive and enjoyable. The tip will appear at the bottom of your Explorer window.
For Netscape Users	Microsoft's support page for Netscape users who are new to Internet Explorer.
Tour	A Web-based tutorial on Internet Explorer 5. Learn about the new features or how to perform basic functions.
Online Support	Search Microsoft's Knowledge Base of technical support. Get answers to support questions on any Microsoft product.
Send Feedback	Tell Microsoft what you think about its product. You can report any bugs you may have found and send e-mail to Microsoft's technical support.
Repair	Automatically detect and repair problems with Internet Explorer.
About Internet Explorer	Version information.

3

Getting Software from Microsoft

Microsoft posts updates, fixes, add-on files, and programs that you can download from the Microsoft Internet Web site. Even though the software is free, downloading software can sometimes take a long time to complete.

SEE ALSO

See "Downloading Files from a Web site" on page 52 and "Downloading Files from an FTP Site" on page 54 for information about downloading files from the Internet.

SEE ALSO

See "Installing Add-Ons and Viewers" on page 96 for information about getting enhancements for Internet Explorer.

Download Free Software Updates

1. Create a folder in which to store the downloaded files.

2. Start Internet Explorer and connect to *http://www.microsoft.com/msdownload/*.

   To avoid problems, read and follow the download and installation instructions carefully.

3. Click a link to the category of free software, or scroll down the page to see the free software choices.

4. Click a link to the software you want to download.

5. Read the Web page, and then follow the download instructions.

6. Download the software setup files into your new folder.

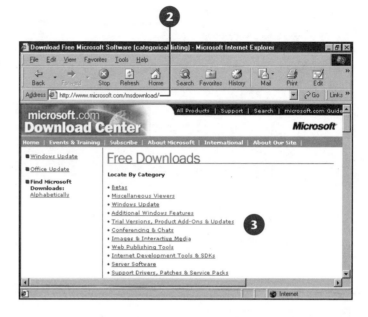

Handling Information with Internet Explorer

IN THIS SECTION

Understanding Common Error Messages

Avoiding Viruses

Downloading Files from a Web Site

Downloading Files from an FTP Site

Copying and Saving Graphics

Copying and Saving Background Graphics

Copying and Pasting Text from a Web Page

Getting Media Clips from the Web

Creating and Using Style Sheets

New **Editing and Updating an Office Web Page**

Printing a Web Page

New **Saving a Web Page**

From time to time you will need to handle various types of information that come from the Internet. With Microsoft Internet Explorer 5, you can:

◆ Download programs, games, and other files to your computer

◆ Copy text and graphics from a Web site to a document stored on your computer

◆ Download a variety of media clips including movies, audio, and MIDI music

◆ Create style sheets that override Web page settings, customizing your view of any Web page on the Internet

◆ Automatically launch Office 2000 programs so you can edit Web pages created in Office 2000

◆ Print virtually any Web page you see, including individual frames

◆ Save entire Web pages for later viewing

Understanding Common Error Messages

Having some trouble connecting to certain Web sites? You're not alone. Because of the way the Internet is constructed, a bad telephone line, a broken server, or an absentminded Web page administrator can come between you and the information you seek. Knowing how to decipher error messages and fix problems will help to make your Internet experience easier.

Internet Explorer groups a lot of common problems under just a couple of error messages—"The page cannot be found" and "The page cannot be displayed." Error messages usually provide some possible reasons that the Web site or Web page was unavailable along with some things to try that might solve the problem (for example, check your spelling or click the Refresh button). If your Web address is for a valid Web site, but the particular Web page doesn't exist, Internet Explorer will provide a link to the site's home page, so you might still find what you are looking for by starting there. Internet Explorer may also list the Internet's actual error code at the bottom of the standard Error Page. These codes are explained in the table on the right.

When downloading files, you might run into the error message, "The request to the host has taken longer than expected" or "Server Busy." This means that the site you are trying to connect to is overloaded with requests from other users. The best thing to do is wait until the network traffic jam subsides, and then try again. Peak

download hours on the Internet are from 4:00 P.M. to 11:00 P.M., so it's best to avoid downloading during those hours.

COMMON ERROR MESSAGES	
Message or Code	**Description**
400 Bad Request	The server doesn't recognize the URL. You can check your spelling, but the page might have been removed.
401 Unauthorized User	You've entered an invalid user name or password for a protected page. Check your spelling, or contact the Web site administrator to verify your authorized account or password.
403 Forbidden Page	You are trying to view a page that is either password protected or is otherwise unavailable.
404 File Not Found	The Web's most common error: It could be a spelling error, or the Web page has been removed by the author.
502 Service Overloaded	There are too many requests at the moment for the server to handle. Try again later.
503 Service Unavailable	You have entered a valid URL, but the server isn't responding at this time. Try again later.

Avoiding Viruses

Using the Internet can expose your computer to a wide variety of viruses through e-mail, file transferring, and even possibly through Java and ActiveX, which are both programming languages used to enhance Web pages. A *virus* is an executable program whose functions range from just being annoying to causing havoc to your computer. A virus may display an innocuous warning on a particular day, such as Friday the 13th, or it may cause a more serious problem, such as wiping out your entire hard disk. Viruses are found in executable (.exe and .com) files, along with Microsoft Word and Microsoft Excel macro files.

When you start downloading files to your computer, you must be aware of the potential for catching a computer virus. You can't catch a virus from just reading a mail message, but you can catch a virus from opening a file attached to a mail message. And even though most viruses take the form of executable programs, data files that have macros or Visual Basic code attached to them, such as Word or Excel files, can also be infected with viruses.

Although the odds are low that you'll catch a virus through sharing disks or downloading files, there are a few things you can do to keep your system safe from the infiltration of viruses.

First, make sure you are using the most up-to-date virus checking software. New viruses and more virulent strains of existing viruses are discovered every day. Unless you update your virus checking software, new viruses can easily bypass outdated virus checking software. Companies such as MacAfee and Symantec offer shareware virus checking programs available for download directly from their Web sites. These programs will monitor your system, checking each time a file is added to your computer to make sure it is not in some way trying to change or damage valuable system files.

Second, be very careful of the sites from which you download files. Major file repository sites, such as FileZ, Download.com, or TuCows, regularly check the files they receive for viruses before posting such files to their Web sites. Don't download files from Web sites unless you are certain that the sites check their files for viruses.

Finally, make sure you activate macro virus checking protection in both Word and Excel. To do so, click the Tools menu, point to Macro on the expanded menu, click Security, and then make sure that the High Security Level option is selected. (In Office 2000, click the Tools menu, click Options, click the General tab, and then make sure the Macro Virus Protection option is selected.) And always elect not to run macros when opening a Word or Excel file that you received from someone who might not be using proper virus protection.

4

Downloading Files from a Web Site

There are thousands of sites on the Internet offering all sorts of files you can download to your computer, from movie trailers to the latest game demos. You can download files from any Web site by finding the file you want, right-clicking the link, and telling Internet Explorer where you want to save the file. Internet Explorer even offers a direct link to the Microsoft's Windows Update Home Page for downloading product updates and exploring member services. Internet Explorer will connect to the appropriate file server and then transfer the file to your computer.

TRY THIS

Access a site with lots of files to download. *Try these sites to find plenty of files to download:* **http://www.download.com** *and* **http://www.shareware.com**.

Download a File from a Web Page

1. Locate the Web page from which you want to download a file.

2. Right-click the link pointing to the actual file, and then click Save Target As on the shortcut menu.

3. Select the folder in which you want to save the file.

4. Click Save.

   The File Download dialog box displays the estimated time to download the file, along with the estimated transfer time.

5. Click OK when the download is complete.

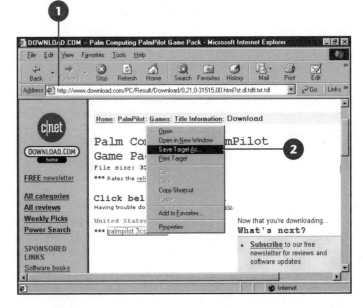

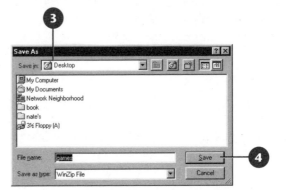

Download a File from Microsoft

1. In the Address bar, enter the following address:
http:// www.microsoft.com/ msdownload.

2. Click the product category for the software you want to download.

3. Click the link for the software you want to download.

4. Follow the instructions for downloading. Some download instructions may include filling out an Online Profile.

5. Click the link to download the file. If necessary, choose a link that is closest to your own location. The File Download Wizard dialog box opens.

6. Click the Save This Program To Disk option button, and then click OK.

7. Click OK.

8. Select the folder in which you want to save the file, and then click Save.

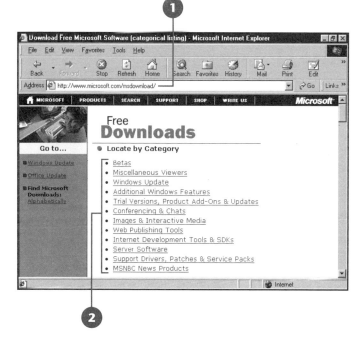

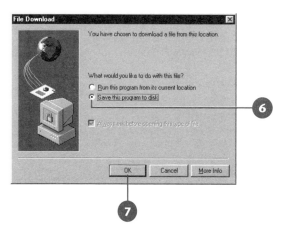

4

Downloading Files from an FTP Site

Sometimes you'll need to connect directly to a File Transfer Protocol (FTP) site to download or transfer a file to a remote computer system. Internet Explorer allows you to easily access and download files from any FTP site, public or private. *Public FTP sites* allow you to access files without requiring that you have an account on the server. *Private FTP sites* expect you to enter your user name and password in order to see the directories and files. When you are connected to an FTP site, Internet Explorer's view of the files is the same as looking at a directory on your local hard disk—complete with folder and file icons. Within this view you can drag onto your desktop or right-click to save the file in a particular folder on your computer.

Download a File from a Public FTP Site

1 In the Address bar, type the URL for the public FTP site.

2 If the site offers it, double-click the link to the Pub directory to display the list of files you can download.

3 Right-click the link for the file you want to download, and then click Copy To Folder.

4 Select the folder in which you want to save the file.

5 Click OK.

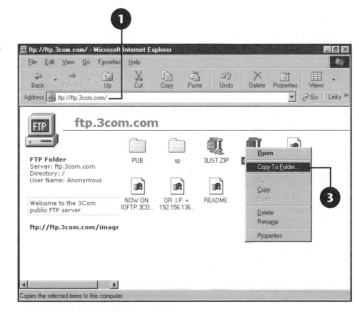

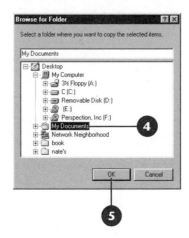

Include your user name and password in the URL for a private FTP site. *For access to a private FTP site, you must supply your user name and password in the URL. The correct syntax to use is: **ftp:// username:password@ftp. server/directory**.*

Get the size of the file before you download. *At an FTP site, right-click the file you want to download, and then click Properties to check the size of the file before deciding to download the file.*

Remember to double-click in folder view. *When viewing files and folders at an FTP site, you need to double-click a folder to move into another folder.*

Access files at a public FTP site. *Most public FTP sites will either display a list of folders or take you directly to the publicly accessible folder. The /pub folder is usually the location in which publicly accessible files are stored.*

Download a File from a Private FTP Site

1. In the Address bar, type the URL for the private FTP site. Include your user name and password in the URL.

2. Press Enter.

   The private FTP server should list the directory you specified.

3. Right-click the link for the file you want to download, and then click Copy To Folder.

4. Select the folder in which you want to save the file.

5. Click OK.

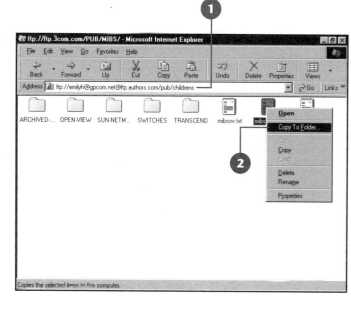

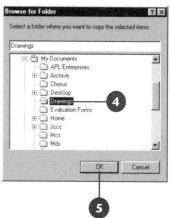

4

Copying and Saving Graphics

Using Internet Explorer, you can copy just about any graphic you see on a Web page to an application or document of your choice. You can also save the graphics that many Web sites include on their pages to your computer's hard disk.

Most Internet graphics are relatively small in size, occupying no more than 50 KB, and are saved in GIF format. GIF and JPEG files can be opened with a wide variety of graphics programs, such as Microsoft Photo Editor, Image Composer, Adobe Photoshop, or Microsoft FrontPage.

When you save a graphic from a Web page, you can save it in a different file format so you can modify it as you like.

Copy and Paste a Graphic

1. Open the Web page containing the graphic you want to copy.

2. Right-click the graphic, and then click Copy on the shortcut menu.

3. Open the application or document in which you want to paste the graphic.

4. Position the insertion point where you want to place the graphic.

5. Click the Edit menu, and then click Paste.

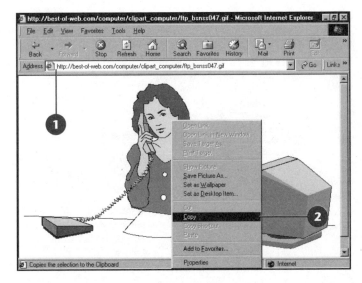

It's easy to copy just about anything on the Internet. *But sometimes it's not legal. Before you copy any text or before you include text on your own Web page, make sure you have permission from the original author of the text. If the original copyright holder finds you have violated the copyright, you could have a costly legal problem on your hands.*

Convert graphics formats at the time of download. *Only GIF and JPEG graphics formats are supported on the Web. If you want your downloaded picture to be in a bitmap format, click the Save As Type drop-down arrow, and click Bitmap. Internet Explorer will convert the GIF or JPEG image to a bitmap image.*

Find out how much space the graphic file will occupy. *Right-click the graphic, and then click Properties on the shortcut menu. The size of the graphic appears in the Properties dialog box.*

Save a Graphic

1. Open the Web page containing the graphic you want to save.

2. Right-click the graphic you want to save, and then click Save Picture As on the shortcut menu.

3. Select the folder in which you want to save the graphic.

4. If you want, type a new filename for the graphic.

5. If you want, click the Save As Type drop-down arrow to save the graphic as a bitmap. Otherwise, Internet Explorer will save the graphic as a GIF or JPEG file.

6. Click Save.

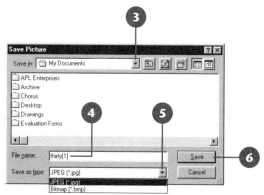

4

Copying and Saving Background Graphics

Some Web sites use interesting graphic images for the background of a Web page. These graphics are also available for copying and using in your other applications. Background images are typically small images consecutively tiled across a Web page. When you copy or save these background images, only a single image is copied or saved. If you copy a background image, you can paste the image into another application or document immediately. When you save a background image, you can choose the file format in which you want to save the image, and then open the file in a graphics program to modify it as you like.

Copy and Paste a Background Graphic

1 Open the Web page containing the background graphic you want to copy.

2 Right-click the background of the Web page, and then click Copy Background on the shortcut menu.

3 Open the application or document in which you want to paste the background graphic.

4 Position the insertion point where you want to place the background graphic.

5 Click the Edit menu, and then click Paste.

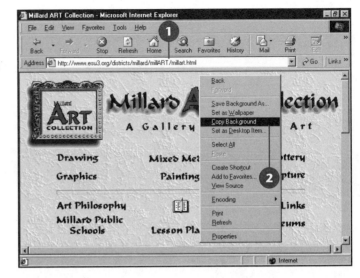

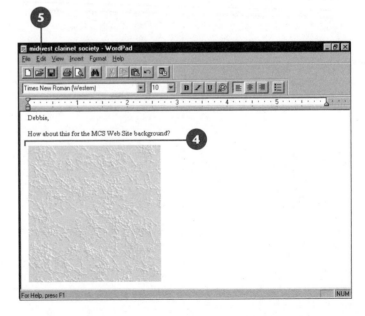

Open a graphic that you saved. *Internet Explorer and FrontPage Express can open files saved in JPEG or GIF formats. If you saved a graphic as a bitmap file, use Microsoft Paint or Microsoft Photo Editor to open and edit the file.*

Rename the graphic when you download. *When the Save Picture dialog box is open during the saving of a background graphic, you can change the name of the file. Just be sure to not change the file extension. Internet Explorer will assign the proper extension when you click the Save button.*

Turn a favorite background into a desktop pattern. *Right-click the graphic you want to use as a background on your desktop, and then click Set As Wallpaper on the shortcut menu. Go to your desktop and then right-click an empty area on it, click Properties, and then click the Display drop-down arrow to choose whether the graphic is centered, tiled, or stretched across your desktop.*

Save a Background Graphic

1. Right-click the background of the Web page, and then click Save Background As on the shortcut menu.

2. Select the location in which to save the file.

3. Type the filename you want for the graphic, or accept its original filename.

4. Click the Save As Type drop-down arrow, and then select a file type.

5. Click Save.

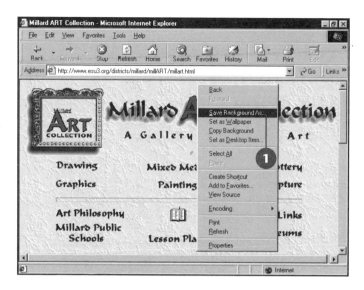

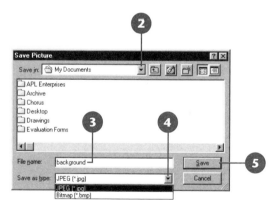

Copying and Pasting Text from a Web Page

Maybe you've found an interesting story or a great joke on the Web that you'd like to pass along to your friends and relatives. Using Internet Explorer, you can easily copy information from a Web page into a mail message or a Word, Excel, or PowerPoint document with a few clicks of the mouse. When you select a range of text that includes images, only the text within the selection can be copied. Text and graphics are independent elements.

TIP

Select and copy all the text on a Web page. *Right-click an empty area of the Web page, click Select All on the shortcut menu, right-click the selected text, and then click Copy on the shortcut menu.*

Copy and Paste Text from a Web Page

① Open the Web page containing the text you want to copy.

② Use the mouse to highlight the text you want to copy.

③ Click the Edit menu, and then click Copy.

④ Open the application or document in which you want to paste the text.

⑤ Click to position the insertion point at the location where you want to place the copied text.

⑥ Click the Edit menu, and then click Paste.

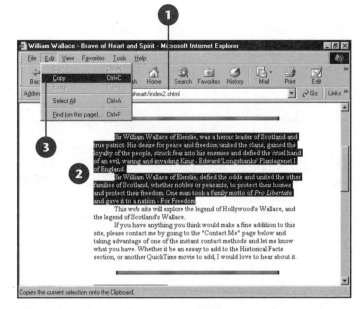

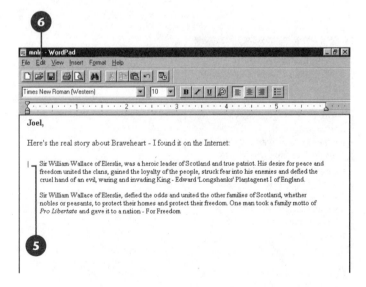

Getting Media Clips from the Web

To take advantage of the hundreds of images and sounds on the World Wide Web, you can find and download these media files from the Microsoft Site Builder Network Web site or from other Web sites on the Internet. You can use these files to create your own Web pages or include them in other documents or applications.

TRY THIS

Visit a site with lots of clip art. *Download clip art from http://www.aplusart.com. Bullets, backgrounds, icons, and animated GIFs are available for use in your Web pages or other documents.*

Find and Download a Media Clip from the Microsoft Gallery

1. In the Address bar, enter the following address: **http:// www.microsoft.com/ gallery**.

2. Click the Images or Sounds link.

3. Click the media category from which you want to download a file. If you choose an image link, click the link to display it in the right pane.

4. Right-click the image or sound file link.

5. If you chose an image, click Save Picture As on the shortcut menu. If you chose a sound, click Save Target As.

6. If you are downloading a program, click the Save This Program To Disk option button, and then click OK.

7. Select the folder in which you want to save the file, and then click Save.

8. If necessary, click OK when the download is complete.

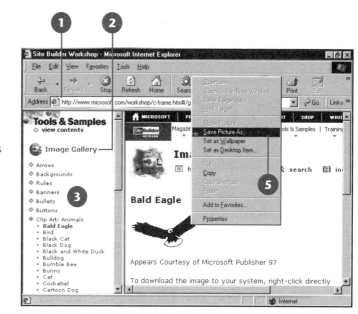

Creating and Using Style Sheets

Using style sheets is a convenient way to make Web pages more readable, regardless of the formatting used by the original Web page designer. A style sheet allows you to override the settings of the Web pages you browse with settings of your own, so that you can view pages in the format you prefer. With a style sheet, you can specify font styles, sizes, and colors, text alignment, indentation, and other layout information. When you activate the Internet Explorer style sheet option, all Web pages you view will be displayed using the features defined in your style sheet.

TIP

A style sheet does not affect the size of graphics. *Only the text, background color, and font sizes of text on a Web page are affected by the use of style sheets.*

Create a Style Sheet

1. Open the Web page you want to use as a style sheet.

2. Click the Tools menu, and then click Internet Options.

3. Click the General tab.

4. Click Colors, select the colors to be used for the text and background and for the visited and unvisited links, and then click OK.

5. Click Fonts, select the fonts to be used for the style sheet, and then click OK.

6. Click OK.

7. Click the File menu, and then click Save As to save the page to your local hard disk.

8. Select the folder in which you want to save the style sheet.

9. Type the filename for the style sheet, or use the default filename.

10. Click the Save As Type drop down arrow, and then click Web Page, HTML Only.

11. Click Save.

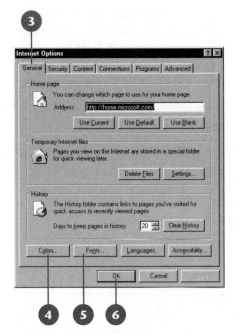

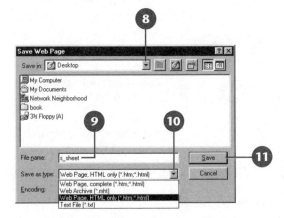

Use a Style Sheet

1. Open a Web page in the Internet Explorer window.

2. Click the Tools menu, and then click Internet Options.

3. Click the General tab.

4. Click Accessibility.

5. In the Formatting section, click to select any or all of the three check boxes for ignoring colors, font styles, and font sizes used on Web pages.

6. Click to select the Format Documents Using My Style Sheet check box.

7. Type the path to the style sheet you want to use, or click Browse to search for it. Click the Files Of Type drop-down arrow, and then click All Files to select from all file types. Locate the file you saved as a style sheet on your local hard drive, and then double-click the file to use it as the style sheet.

8. Click OK.

9. Click OK.

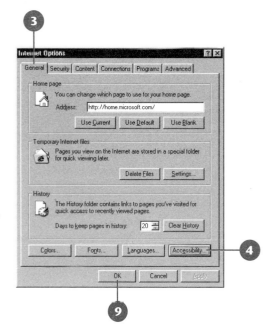

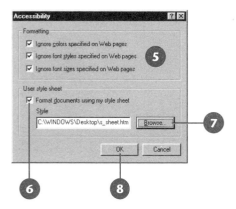

Editing and Updating an Office Web Page

For those of you who have Office 2000 installed on your computer, you can edit an Office Web page—a Web page saved in an Office program—with the help of Internet Explorer. With an Office Web page displayed in the Internet Explorer window, you can launch the Office program that was used to create the Web page. This makes editing Web pages seamless and easy.

Edit an Office Web Page

1. Open the Office Web page you want to edit.

2. Click the Edit button on the Standard toolbar.

   The toolbar button icon indicates the Office program associated with the Web page.

3. Begin editing the Web page in the Office program as usual.

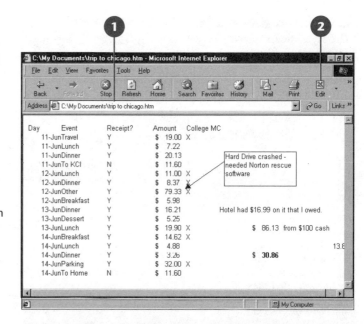

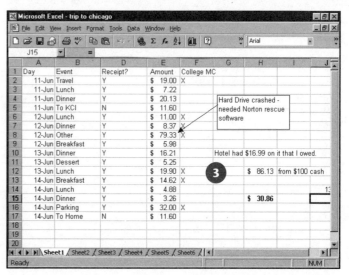

Edit an Office Web page in another program. *You can edit an Office Web page in more than one program; a drop-down arrow appears next to the Edit button. When you click the Edit drop-down arrow, a list of programs from which you can edit the Office Web page appears .*

See "Starting FrontPage Express" on page 186 for information on using the Edit button for non-Office Web pages.

Save a Web page in an Office program. *In the Office program, click the File menu, click Save As Web Page, enter a filename, and then click Save.*

Update an Office Web Page

1. If necessary, open the Office Web page in the Office program.

2. Click the Save button on the Standard toolbar.

   When you're done making changes to the Web page, you can close the Office program.

3. Switch back to Internet Explorer.

4. Click the Refresh button on the Standard toolbar.

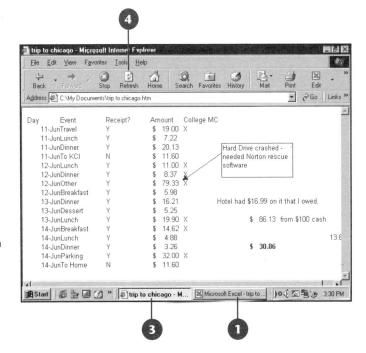

Printing a Web Page

Web pages are designed to be viewed on a computer screen, not printed on paper. Nevertheless, Internet Explorer provides many options for printing Web pages. On framed Web sites, you can print the page just as you see it, or you can elect to print a particular frame. You can even use special page setup options to include the date, time, or window title on the printed page. To print a Web page, first set up Internet Explorer so that it prints the Web page as it is displayed on your screen. This involves making sure that pictures and graphics on the site are displayed and that the option to print the back-ground pictures and colors is activated. Just make sure you have adequate printing resources before turning this option on.

Set the Printing Options

1. Click the Tools menu, and then click Internet Options.

2. Click the Advanced tab.

3. Scroll, if necessary, to the Multimedia area, and make sure that the Show Pictures check box is selected.

4. Scroll to the Printing area, click to select the Print Background Colors And Images check box.

5. Click OK.

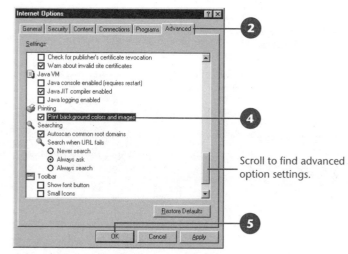

Scroll to find advanced option settings.

Specify the Page Setup

1. Click the File menu, and then click Page Setup.

2. Do one or more of the following.

   ◆ Click the Size drop-down arrow, and then select a paper size.

   ◆ Enter a header or footer or both in the Header and Footer boxes, respectively.

   ◆ Click the Portrait or Landscape option button.

   ◆ Specify the margins.

3. Click OK.

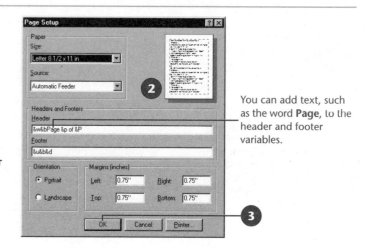

You can add text, such as the word **Page**, to the header and footer variables.

Change header and footer variable options. *The following are the variables you can enter in either the Header box or Footer box displayed in the Page Setup dialog box:*
&w – prints the window title
&u – prints the page address
&d – prints the short date
&D – prints the long date
&t – prints the time
&T – prints the time in 24-hour format
&p – prints the page number
&P – prints the total number of pages
&& – prints a single ampersand symbol

Make sure of your print options. *In the Print dialog box, don't select the Print All Linked Documents check box unless you know only a few documents are linked. Otherwise, you might end up printing more than you expected.*

What is a frame? *A frame is a separate Web window within a Web page. Frames give you the ability to show more than one Web page at a time.*

Print the Current Page

1. Click the File menu, and then click Print.

2. Click the Name drop-down arrow, and then select the printer you want to use.

3. Set any additional options, such as the Print Range and Number Of Copies.

4. Click OK.

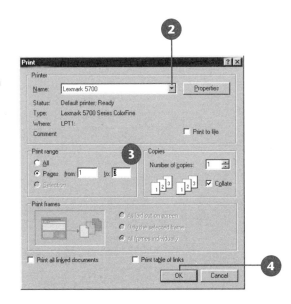

Print the Contents of a Selected Frame

1. Open the Web page, and then click the frame to select it.

2. Click the File menu, and then click Print.

3. Click the Only The Selected Frame option button.

4. Set any additional options, such as the Printer Name, Print Range, and Number Of Copies.

5. Click OK.

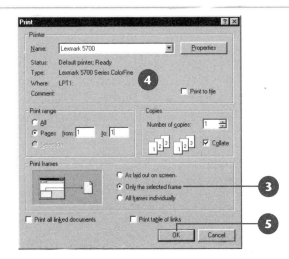

Saving a Web Page

Unlike word processing or desktop publishing documents, Web pages are made up of separate elements (such as text, pictures, style sheets, and so forth). When you save a Web page, Internet Explorer allows you to save just the text from the Web page or save all the separate elements of a Web page in a new folder. Internet Explorer will also alter the HTML coding of the page to reflect its new home on your hard disk. All HTML references to graphics or other elements will be changed to point to the folder that was created when you saved the Web page.

TIP

Save only the text from a Web page. *When saving a Web page, click the Save As Type drop-down arrow, and then specify to save the file as a HTML or text file. This will not save the pictures, but it will store a copy of either the HTML coding for the page or just the words from the page.*

Save an Entire Web Page

1. Open the Web page you want to save.

2. Click the File menu, and then click Save As.

3. Specify the drive and folder in which to save the file.

4. Type the name you want for the file, or use the default filename.

5. Click the Save As Type drop-down arrow, and then select the file format type you want.

   Refer to the table for information on file formats.

6. If necessary, click the Encoding drop-down arrow, and then select the language encoding type you want.

7. Click Save.

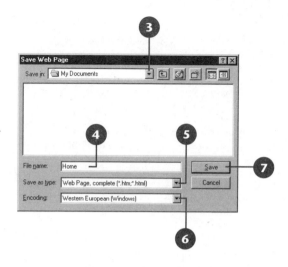

SAVE AS TYPES	
File Format Type	**Description**
Web Page, complete (*.htm,*.html)	Saves all the files needed to display the current Web page, including graphics, frames, and style sheets.
Web Archive for email (*.mht)	Saves all the information needed to display the current Web page in a single e-mail file.
Web Page, HTML only (*.htm,*.html)	Saves the HTML coding for the current Web page excluding the graphics, sounds, or other files.
Text File (*.txt)	Saves the text from the current Web page.

Personalizing Internet Explorer

IN THIS SECTION

Customizing the Microsoft Home Page

Adding the Address and Links Bars to Your Taskbar

Modifying the Links Bar

Modifying the Internet Explorer Window

Understanding Security

Creating Security Zones

Setting Ratings Using the Content Advisor

Storing Personal Information

New **Shopping on the Internet**

Adding a Language

Changing Colors and Font Settings

Improving Performance

Choosing Programs to Use with Internet Explorer

Microsoft Internet Explorer 5 is fully customizable. You can change a wide variety of options to make Internet Explorer work in the best way for you. Some of the ways you can personalize Internet Explorer include:

◆ Creating your own personalized home page

◆ Configuring the Links bar to contain the items you use the most

◆ Selecting which external programs, such as e-mail and newsgroup readers, will work with Internet Explorer

◆ Creating security zones so site contents can be checked for information that could potentially damage your computer

◆ Setting security options so important information is relayed only to those sites you allow

◆ Setting rating options that prevent children from seeing inappropriate sites

◆ Changing the colors, fonts, and languages used while you browse the Web

◆ Changing the language used to display Web pages

Customizing the Microsoft Home Page

The Microsoft (MSN) Home Page is the default page displayed as your home page when you click the Home button on the Standard toolbar. You can customize the MSN Home Page, choosing which items you want displayed, such as the day's top headlines, stock quotes, financial news, and so on. You can also specify which links you want to access directly from this page. Customizing the MSN Home Page takes just a few minutes, and you can change options at any time.

Customize the MSN Home Page

1. Make sure you are connected to the Internet. Customizing the MSN Home Page will only work while you are online.

2. Click the Home button on the Standard toolbar.

   If *home.microsoft.com* isn't your home page, click the View menu, and then click Internet Options to change your home page.

3. Click Personalize.

4. Click the Show On MSN.COM Home Page check box to add or remove information sources. For e-mail, if you don't have a Hotmail account (Microsoft's free e-mail provider), you can choose to remove the entire section from your home page.

5. Select the information category and use the position arrows to move it higher or lower on the page.

6. Click Update to store your choices with MSN.com.

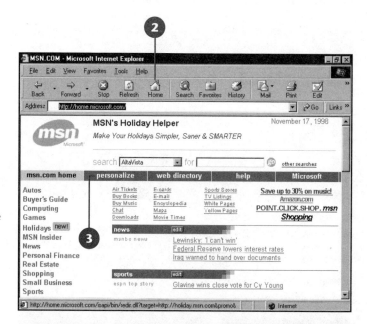

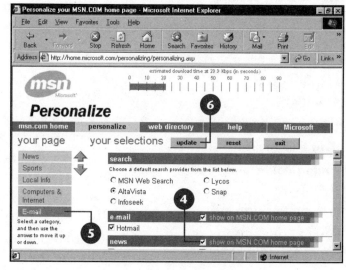

Adding the Address and Links Bars to Your Taskbar

By placing an Address bar on the taskbar, you can enter a URL and launch Internet Explorer with any Web page you choose. You can also make the Links bar part of the taskbar and quickly launch Internet Explorer to any of your favorite Web sites. Resize the taskbar as necessary to display all the toolbars you use.

TIP

Double the height of your taskbar. *Drag the top of the taskbar upward to stretch it to double the height. After resizing the taskbar, you can click the left edge of any of the bar icons, and then drag the bar to one of the new rows.*

SEE ALSO

See "Searching for Information on the Internet" on page 32 for information on entering search requests using the Address bar.

Add the Address Bar to the Taskbar

1. Right-click a blank area on the taskbar.

2. Point to Toolbars.

3. Click Address.

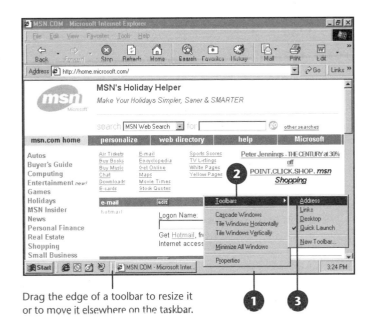

Drag the edge of a toolbar to resize it or to move it elsewhere on the taskbar.

Add the Links Bar to the Taskbar

1. Right-click a blank area on the taskbar.

2. Point to Toolbars.

3. Click Links.

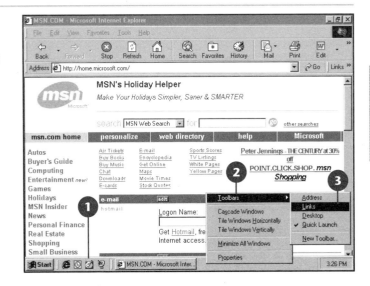

Modifying the Links Bar

The Links bar provides you with access to your favorite Web sites with the click of a button. You can add a link button that links you to a favorite, or you can remove a link button when you no longer need quick access to a site. You can even add a folder of favorites to the Links bar. When you click the folder icon on the Links bar, a list of Web links you've placed in the folder appears.

TIP

Links on the Windows taskbar? *If you modify your Links bar in Internet Explorer, the changes will be reflected on the Links bar you might have added to the Windows taskbar.*

SEE ALSO

See "Modifying the Internet Explorer Window" on page 74 for information on how to display or hide the Links bar.

Display the Links Bar as a Separate Bar

1. Position your mouse pointer over the word **Links** at the left end of the Links bar, and then click. The mouse changes to a four-headed arrow.

2. Drag the Links bar below the Address bar.

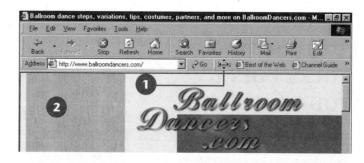

Add or Remove a Link Button from the Links Bar

1. Open the Web page or display the folder you want to add to the Links bar.

2. Drag the Web page or folder icon in the Address bar to the Links bar.

3. Release the mouse button to position the new item.

4. To remove a link, right-click the item you want to delete.

5. Click Delete on the shortcut menu.

6. Click Yes to confirm the deletion.

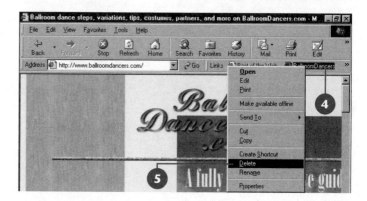

Rearrange items on the Links bar. *Drag an item to the left or right of another on the Links bar. The item will be placed in the location where you release the mouse button.*

Add a site from your Favorites folder to the Links bar. *Click the Favorites button on the Standard toolbar. Drag a favorite Web site link from the Favorites pane to the Links bar, and then release the mouse button when the link is positioned correctly.*

Change the name of a Links bar button. *Right-click the link button you want to change, click Rename on the shortcut menu, and then type the new name you want for the button. Changing the button name doesn't affect the button's link to the URL.*

Create a desktop shortcut for a link. *You can create a desktop shortcut for any Links bar link so that you can access the site right from your desktop. Simply drag any Links bar link to the desktop.*

Add a Folder of Links to Your Links Bar

1 Click the Favorites menu, and then click Organize Favorites.

2 Drag the Media folder to the Links folder.

3 After the Links folder opens, drop the Media folder into the Links folder by releasing the mouse button.

4 Click Close.

Internet Explorer displays the Media folder on the Links bar or the Links bar list, depending on how many links you have and how wide your screen is.

5 Click the Media folder link, and then select a Web site

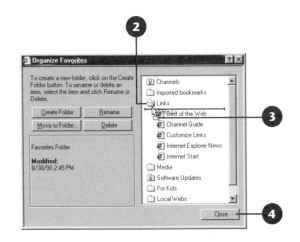

Drag the Links bar here to display more link buttons.

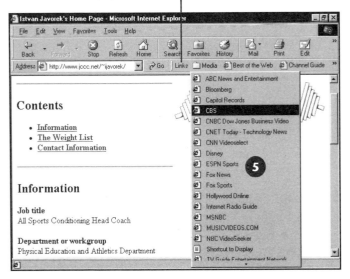

Modifying the Internet Explorer Window

There are many options you can select to customize the appearance of the Internet Explorer window. Some options provide you with more space on the screen to display Web pages, whereas others allow you to display or hide the status bar and the different toolbars. You can also modify a toolbar by adding or removing buttons. You can move the toolbar buttons to reposition them in whatever arrangement works best for you. You can even change the appearance of a toolbar by making the icons smaller, if you want.

Turn On or Turn Off Full Screen Mode

1. Click the View menu, and then click Fullscreen.

   The menu bar, window title bar, Address bar, and Links bar disappear. A minimized Standard toolbar now appears at the top of the screen.

2. Press the F11 key to return to the normal view.

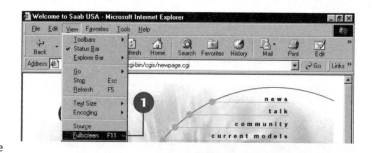

Show or Hide a Toolbar

1. Click the View menu, and then point to Toolbars.

2. Click the toolbar you want to show or hide.

   A toolbar that is displayed on the screen has a check mark to its left on the Toolbars submenu.

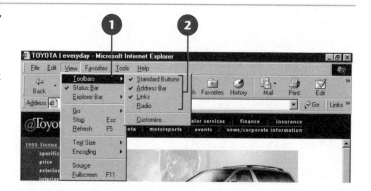

TRY THIS

Add toolbars to your full screen status bar. *Right-click the minimized Standard toolbar when you are in full screen mode and choose to display the menu bar, Address bar, or the Links bar.*

TRY THIS

Switch to smaller toolbar buttons. *Click the View menu, point to Toolbars, click Customize, click the Icon Options drop-down arrow, click Small Icons, and then click Close. The buttons on the Standard toolbar shrink, and their labels no longer appear below them.*

TIP

Hide the status bar. *Click the check mark to the left of the option. The check box indicates if the status bar is currently displayed on the screen.*

SEE ALSO

See "Changing Advance Options" on page 90 for information on other ways to customize a toolbar.

Customize the Standard Toolbar

1. Click the View menu, point to Toolbars, and then click Customize.

2. To add a button to the current toolbar, click a button in the Available Toolbar Buttons box, and then click Add.

3. To make changes to the toolbar, click the button you want to change, and then do one of the following.

   ◆ Click Remove to remove the selected button.

   ◆ Click the Move Up or Move Down button to reposition the selected button on the toolbar.

4. To display labels on the toolbar buttons, click the Text Options drop-down arrow, and then select Show Text Labels.

5. To shrink the size of the toolbar buttons, click the Icon Options drop-down arrow, and then select Small Icons.

6. To return a toolbar to its original settings, click Reset.

7. When you're done, click Close.

Click to select an available button to add to the toolbar.

Click to remove the selected button from the toolbar.

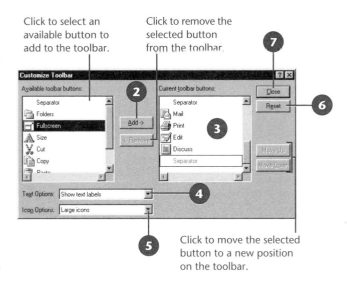

Click to move the selected button to a new position on the toolbar.

Understanding Security on the Internet

No other Web browser offers as many customizable features as Internet Explorer does, particularly advanced security features that are built into the program. To understand all the Internet Explorer security features, you first have to learn about security on the Internet in general.

When you send information from your computer to another computer, the two computers are not linked directly together. Your data may travel through multiple networks as it works its way across the Internet. Since your data is broadcast to the Internet, any computer on any of these networks could be listening in and capturing your data (they typically aren't, but they could be).

In addition, on the Internet it's possible to masquerade as someone else. E-mail addresses can be forged, domain names of sites can easily be misleading, and so on. You need some way to protect not only the data you send, but also yourself from sending data to the wrong place.

Furthermore, there is always the potential that someone (referred to as a "hacker") or something, such as a virus, could infiltrate your computer systems. Once infiltrated, a hacker or virus can delete, rename, or even copy valuable information from your computer without your knowledge.

Security Zones

Through the use of *security zones,* you can easily tell Internet Explorer which sites you trust to not damage your computer and which sites you simply don't trust. In your company's intranet you would most likely trust all the information supplied on Web pages through your company's network, but on the Internet you may want to be warned first of potential dangers a site could cause your system. You can set up different levels of security based on different zones.

Certificates

When shopping on the Internet, you want to do business with only those companies that offer a certain level of security and promise to protect your buying information. In turn, those companies want to do business with legitimate customers only. A *certificate* (also called a *digital ID*) provides both the browser and the company with a kind of guarantee confirming that you are who you say you are and that the site is secure and genuine, not a fraud or scam.

An independent company, called a *credentials agency,* issues three types of certificates: personal, authority, and publisher. A *personal certificate* identifies you so that you can access Web sites that require positive identification, such as banks that allow online transactions. You can obtain a personal certificate from a credentials agency called VeriSign using the Security tab of the Options dialog in Outlook Express. An *authority certificate* ensures that the Web site you are visiting is not a fraud. Internet Explorer automatically checks site certificates to make sure that they're valid. A *publisher certificate* enables you to trust software, such as ActiveX controls, that you download.

Internet Explorer maintains a list of software companies whose certificates are valid and trustworthy. You can view your certificate settings on the Content tab of the Internet Options dialog box.

Content Advisor

Just about everyone can find objectionable material on the Internet. Parents might not want to subject their children to some of this material, such as strong language, violence, and other adult themes. However, most parents cannot spend every online minute with their children, censoring sites that are objectionable. In such cases, you can employ Internet Explorer's *Content Advisor* to screen out inappropriate sites, preventing youngsters from seeing things they shouldn't.

The Content Advisor works with different rating bureaus, such as the Recreational Software Advisory Council (RSAC), to rate sites within certain ranges. The RSAC's rating system is based on research that compiled a rating system to reflect different levels of violence, strong language, and so on. You decide exactly what kind of sites can be accessed, what ratings systems are used, which ranges are available to users within those sites, and whether users of your computer can see unrated sites.

You can also assign a supervisor password to allow a user to view such sites. As long as the user supplies the password you specified when you initially set up the content rating systems, the user can view sites where the material rates above the level chosen. You can turn off the Content Advisor at any time, opening up all sites on the Internet for viewing by any user without having to enter a password.

In order for the rating system to work, sites must subscribe to the system so that their ratings are passed to your computer when you access the sites. Most sites that want to offer quality information for children and those adult sites interested in making sure only individuals 18 years old or older are accessing their sites subscribe to rating systems like the RSAC. A site that voluntarily rates itself usually displays the RSAC logo on its home page. This logo is your indication that the site has properly rated itself and offers only materials that are appropriate to its rating.

Content Advisor dialog box

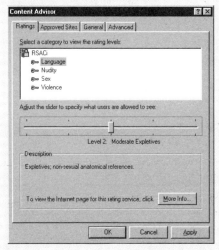

Creating Security Zones

Internet Explorer lets you create security zones based on where information comes from. For example, you may want to restrict access to Web pages that can be viewed from the Internet, but you don't want any restrictions applied to those sites within your company's intranet. You can specify the level of security for each of the four available security zones:

◆ **Local Intranet**—sites within your company's network

◆ **Trusted Sites**—sites you know and trust

◆ **Restricted Sites**—sites you don't trust or that need high security

◆ **Internet**—by default, anything not assigned to one of the other security zones

Select a Security Zone and Its Security Level

1 Click the Tools menu, and then click Internet Options.

2 Click the Security tab.

3 Click the zone to which you want to assign security options.

4 If you want, click Default Level to reset the settings to Microsoft's suggested level.

5 Move the slider to the level of security you want to apply.

6 If you want to specify individual security options, click Custom Level.

7 Scroll to a settings area, and then click the Enable, Prompt, or Disable option button.

8 Click OK.

9 Click OK.

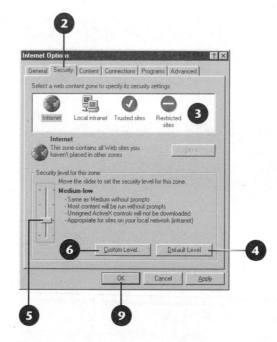

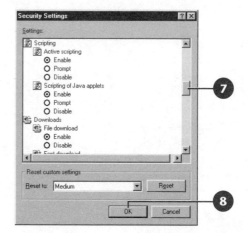

Remove a site from your Restricted Sites zone. *Click the Tools menu, click Internet Options, and then click the Security tab. Click Restricted Sites, and then click the Sites button. In the Web Sites box, click the site you want to remove, click Remove, and then click OK. Click OK to close the Internet Options dialog box.*

See "Understanding Security on the Internet" on page 76 for more information on security zones.

Reset default settings for security options. *To return each option to its default settings for a specified security level, click the Reset Custom Settings drop-down arrow, select a security level, and then click Reset.*

How do you know a Web site is secure? *Internet Explorer displays a padlock icon in the status bar.*

Add Sites to Your Restricted Sites Zone

1. Click the Tools menu, and then click Internet Options.
2. Click the Security tab.
3. Click Restricted Sites.
4. Click Sites.
5. Type the full URL for the site.
6. Click Add.
7. Click OK.
8. Click OK.

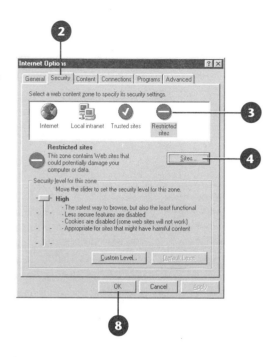

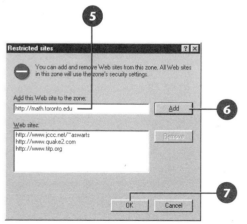

Setting Ratings Using the Content Advisor

If you have children who surf the Internet and you don't want to subject them to strong language, violence, or sexually explicit material, you can use the Content Advisor to restrict their access to inappropriate Web sites. If a rated site matches your ratings specifications, the site can be viewed. If the site is rated above the level you've set, or if the site is not rated and you've restricted access to unrated sites, the site can be viewed only when the supervisor password is supplied.

TIP

Use the Content Advisor for the first time. *When you click Enable, the Content Advisor dialog box appears. Set your initial ratings, and then click OK. Type a password, retype the password, click OK, and then click OK again.*

Set the Content Advisor Ratings

1️⃣ Click the Tools menu, and then click Internet Options.

2️⃣ Click the Content tab.

3️⃣ Click Enable. This button toggles between Enable and Disable.

4️⃣ Type a supervisor password, and then click OK.

For security, an asterisk (*) appears for each character you type. If necessary, retype the password to confirm it.

5️⃣ Click OK to confirm the Content Advisor has been turned on.

6️⃣ Click Settings. If necessary, type the supervisor password and click OK.

7️⃣ Click the category for which you want to set the rating.

8️⃣ Move the Rating slider to the rating level you want.

9️⃣ Click OK.

🔟 Click OK.

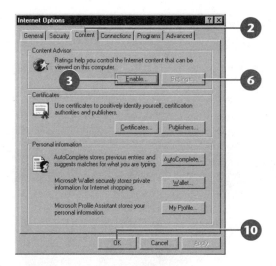

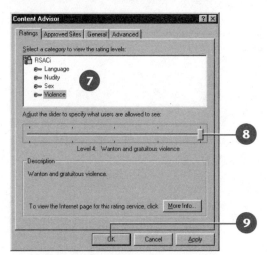

Storing Personal Information

Using Internet Explorer, you can store personal, home, business, and other information in a single location to make communicating and shopping on the Internet quick and easy. The *Profile Assistant* stores your name, address, and other important information. To make sure your information is safe and secure, Internet Explorer uses a feature called Microsoft Wallet. If you plan to shop over the Internet, you can securely store your personal information in a personal certificate to protect yourself from theft and fraud.

SEE ALSO

See "Shopping on the Internet" on page 82 for information on using the Microsoft Wallet.

Enter Information About You Using the Profile Assistant

1 Click the Tools menu, and then click Internet Options.

2 Click the Content tab.

3 Click My Profile.

4 If necessary, click the option button you want to create a new profile or select an existing one, and then click OK.

5 Click each tab to enter the information

6 Enter or modify the necessary information in the boxes.

7 Click OK.

8 Click OK.

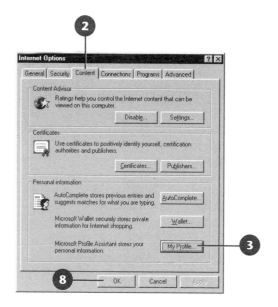

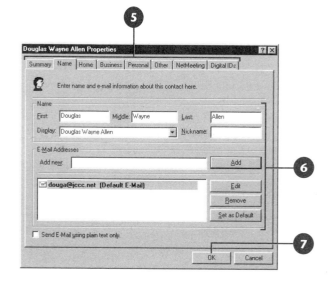

Shopping on the Internet

Microsoft Wallet offers a secure way to keep track of personal information related to Internet shopping so that when you shop online, you don't have to worry about the information falling into the wrong hands. You only need to enter your address and payment information once, and then you transmit it to Wallet-enabled Internet stores as you shop. You define a unique password for each payment method so that only you can use it. You use the Wallet's Addresses option to store and access addresses that can be referenced for shipping and billing. You use the Wallet's Payments option to store and access payment methods for your online purchases.

Add an Address to the Wallet

1. Click the Tools menu, and then click Internet Options.

2. Click the Content tab.

3. Click Wallet.

4. Click the Addresses tab.

5. Click Add.

6. If you want, click Address Book, select a name from the list, and then click OK.

7. Enter the necessary information in the boxes. If necessary, make changes to the information supplied by the Address Book.

8. Accept the default display name shown, or type a new name to define this entry in the Address Book.

9. Click the Home icon or the Business icon.

10. Click OK.

11. Click Close.

12. Click OK.

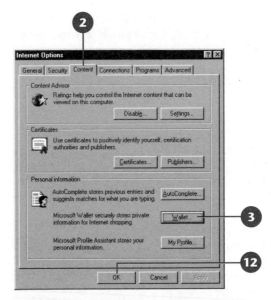

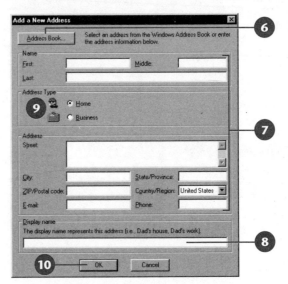

TIP

Remove a card from your wallet. *Click the Tools menu, and then click Internet Options. Click the Content tab, click Wallet, click the Payments tab, click a card, and then click Delete.*

TIP

Manage your receipts. *You can view details, track orders, and delete receipts from purchases you've made over the Internet. Click the Tools menu, and then click Internet Options. Click the Content tab, click Wallet, click the Receipts tab, and then type a password. Click the receipt you want to manage, and then click the button you want. When you're done, click Close, and then click OK.*

SEE ALSO

See "Getting a Personal Certificate" on page 158 for information on personal certificates and Internet security.

Add a Payment Method to the Wallet

1. Click the View menu, and then click Internet Options.

2. Click the Content tab.

3. Click Wallet.

4. Click the Payments tab.

5. Click Add, and then select the type of card you want to add. Click Next to continue.

6. Click I Agree on the license agreement. Click Next to continue.

7. Enter the name, expiration date, and the card number. Accept the default display name shown, or enter a new one. Click Next to continue.

8. Enter the billing address information for the card. If you want, click the New Address button and enter a new billing address, or select one from the Address Book. Click Next to continue.

9. Enter a password, press Tab, and then retype the password.

10. Click Finish.

11. Click Close, click OK, and then click OK again.

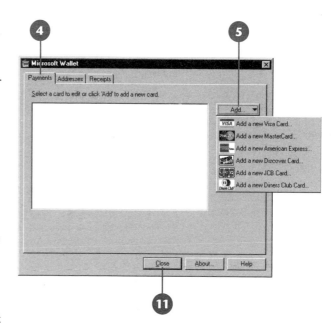

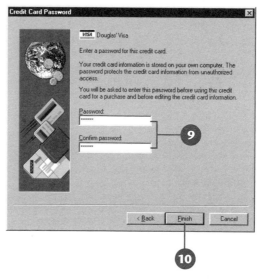

Adding a Language

In order to see Web pages written in a different language, you must first add the language character set to your Internet Explorer options. When you add a language character set, you enable Internet Explorer to display the correct characters for that language. This means that special characters, such as the tilde (~) in Spanish, will be displayed properly on the page.

TIP

You may still need a font.
Many languages have different characters from those found in the standard font set. You may need to download a multi-language support pack to display pages in a particular language.

SEE ALSO

See "Getting Updates to Internet Explorer" on page 258 for information on installing the Multi-Language Pack For Internet Explorer.

Add a Language Character Set

1. Click the Tools menu, and then click Internet Options.

2. Click the General tab.

3. Click Languages.

4. Click Add.

5. Click the language you want to add from the list of available languages.

6. Click OK.

7. Click OK.

8. Click OK.

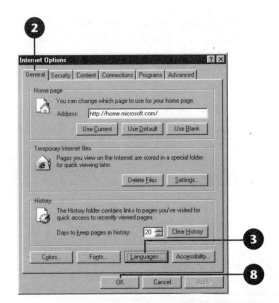

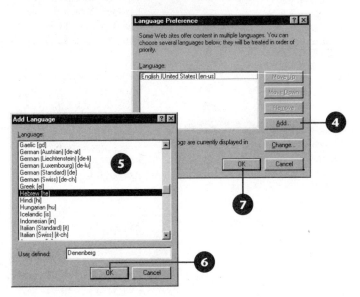

TIP

If you speak more than one language. *If a Web page is offering content in multiple languages, Internet Explorer will display the content in the language with the highest priority. If you want to see support for other languages on a particular Web page, you will need to both add the language and rank it higher than other languages offered on the Web page.*

TIP

Delete a language. *To delete a language you no longer use, select the language to be deleted in the Language Preference dialog box, click the Remove button, and then click OK.*

TIP

Change language setting for Office 2000 programs. *Click the Start button, point to Programs, point to Microsoft Office Tools, and then click Microsoft Office Language Settings. Click to enable or disable the languages you want, and then click OK.*

Specify the Priority of Languages

1 Click the Tools menu, and then click Internet Options.

2 Click the General tab.

3 Click Languages.

4 Click the language you want to move.

5 Click the Move Up button or the Move Down button to change the position of the language in the list.

The language at the top of the list has the highest priority; that is, it is used first on pages where content is displayed in multiple languages.

6 Click OK.

7 Click OK.

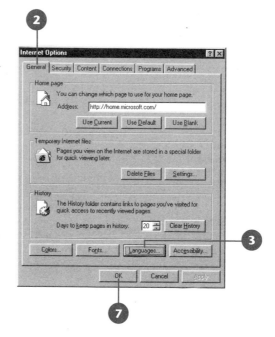

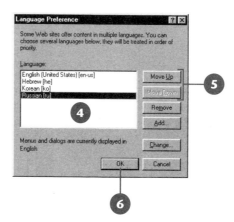

Changing Colors and Font Settings

Sometimes the color schemes and fonts of certain Web pages can make the information on the pages difficult to read. For example, the font might be too small or the color contrast too severe with the background of the Web page. In such cases, you can select the color, font size, background color, and even the character set used on the page. You can make these types of changes only if the default settings of the specific Web page can be overridden.

SEE ALSO

See "Creating and Using Style Sheets" on page 62 for information on displaying Web pages with the fonts and colors of your choice.

Change the Font Size

1. Click the View menu, and then point to Text Size.

2. Click the font size you want to use, either larger or smaller, for the text on the Web page.

   The text automatically changes to the size you specify.

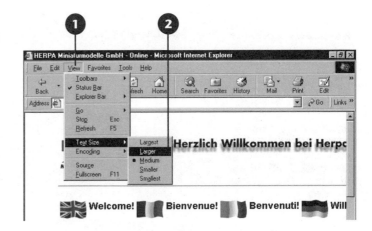

Change the Font Type

1. Click the Tools menu, and then click Internet Options.

2. Click the General tab.

3. Click Fonts.

4. Click the Language Script drop-down arrow, and select the character set you want to use.

5. Click the Web page font you want to use.

6. Click the plain text font you want to use.

7. Click OK.

8. Click OK.

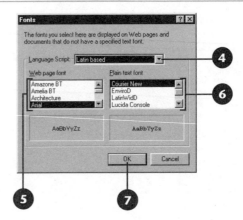

What's the difference between the Web page font and the plain text font? *A Web page font is a proportional font. With a proportional font, the width of each character differs with the character's shape. For example, the letter "m" is wider than the letter "i." A plain text font is a fixed-width font, which gives the same amount of space to each character, like text typed on a typewriter.*

See "Changing Advanced Options" on page 90 for information on changing underlining options used while you browse the Internet.

Hover in color. *If you want a link to change color as you hold your mouse pointer over it before deciding to click the link, click to select the Use Hover Color check box, select a hover color, and click OK.*

Change Text and Background Colors

1. Click the Tools menu, and then click Internet Options.

2. Click the General tab, and then click Colors.

3. Click to clear the Use Windows Colors check box.

4. Click the Text box.

5. Click the color you want to use, and then click OK.

6. Click the Background box, click a color you want to use, and then click OK.

7. Click OK.

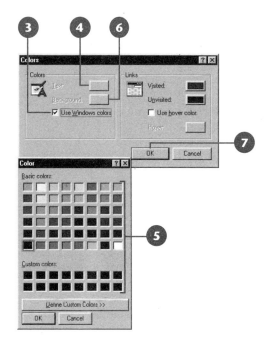

Change Link Colors

1. Click the Tools menu, and then click Internet Options.

2. Click the General tab, and then click Colors.

3. Click the Visited box, click the color you want to use, and then click OK.

4. Click the Unvisited box, click the color you want to use, and then click OK.

5. Click OK.

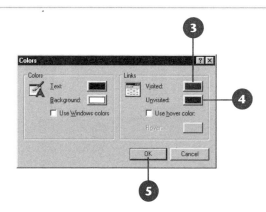

Improving Performance

Sometimes the Internet can be sluggish, especially if the Web site you are viewing is full of multimedia options such as streaming video, sound files, or lots of images. Internet Explorer allows you to improve system performance by turning off options that might take too long to load or slow down your system. You can also improve performance by increasing the storage of temporary files on your computer so Web pages don't have to be reloaded every time you go back to visit a site.

TIP

Text-only surfing. *If you turned off multimedia components from loading with Web pages, you will see a series of image placeholders and no images. But the Web pages will load faster, and you'll still see all the text information.*

Turn Off Multimedia Options

1 Click the Tools menu, and then click Internet Options.

2 Click the Advanced tab.

3 Scroll to the Multimedia area.

4 Click to clear the check boxes for:

◆ Show Pictures

◆ Play Animations

◆ Play Videos

◆ Play Sounds

◆ Smart Image Dithering

5 Click OK.

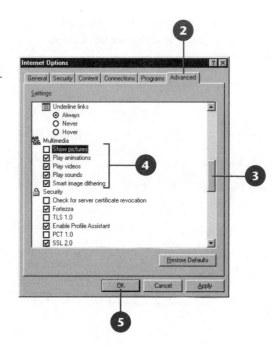

Let Internet Explorer decide when to update pages from the Internet.

The Automatically option for checking for newer versions of Web pages enables Internet Explorer to track the changes in a Web page over time. If Internet Explorer determines that a page doesn't change very often, it won't bother to go to the Internet for a newer version.

View the temporary files stored on your computer.

Click the Tools menu, and then click Internet Options. Click the General tab if necessary, and then click Settings in the Temporary Internet Files section. Click the View Files button to view those files temporarily stored on your computer.

See "Viewing Your Favorites Offline" on page 40 for more information on viewing pages directly from your hard disk at top speed.

Increase the Storage of Temporary Internet Files

1. Click the Tools menu, and then click Internet Options.

2. Click the General tab.

3. Click Settings.

4. If you want, click the Never option button so that Internet Explorer won't check each Web site visited for a newer version of the page.

5. Use the slider to increase the amount of hard disk space used to store temporary files.

6. Click OK.

7. Click OK.

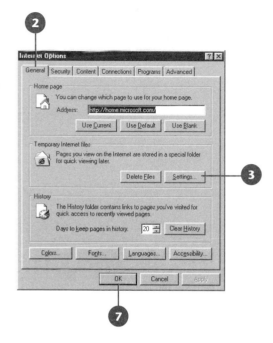

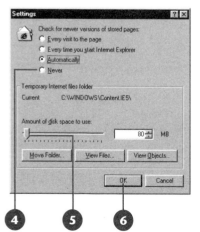

Changing Advanced Options

You can fine-tune Internet Explorer to your liking by changing many of the advanced options. For example, you can have Internet Explorer synchronize offline items on a schedule, use AutoSuggest in forms, automatically check for updates to Internet Explorer, or modify the look of a toolbar. These are just some of the advanced features you can take advantage of to further customize your Internet Explorer environment. The changes you make take effect immediately unless it is otherwise noted.

TIP

Not sure what an option does? *Click the Help button on the dialog box, and then click the option with the Help pointer. A definition box appears with a brief description of the option's purpose.*

Change Advanced Options

1. Click the Tools menu, and then click Internet Options.

2. Click the Advanced tab.

3. Scroll to display the options you want to change.

4. Click to select or clear the options you want to turn on or off.

5. Click OK.

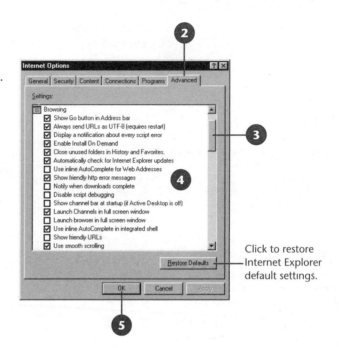

Click to restore Internet Explorer default settings.

Choosing Programs to Use with Internet Explorer

Internet Explorer relies on other, external programs to provide you with connections to your e-mail, newsgroups, Internet telephones, calendars, and contact lists. You have full control over what programs are used for each option. Although Internet Explorer comes with a full suite of add-on programs—such as Outlook Express for reading e-mail and newsgroup messages, and Microsoft NetMeeting for conversing with others over the Internet using speakers and a microphone—you can choose other applications to provide you with the same options.

SEE ALSO

See "Understanding Newsgroups" on page 143 for more information on what a newsgroup is.

Choose Programs to Use with Internet Explorer

1. Click the Tools menu, and then click Internet Options.

2. Click the Programs tab.

3. Do one or more of the following.

   ◆ Click the E-Mail drop-down arrow, and then select the e-mail program you want to use.

   ◆ Click the Newsgroups drop-down arrow, and then select the newsgroup reader program you want to use.

   ◆ Click the Internet Call drop-down arrow, and then select the program you want to use for Internet calls.

   ◆ Click the Calendar drop-down arrow, and then select the program you want to use for scheduling.

   ◆ Click the Contact List drop-down arrow, and then select the Internet contacts or address book program you want to use.

4. Click OK.

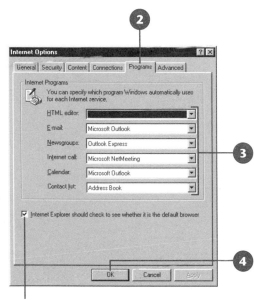

Select to have Internet Explorer check to make sure it's the default browser.

IN THIS SECTION

Understanding Add-Ons, Plug-Ins, and Viewers

Finding Add-Ons, Plug-Ins, and Viewers on the Web

Working with Add-Ons and Viewers

Understanding Java and ActiveX

Using ActiveX Controls

Running Java Applets

Controlling ActiveX and Java Content

New **Playing Sounds and Videos**

Changing Sound and Video Properties

Broadcasting Audio and Video with NetShow

Playing a VRML Animation

Playing an Internet Game

6

Expanding Functionality with Internet Explorer

The popularity of the Internet has resulted in an explosion of technology to deliver information to you in all forms—text, images, audio, and video. These new media types need to somehow use your Web browser to travel to your desktop. When you plug in and add on functions to support these exciting capabilities, Microsoft Internet Explorer 5 allows you to see information in a whole new light.

Multimedia adds another dimension to the Internet. Many Web sites include multimedia sound, video, and animation, in addition to text and graphics, to add interest and to increase understanding. Using Internet Explorer's built-in and add-on functionality, you can access the World Wide Web to listen to prerecorded or live radio programs, watch movies or videos, view the output of live video cameras, or play 3-D interactive animations and games over the Internet.

Understanding Add-Ons, Plug-Ins, and Viewers

Since no one is in charge of the Internet, no one is coordinating the development of all of the applications Internet users are demanding. The solution has been for the major Internet players (Microsoft and Netscape) to design their Web browsers to be *extensible*. An extensible program, like Internet Explorer, has specific functions that allow computer programmers to add functionality to what it can already do. This means that companies can develop new Internet programs directly for Internet Explorer. Without an extensible browser, new Internet programs would have to run separately from the browser, making installation and operation more difficult.

The term *plug-in* was coined by Netscape to refer to programs that take advantage of Netscape Communicator's extensibility. Microsoft uses the term *add-on* to refer to programs that take advantage of Internet Explorer's extensibility.

A *viewer* is a particular type of add-on that allows you to read documents created by applications like word processors, spreadsheets, and presentation programs. For example, many companies have documents stored in Microsoft Word format that they would like to offer to people visiting their Web sites. Internet Explorer can read and display Word documents with a viewer for Word.

Microsoft offers viewers for Microsoft Excel and Microsoft PowerPoint, also. Other companies, such as Adobe, offer viewers for their applications that you can

view with Internet Explorer. Viewers are most useful for people who do not have the original application that was used to create the document.

ActiveX Viewer Web page

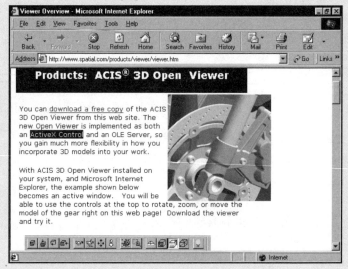

Finding Add-Ons, Plug-Ins, and Viewers on the Web

The best place to find add-ons, plug-ins, and viewers is the World Wide Web. Add-ons are available from several places on the Web, but the best place to go is to the company that created Internet Explorer—Microsoft. Microsoft's Web site contains add-ons and viewers on several different pages:

* *http://www.microsoft.com/msdownload/*

* *http://windowsupdate.microsoft.com*

* *http://computingcentral.msn.com/downloads*

You can also find add-ons, plug-ins, and viewers at software collection sites. These are Web sites that maintain large libraries of software available for downloading to your computer. Some popular sites are:

* *http://www.shareware.com*

* *http://www.jumbo.com*

* *http://browserwatch.internet.com*

* *http://www.cooltool.com*

* *http://www.tucows.com*

* *http://www.download.com*

When you are at one of these sites, use the local search engine to locate add-ons. Keywords to use

include *activex*, *add-on*, *viewer*, and *plug-in*. Finally, many vendors that develop add-ons, plug-ins, and viewers offer their products for downloading from their own individual Web sites. For example, if you want the RealPlayer, you can go to *http://www.real.com*, or if you want Adobe's PDF viewer, you can go to *http://www.adobe.com*.

BrowserWatch Plug-In Plaza Web page

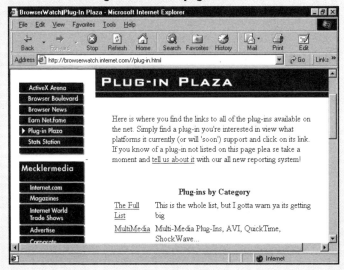

6

Installing Add-Ons and Viewers

Installing add-ons or viewers for Internet Explorer is a two-step process: download the program from the Internet, and then run the setup program to add the functionality. The files that you download are typically setup programs. You can run these setup programs by double-clicking the setup file in Windows Explorer or by using the Run dialog box that you open from the Start menu.

Install the RealPlayer Add-On

1. Create a new folder in which to store the downloaded files.

2. In the Address bar, type **http://www.real.com**.

3. Locate and then click the link for downloading the RealPlayer add-on. Follow the instructions, and then click the location from which to download.

4. Click the Save This File To Disk option button, and then click OK.

5. Click OK.

6. Save the software setup files in your new folder.

7. When the download is complete, click OK.

8. Start Windows Explorer, and then double-click the RealPlayer setup file.

9. Follow the instructions for installing the RealPlayer.

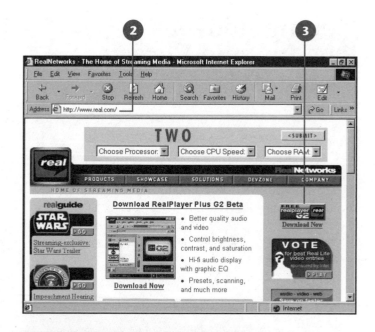

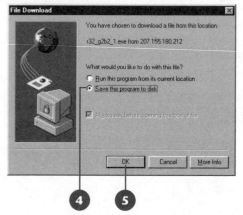

TIP

Install a plug-in. *To install a plug-in, you use the same procedure you use for installing an add-on.*

TIP

What is a PDF viewer? *PDF stands for Portable Document Format. This is a method of storing a printable document on the Web that any computer can read—no matter what kind of computer it is. Adobe has developed PDF viewers for Macintosh, UNIX computers, and, of course, Windows.*

SEE ALSO

See "Using Add-Ons and Viewers" on page 98 for information about using Internet Explorer add-ons and viewers.

SEE ALSO

See "Understanding Add-Ons, Plug-Ins, and Viewers" on page 94 for information on the functionality of add-ons, plug-ins, and viewers.

Install the Acrobat PDF Viewer

1. Create a new folder in which to store the downloaded files.

2. In the Address bar, type **http://www.adobe.com**.

3. Locate and click the Get Acrobat Reader link.

4. Follow the instructions for registering and choosing a reader, and then click the Download button.

5. Click the Save This File To Disk option button, and then click OK.

6. Click Save to save the software setup files in your new folder.

7. Click OK to complete the download.

8. Start Windows Explorer, double-click the Acrobat PDF viewer setup file, and then click Yes to continue.

9. Follow the instructions for installing the Acrobat PDF viewer.

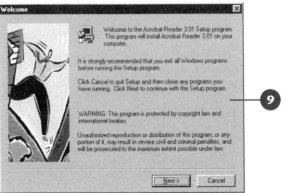

Using Add-Ons and Viewers

To take advantage of an add-on or viewer, all you have to do is visit a Web site that contains content that requires the add-on or viewer for proper delivery. Because the installed add-on or viewer becomes an integral part of Internet Explorer, you don't need to start the add-on or viewer as a separate program. In most cases, viewers are also separate programs that you can use as stand-alone programs to view documents you receive from places other than the Internet.

> **TIP**
>
> **What is streaming?** *Instead of making you download a large audio clip before playing it, many Web sites will* stream *the content. Your computer downloads and buffers a few seconds worth of audio and then begins playing the stream.*

Play Streaming Audio and Video Using the RealPlayer Add-On

1 Connect to a Web site containing a RealMedia sound or video.

Try connecting to **http:// www.dailybriefing.com** to locate news stories delivered through RealMedia.

2 Click a link to play RealAudio or RealVideo. The RealPlayer appears on your screen in its own window.

3 To use RealPlayer, click the appropriate buttons to play, pause, or stop the video. You can also control the volume.

Click the Real logo to see streaming content.

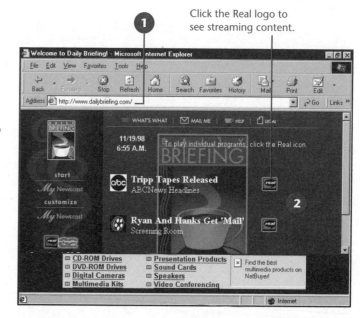

Pause

Play   Stop   Move the frame slider to review previous parts of the video.

Click to hide all controls, leaving only the video screen displayed.

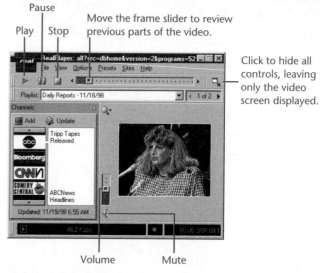

Volume   Mute

TIP

Acrobat may leave a window open. *When you view a PDF document, Acrobat will be launched in a separate window even though it displays the document in Internet Explorer. You can close the Acrobat program at any time.*

TRY THIS

Check out these RealAudio Web sites. *Connect to the following RealAudio Web sites:* **http://www.audionet.com** *or* **http://www.abc.com**.

TRY THIS

Check out an Acrobat PDF Web site. *Connect to the following Acrobat PDF Web site:* **http://thomas.loc.gov**.

TRY THIS

Get your tax forms in PDF format. *Tax forms in PDF format are available at* **http://www.efs.com/irs-pdf.htm**.

SEE ALSO

See "Finding Add-Ons, Plug-Ins, and Viewers on the Web" on page 95 for Web sites where you can find Internet Explorer add-ons, plug-ins, and viewers.

View a PDF Document with the Acrobat PDF Viewer

1. Connect to a Web site containing an Acrobat PDF document.

   Try connecting to **http://www.pdfzone.com**, and then click the PDF Showcase link to locate a Web site with an Acrobat PDF document.

2. Click a link to open an Acrobat PDF document. Many times the link to a PDF document has the Adobe PDF logo.

   The Acrobat PDF document opens.

3. Use the Acrobat toolbar to view the document.

Acrobat toolbar

Understanding Java and ActiveX

Java is a computer language developed by Sun Microsystems that allows programmers to write interactive programs for Web browsers. Standard Web authoring tools are limited to the activities and functions that are available from a Web page. With a complete programming language like Java, there are very few limitations to the number of functions that a Web page can have. Here are a few of the things that Internet programmers have been able to implement using the Java programming language:

- Scrolling stock tickers

- Automobile design shifter

- Rotating 3-D images of molecules

- Auto-changing advertising banners

A Java program is called an *applet*. Applets are stored with the Web page on the Web server. When you visit a Web page containing Java enhancements, the Java applet is downloaded to your computer automatically along with the Web page—you don't have to do anything special. Internet Explorer knows how to run Java applications, so an applet begins to run as soon as it arrives at your computer. To keep your computer safe, Internet Explorer introduces a Java security model that allows you to run powerful Java applets without worrying about harming your computer or threatening your privacy.

Java information Web site

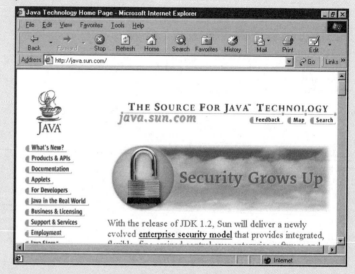

Javascript is a much simpler computer language that is used to add enhancements to Web pages. Javascript was developed by Netscape and unlike Java, it can't be used to write programs or applets. Javascript is used for simple tasks, such as highlighting a word when your mouse hovers over it or making a button look like it was pressed when you click it with a mouse. Internet Explorer supports Javascript and will render JavaScript-enhanced Web pages. While Javascript is generally transparent to end-users, you may encounter error messages about Javascript code not running properly in your Web browser.

Microsoft likes to describe ActiveX as a set of technologies for creating interactive Web sites. Unlike Java, Microsoft's ActiveX is not a programming language, but a set of software components that other programming languages (such as Java) can use. Just as add-ons and plug-ins extend the capabilities of Internet Explorer, ActiveX extends the capability of Java.

ActiveX programs are called *controls*. Just like Java applets, controls are downloaded and run on your computer when you visit a Web page that contains ActiveX. In the lower left corner of Internet Explorer window, you will see the words **Installing components while the ActiveX control is being downloaded**. Sometimes you might be presented with an on-screen certificate and asked if you would like the ActiveX control downloaded to your computer.

ActiveX is one of the technologies that is part of Microsoft's Component Object Model (COM) of programming. This model allows programmers to create individual programs for Web pages or applications that perform specific functions. Once written for one application, they can be reused in others. Here are some applications that run inside Internet Explorer utilizing ActiveX:

◆ PowerPoint presentations

◆ Interfaces to corporate databases

◆ International clocks

◆ Interactive subway maps

One big advantage that both Java and ActiveX have over plug-ins, add-ons, and viewers is that they work automatically. You don't need to go to the plug-in site, fill out a registration form, download a program, and run the installation program. Since Internet Explorer already has Java and ActiveX support installed, all you have to do is wait for the applet or control to automatically download; as soon as it arrives at your computer, it will begin executing.

ActiveX information Web site

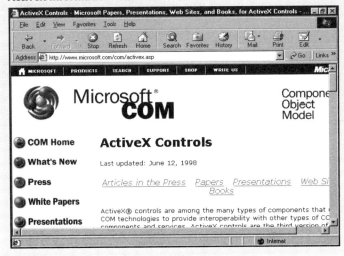

6

Using ActiveX Controls

ActiveX controls bring Web pages alive with effects such as live audio, scrolling banners, and much more. If you encounter a Web site that has an ActiveX control, Internet Explorer checks to see whether the control has been digitally signed. A *digitally signed control* has been independently certified to be free from computer viruses or destructive effects. You'll see a certificate indicating it's safe to install this software or a warning indicating it's not safe to continue.

SEE ALSO

See "Understanding Java and ActiveX" on page 100 for more information on ActiveX controls.

SEE ALSO

See "Controlling ActiveX and Java Content" on page 104 for information on security issues.

Use an ActiveX Control

1 Connect to a Web page containing an ActiveX control.

Try connecting to *http://carpoint.msn.com*.

2 Click a sound or video link.

3 If necessary, click Yes to accept the ActiveX control.

The ActiveX control downloads and executes.

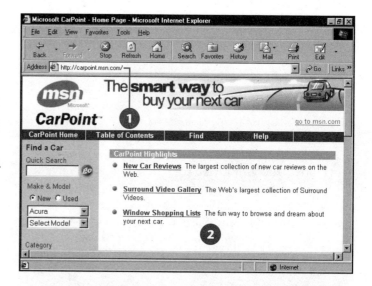

3-D surround video of current automobiles

Running Java Applets

Internet Explorer runs a Java applet while a Web page containing a Java applet is being displayed. There are thousands of Java applets on the Web. Examples include scrolling stock tickers, banners, spreadsheet-like calculators, and many more. Internet Explorer includes a *Just-In-Time* (JIT) compiler that speeds up the display and execution of Java applets. The JIT compiler turns on by default. If you encounter problems with a Java applet, you can turn off the JIT compiler option in the Advanced tab of the Internet Options dialog box.

SEE ALSO

See "Understanding Java and ActiveX" on page 100 for more information on Java.

SEE ALSO

See "Controlling ActiveX and Java Content" on page 104 for information on setting security when running Java applets.

Run a Java Applet

1 Connect to a Web page containing a Java applet.

Try connecting to *http:// www.gamelan.com* or *www.javasoft.com*.

2 Click to select a category, and then click a Web page with a Java applet.

The Java applet downloads and executes.

3 If necessary, enter information or select options associated with the Java applet.

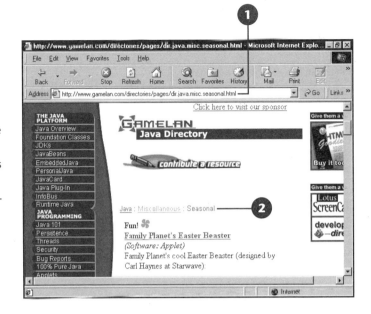

Turn Off the JIT Compiler

1 Click the Tools menu, and then click Internet Options.

2 Click the Advanced tab.

3 Scroll down to the Java VM area.

4 Click to clear the Java JIT Complier Enabled check box.

5 Click OK.

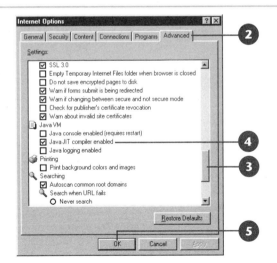

6

Controlling ActiveX and Java Content

With Internet Explorer you can control exactly how ActiveX controls and Java applets interact with your computer system. Using security zones, users and administrators can decide in advance what capabilities and levels of access to give to ActiveX controls and Java applets. For example, you can give broad access to Java applets from sources you trust, while restricting applets from unknown sources to safe places where they can't harm files.

SEE ALSO

See "Inserting ActiveX Controls" on page 234 for information on how to use ActiveX on your own Web pages.

SEE ALSO

See "Creating Security Zones" on page 78 for information on ways to secure the information that comes from the Internet to your computer.

Change ActiveX Security

1. Click the Tools menu, and then click Internet Options.

2. Click the Security tab.

3. Click the appropriate zone.

4. Drag the slider up for a higher level of security, or drag the slider down to lessen security.

5. To change specific settings, click Custom Level.

6. To control content, click the Enable, Prompt, or Disable option button for each of the following security levels.

   ◆ Script ActiveX Controls Marked Safe For Scripting

   ◆ Run ActiveX Controls And Plugins

   ◆ Download Signed ActiveX Controls

   ◆ Download Unsigned ActiveX Controls

   ◆ Initialize And Script ActiveX Controls Not Marked As Safe

7. Click OK.

8. Click OK.

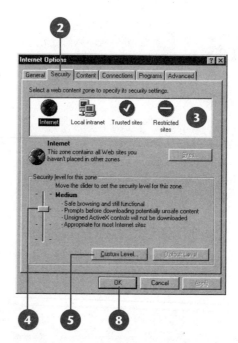

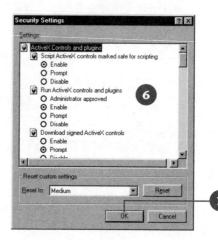

TIP

Reset security to Microsoft's recommended settings. *Click the Tools menu and then click Internet Options. Click the Security tab. Select the zone for which you want to reset the security settings. Click the Reset To Recommended Settings option.*

TIP

Problems with Java? *Some Web pages contain Java applets that are either poorly written or designed for specific functions that are provided by other browsers. Changing the Java settings may not make a difference. If you experience problems with a particular page, send e-mail to the page author or the Web site's Webmaster, about what happened.*

SEE ALSO

See "Understanding Java and ActiveX" on page 100 and "Running Java Applets" on page 103 for more information about Java.

Change Java Security Permissions

1 Click the Tools menu, and then click Internet Options.

2 Click the Security tab.

3 Select the zone for which you want to change security.

4 Click Custom Level.

5 Scroll down to the Java area.

6 Click one of the following security option buttons.

◆ Custom

◆ Low Safety

◆ Medium Safety

◆ High Safety

◆ Disable Java

7 Click OK.

8 Click OK.

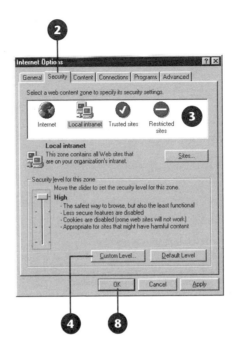

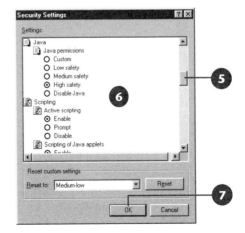

Playing Sounds and Videos

Internet Explorer comes with a built-in sound and video player called *Windows Media Player,* which can play most of the sounds and videos that you'll encounter on the Internet. You can sometimes recognize a hyperlink to a sound or video clip by its QuickTime or RealAudio logo or by a multimedia file extension. When you play a sound or video, a small control appears containing buttons that you can use to start and stop the media clip. You can also play the radio, also known as streaming audio, from the Internet using a built-in player called *Windows Media Radio.* You can access radio controls to play, stop, or control volume by displaying the Radio toolbar.

Play a Sound or Video from the Internet

1. Connect to a Web page containing a sound or video.

   Try connecting to *http://www.nba.com /theater.*

2. Click the sound or video link you want to play.

   The Windows Media Player appears in its own window.

3. Click the available buttons to play, pause, or stop the video. Drag the slider to control volume.

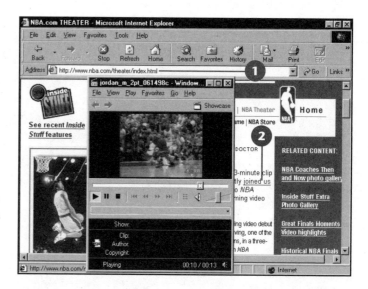

Play the Radio from the Internet

1. Click the View menu, point to Toolbars, and then click Radio. If you want, drag the Radio bar down to display the entire toolbar.

2. Click Radio Stations on the Radio bar, and then click Radio Station Guide.

3. Click the link to the radio station to which you want to listen.

   The radio sound is loaded and starts to play.

Currently selected radio station

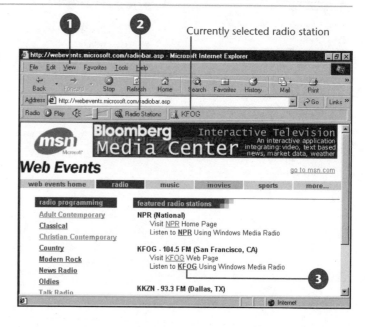

Play a Sound from Disk

1 In the Address bar, type **http://www.lycos.com/picturethis**.

2 Click the Sounds option button.

3 Enter a keyword for searching.

4 Click Go Get It.

If necessary, click Yes to acknowledge the warning message.

5 On the search results page, right-click the sound link you want to save, and then click Save Target As on the shortcut menu.

6 Specify the location to which you want to save the sound or video file.

7 Click Save.

8 Click OK when the download is complete.

9 Start Windows Explorer, and then double-click the sound file to listen to it.

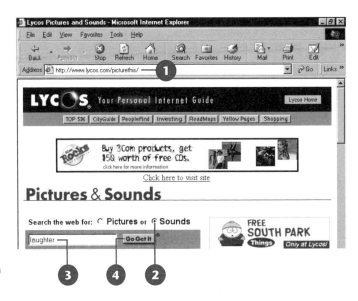

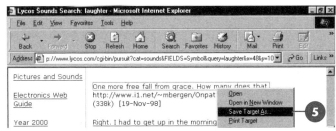

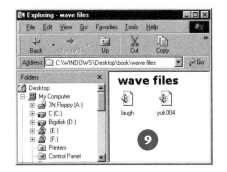

Changing Sound and Video Properties

Windows Media Player gives you control over how a sound or video clip plays. You can change the volume and timing, display size, control panel options and colors, and other advanced settings. You can also organize your favorite media clips just like you organize your favorite Web pages. If you decide that you do not want Web pages to display sounds, videos, or animations in Internet Explorer, you can turn off the corresponding functions. When you turn off these options, Web pages load much faster.

TIP

Start the Windows Media Player. *Click the Start button on the taskbar, point to Programs, point to Internet Explorer, and then click Windows Media Player.*

Change Sound and Video Properties

1. While listening to or viewing a media clip using Windows Media Player, click the View menu, and then click Options.

2. Click the Playback tab to change the volume, balance, size, and number of time the clip repeats.

3. Click the Player tab to choose player options.

4. Click the Custom Views tab to change the settings for compact and minimal viewing modes.

5. If necessary, click the Advanced tab, click Change, make changes to the buffer, protocol, and other advanced settings, and then click OK.

6. Click OK.

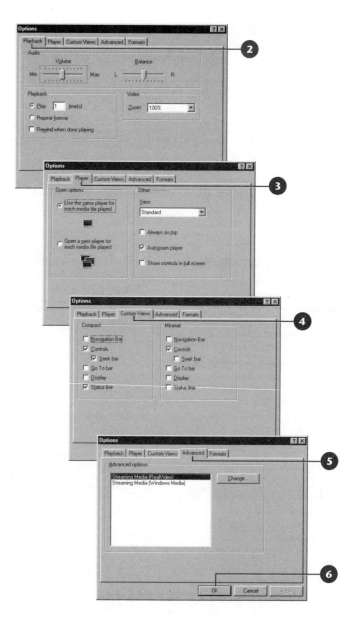

SEE ALSO

See "Playing Sounds and Videos" on page 106 for more information about Windows Media Player.

TIP

Display video statistics. *If you are curious about the speed or quality of the video you are watching, you can display the video frame-rate and network bandwidth. While playing a movie, right-click the Windows Media Player video screen, and then click Statistics.*

TRY THIS

Modem too slow for multimedia? *To improve performance, click the Tools menu, click Internet Options, click the Advanced tab, and then scroll to the Multimedia area. Click to deselect any of the following check boxes so the media will not play when the Web page is displayed:*
- ◆ *Play animations*
- ◆ *Play videos*
- ◆ *Play sounds*

SEE ALSO

See "Broadcasting Audio and Video with NetShow" on page 110 for information about NetShow.

Organize Your Media Favorites

1. While listening to or viewing a media clip using the Windows Media Player, click the Favorites menu, and then click Organize Favorites.

2. Click a favorite.

3. To move the selected favorite into another folder, click Move To Folder, and then select a folder.

4. To change the name of your selected favorite, click Rename, type a new name, and then press Enter.

5. To delete the selected favorite, click Delete and then click OK to move the file to the Recycle Bin.

6. When you're done, click Close.

7. Continue listening to or viewing the media clip, and when you're done, close the file.

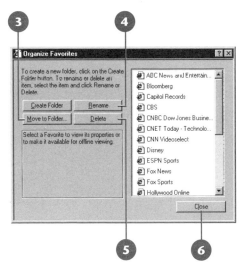

6

Broadcasting Audio and Video with NetShow

Some Web sites offer *NetShow Services* to provide an easy, powerful way to broadcast, or "stream," multimedia across the Internet and intranets. *Streaming* allows content to be delivered to the visitor as a continuous flow of data with little wait before the playback begins. You can view and listen to live or recorded broadcasts with the benefit of instant play—no waiting for content to download. Internet Explorer uses the Media Player to play NetShow content. All you need to do is visit a Web site containing NetShow Services and click a NetShow link.

Display NetShow Content

1 Connect to a Web site that uses NetShow.

Try connecting to the CBS NetShow Web site at *http://www.cbs.com/netshow.*

2 Click a link to play the NetShow content, choosing the appropriate speed for your link.

3 If necessary, click Yes to accept the Security Warning message.

4 Watch the NetShow clip using Media Player.

The NetShow content plays continuously.

5 When you're done watching the clip, click the Close button.

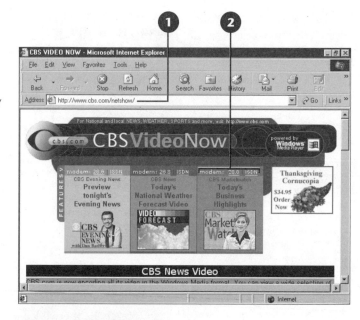

Having trouble playing NetShow content? *Start the Windows Media Player, click the Help menu, and then click Help Topics. Click the Index tab, type* **troubleshooting** *and then click Display. Follow the Help information.*

Shrink the player without shrinking the video screen. *While you are watching a NetShow clip, click the View menu, and then click Minimal.*

Look for upcoming NetShow events. *Start the Windows Media Player, and then click the Web Events button. Internet Explorer will display the MSN Web Events Web page.*

See "Using Add-Ons and Viewers" on page 98 for more information about viewing videos.

Display NetShow Content with the NetShow Player

1. Click the Start button on the taskbar, point to Programs, and then point to Internet Explorer.

2. Click Windows Media Player.

3. Click the File menu, and then click Open.

4. Type the location of the ASF or ASX file that you want to view, or click the Browse button to find the exact file location.

5. Click OK.

   The NetShow content plays continuously.

6. When you're done, click the Close button to quit Windows Media Player.

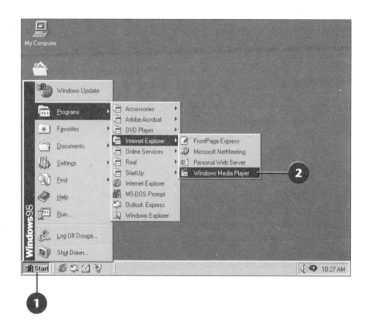

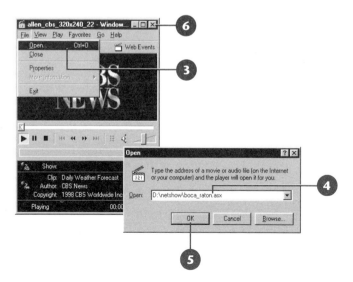

Playing a VRML Animation

VRML (*Virtual Reality Modeling Language*) is a graphic format that places viewers "inside" a scene and allows them to change their point of view and relative location. Microsoft VRML is an Internet Explorer add-on program that displays 3-D interactive animation within Internet Explorer.

TIP

Get more information about VRML. *Visit Microsoft's Virtual Support Web page at* **http://www.microsoft.com /vrml** *for general and download information.*

TRY THIS

Check out these VRML Web sites. *Connect to the following VRML Web sites:*
http://www.microsoft.com/vrml
http://www.planet9.com
http://www.refraction.com/vrml
http://www.virtpark.com/theme /proteinman/
http://www.meshmart.org/wow/
http://www.vrvision.com/

Play a VRML Animation

1. Connect to a Web page containing a VRML animation.

   Try connecting to *http:// www.refraction.com/vrml*.

2. If necessary, click a VRML index link to display a list of animations.

3. Click a link to a VRML animation.

   You may need to download and install the VRML viewer.

4. Click any of the following buttons along the edge of the VRML animation to navigate.

   ◆ W to walk

   ◆ P to pan

   ◆ T to turn

   ◆ R to roll

   ◆ G to go to a location

   ◆ S to study objects

   ◆ Z to zoom out

   ◆ Up to straighten up

   ◆ V to view right or left

   ◆ R to restore the view

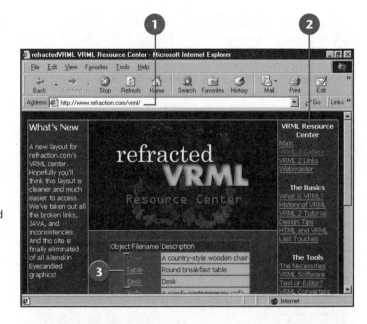

Playing an Internet Game

Using Microsoft's DirectX multimedia technology, you can play games over the Internet. For example, the Microsoft Internet Gaming Zone Web site is an easy-to-use and free Internet-based multiplayer gaming service that offers a wide variety of great games. If you are running Internet Explorer under Windows 95, you may need to install the DirectX component. If you are running Windows 98, you can get right to the gaming—DirectX comes installed.

TRY THIS

Check out these Internet gaming Web sites. *Connect to the following Internet gaming Web sites:*
http://www.gamesville.com
http://www.playsite.com

Find a Gaming Web Site and Play a Game over the Internet

1 Connect to a Web site that offers online games.

Try connecting to *http://www.zone.com.*

2 Click the Play Games link.

3 Accept any security warnings for components that may be required for game play.

4 Click the game category and select a game to play.

5 Follow the instructions to sign up for a free account.

6 Click Install. Accept the default directory for program installation.

7 Click Yes to accept the Gaming Zone License agreement. Additional files may be downloaded at this time.

8 Click Yes if you want a link to the Gaming Zone placed on the desktop.

9 Sign in with your member name and password to begin game play.

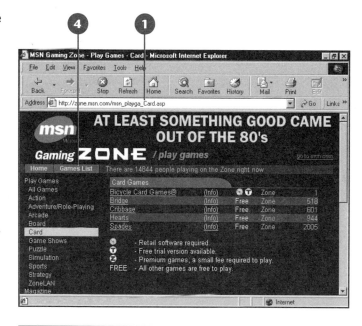

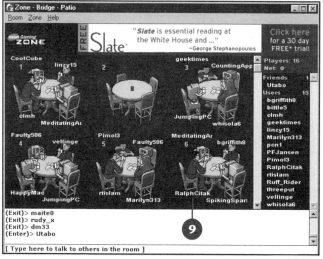

Exchanging E-Mail Using Outlook Express

IN THIS SECTION

Starting Outlook Express

New **Setting Up Your Account**

New **Viewing the Outlook Express Start Page and Window**

Adding Contacts to the Address Book

Composing and Sending E-Mail

Reading and Replying to E-Mail

Attaching a File to E-Mail

Deleting Your E-Mail

Managing Your E-Mail

New **Creating E-Mail Stationery**

New **Diverting Incoming E-Mail**

New **Working with Multiple Accounts**

Finding People on the Web

Printing in Outlook Express

f you're like many people today who are using the Internet to communicate with friends and business associates, you probably have piles of information from names to e-mail addresses that you often need at your disposal. Unless this information is in one convenient place that allows you immediate access to exactly what you need, the information becomes ineffective and you become unproductive. Microsoft Outlook Express solves these problems by integrating management and organization tools into one simple system.

Using Outlook Express, you can:

◆ Create and send mail messages

◆ Manage multiple accounts with different Internet service providers

◆ Use the Windows Address Book to store and retrieve e-mail addresses

◆ Create stationery or add a personal signature to your e-mail messages

◆ Attach a file to your e-mail message

◆ Find people you know on the Web

◆ Print mail messages

Starting Outlook Express

Once you are at your computer's desktop, you can start Outlook Express. You can start Outlook Express by using the Launch Microsoft Outlook button on the Quick Launch toolbar or by using the Start menu on the taskbar. Starting Outlook Express with the Quick Launch button is the easiest since it takes only one click.

TIP

Add the Quick Launch toolbar to your screen. *If you do not see the Quick Launch toolbar on the taskbar, right-click the taskbar, point to Toolbars, and then click Quick Launch.*

TIP

Remove your Outlook Express Desktop Icon. *The installation of Internet Explorer may have placed an icon on your desktop for Outlook Express. Delete the icon from your desktop by dragging it to the Recycle Bin.*

Start Outlook Express from the Quick Launch Toolbar

1. Click the Launch Outlook Express button on the Quick Launch toolbar.

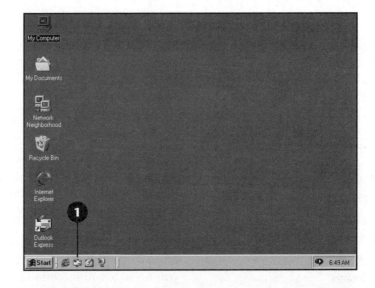

Start Outlook Express from the Start Menu

1. Click the Start button on the taskbar.

2. Point to Programs.

3. Click Outlook Express.

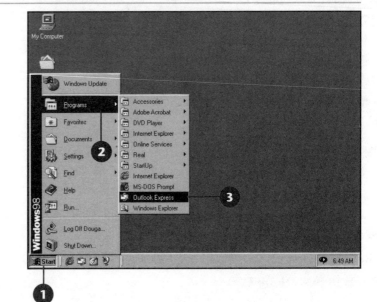

Setting Up Your Account

When you first start Outlook Express, the Internet Connection Wizard begins, asking you about your account setup information. You will need to get most of this information from your Internet service provider (ISP). Your ISP will support either Post Office Protocol (POP) or Internet Message Access Protocol (IMAP). POP is the more common but older protocol. IMAP is the preferred way of handling e-mail. Before you start Outlook Express for the first time, ask your ISP for necessary IMAP or POP configuration information.

SEE ALSO

See "Working with Multiple Accounts" on page 134 for information on how to set up more than one e-mail account.

Set Up an Account from the Internet Connection Wizard

1. Start Outlook Express for the first time, and the Internet Connection Wizard automatically begins.

2. Type your name. Click Next to continue.

3. Enter your e-mail address. Click Next to continue.

4. Click the drop-down arrow, and then select the incoming mail server you want to use.

5. Enter the name of the incoming mail server.

6. Enter the name of the outgoing mail server. Click Next to continue.

7. Enter your account name, and then enter a password. Click Next to continue.

8. Click Finish.

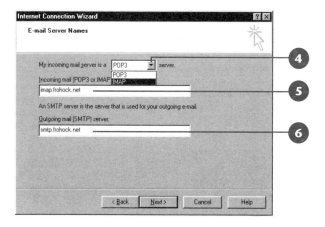

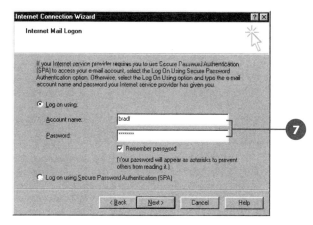

Viewing the Outlook
Express Start Page

E-Mail
The Create A New Mail Message link jumps you to the Create
Message dialog box. The Read Mail link jumps you directly
to mail messages you haven't read and to your Inbox.

Newsgroups
The Setup A Newsgroups
Account link contains Internet
newsgroups that you can
view. You can also subscribe
to them from here.

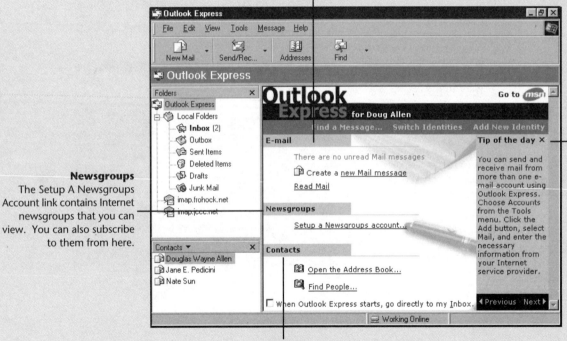

Tip of the Day
This window provides
helpful information about
Outlook Express features
and tasks.

Contacts
The Open The Address Book link makes entering or
editing contact information fast and easy. The Find
People link allows you to quickly find the information
on the people you communicate with.

Viewing the Outlook
Express Window

Menu bar
The menu bar gives you access to all Outlook Express options.

Toolbar
The toolbar contains buttons for commands you can use while you read your mail messages.

Outlook Express start page
Click to return to the Outlook Express start page.

Folder list
The folder list contains all the folders in Outlook Express. If you have an IMAP account, your IMAP folders will also be displayed.

Contacts list
The contacts list displays all the names of the people in your list of contacts.

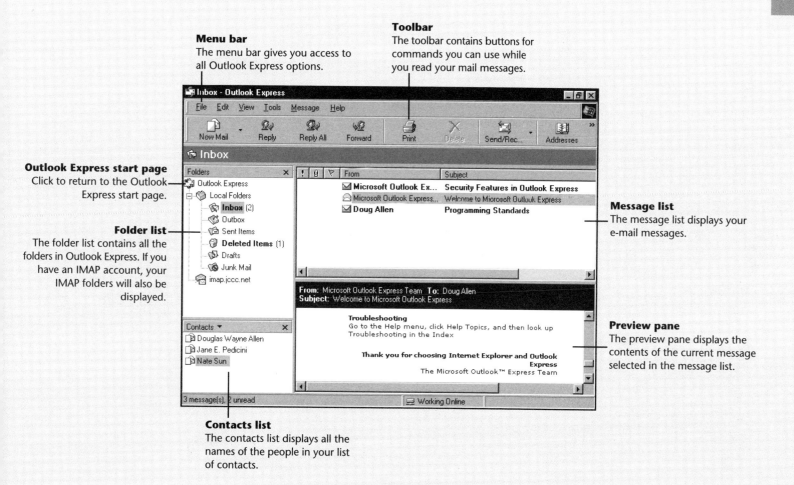

Message list
The message list displays your e-mail messages.

Preview pane
The preview pane displays the contents of the current message selected in the message list.

Adding Contacts to the Address Book

A *contact* is a person or company that you communicate with. One contact can often have several mailing addresses, phone numbers, or e-mail addresses. You can store this information in the Address Book along with other detailed information such as job title, cellular phone number, and Web page addresses. A contact can also be a part of a *contact group*, which is a group of people you communicate with on a regular basis, such as your colleagues at work.

TRY THIS

Organize your contacts in folders. *Click the Address Book button on the toolbar, click the File menu, and then click New Folder. Choose a folder name and then click OK. Click the new folder before adding contacts and they will be stored in the folder.*

Add a New Contact to the Address Book

1. Click the Addresses button on the toolbar, or click the Open Address Book link on the Outlook Express start page.

2. Click the New button on the toolbar.

3. Click New Contact.

4. Enter the new contact's name.

5. Enter the e-mail address, and then click Add.

6. Click the other available tabs to enter additional information about the contact.

7. Click OK.

8. Click the Close button to close the Address Book.

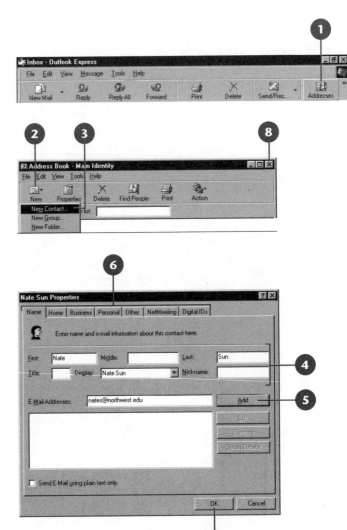

Add a contact from the start page. *When viewing the Outlook Express start page, click New Contact on the Contacts drop-down menu in the contacts list.*

Organize your Address Book. *Sort your Address Book by name, e-mail address, or phone number by clicking on the appropriate column heading. You can switch the sorting method from ascending to descending by clicking the same column heading again.*

Add a contact when creating a group. *To add a new contact while creating a group, simply enter the name and e-mail address in the Add This Entry To The Group section, and then click Add.*

Change information about a contact when creating a group. *To change contact information while creating a group, click the contact name, click Properties, enter the necessary contact information, and then click OK.*

Create a Contact Group

1. Click the Address Book button on the toolbar.

2. Click the New button on the toolbar, and then click New Group.

3. Type a name for the new group.

4. Click Select Members to display your current list of contacts.

5. Click the folder list drop-down arrow, and then choose the folder in which you want to save the contact group.

6. Select each member in the list of contacts you want to add to the new group, and then click Select.

7. Repeat steps 5 and 6 until all contacts have been added.

8. Click OK.

9. To remove a contact from the group, click the contact, and then click Remove.

10. Click OK.

11. When you're done, close the Address Book.

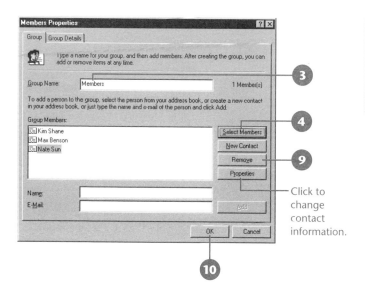

Click to change contact information.

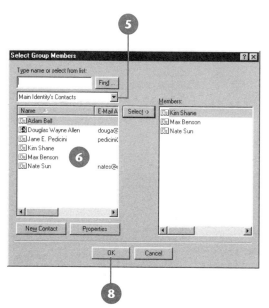

Composing and Sending E-Mail

E-mail messages follow a standard memo format with lines for the sender, recipient, date, and subject. To address an e-mail message, you can enter the nickname you've given to a contact, the contact's real name, or the recipient's complete e-mail address if he or she isn't in your list of contacts. You can also select contact names from the Address Book if you can't remember someone's name or nickname. You can send the same e-mail message to more than one individual or to a contact group.

SEE ALSO

See "Creating E-Mail Stationery" on page 130 for information on how to create a new message using stationery.

TIP

Send and receive from an account. *Click the Send/Recv drop-down arrow, and then click the account you want.*

Compose and Send an E-Mail

1. Click the New Mail button on the toolbar, or click the Create A New Mail Message link on the Outlook Express start page.

2. Type the recipient's name or nickname.

3. If you want, click the To button to open the Select Recipients dialog box.

4. Click a recipient or group.

5. Click one of the following.

   ◆ The To button if you want the recipient to receive the message and to see the addresses in the To and Cc fields.

   ◆ The Cc button if you want the recipient to receive a copy of the message and to see the addresses in the To and Cc fields.

   ◆ The Bcc button if you want the recipient to receive a copy of the message but not be listed as a recipient on any other copy of the message.

6. Click OK.

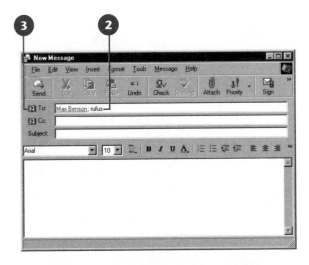

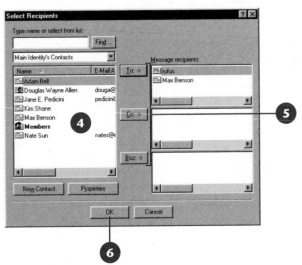

TRY THIS

Add a contact when addressing an e-mail message. *To add a new contact while you are selecting recipients, click the New Contact button. Enter the necessary contact information on each of the appropriate tabs, and then click OK.*

TIP

Send a Web page using Outlook Express. *Open any Web site in Internet Explorer. Click the File menu, point to Send, and then click Page By Email or Link By Email. Outlook Express opens with the Web page as an attached file in the Compose Message dialog box.*

TIP

Three Jacobs in your contact list? *If you have several people with the same first name or similar first names, you can enter that name by itself on the To line. When you click the Send button, Outlook Express will display a list of all contacts that share that name or that part of a name. Click the one you want to send the e-mail message to, and then click OK.*

7 Click in the Subject box, and then enter a brief description of your message.

8 Click in the message box, and type the text of your message.

9 If you want, click the Attach File button on the toolbar to attach a file to the message.

10 If you want, click the Priority button drop-down arrow on the toolbar, and then select a priority level.

11 If you want, use the commands on the Formatting toolbar to format your message.

12 Click the Send button on the toolbar. Or click the File menu, click Send Later, and then click OK to confirm that the message has been placed in your Outbox folder.

13 If you chose to Send Later, click the Send/Recv button on the toolbar to contact the mail server and deliver your message.

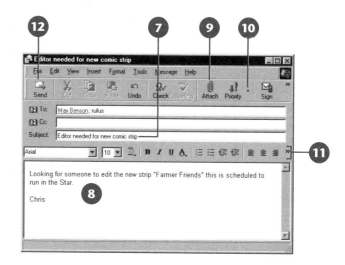

E-MAIL MESSAGE ICONS	
Icon	**Description**
	This message has been read. The message heading text appears in normal text type.
	This message has not been read. The message heading text appears in boldface text type.
	This message has one or more files attached to it.
	The message has been marked as high priority by the sender.
	The message has been marked as low priority by the sender.

Reading and Replying to E-Mail

Mail can be sent to you anytime day or night—even when your computer is turned off. To retrieve your e-mail, you can manually connect to your mail server or set Outlook Express to automatically retrieve your e-mail messages while you are connected to the Internet. New e-mail messages appear in the Inbox along with any messages you haven't yet stored elsewhere or deleted. After reading an e-mail message, you can automatically address a response to the sender or forward the e-mail message on to other appropriate recipients.

SEE ALSO

See "Diverting Incoming E-Mail to Folders" on page 132 for information on how to send your e-mail messages directly to a specified folder.

Retrieve E-Mail

1. Click the Send/Recv button on the toolbar, or click the Send/Recv drop-down arrow, and then click Receive All.

Open and Read an E-Mail

1. Click the Inbox icon in the folder list, or click the Read Mail link on the Outlook Express start page.

2. Double-click the e-mail message you want to read. The message opens in its own window, making it easier to read.

3. Click the Previous or Next button on the toolbar to read additional e-mail messages (if any).

This symbol indicates a high-priority message.

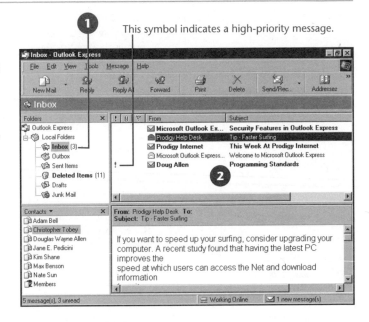

Reply to an E-Mail

1. Open the e-mail message you want to reply to.

2. Click the Reply button to respond to just the sender, or click the Reply All button to respond to the sender and to all other recipients.

TIP

Get new mail quickly. *You can set up Outlook Express to automatically retrieve new e-mail messages. Click the Tools menu, click Options, and then set the appropriate retrieval options on the General and Connection tabs.*

TIP

Forward as an attachment. *You can forward any message as an attachment on another e-mail message. Right-click the message you want to attach, and then click Forward on the shortcut menu.*

TIP

Attachments aren't sent on replies. *When you reply to a message that had an attachment, the attachment isn't returned to the original sender. You can forward the message to the original sender if you need to send the attachment back.*

SEE ALSO

See "Reading News" on page 146 for information on using column buttons to sort e-mail messages.

③ Type your message.

④ Attach any files to send.

⑤ Click the Send button on the toolbar. Or click the File menu, click Send Later, and then Click OK to confirm that the message has been placed in your Outbox folder.

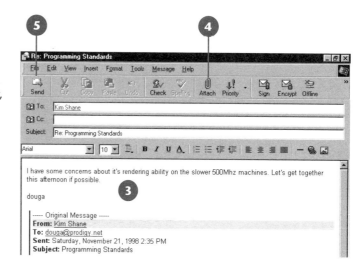

Forward an E-Mail

① Open the e-mail message you want to forward.

② Click the Forward button on the toolbar.

③ Type the name(s) of the recipient(s), or click the To button, and then select the recipient(s).

④ Type your message.

⑤ Attach any files to send.

⑥ Click the Send button on the toolbar. Or click the File menu, click Send Later, and then click OK to confirm the message has been placed in your Outlook folder.

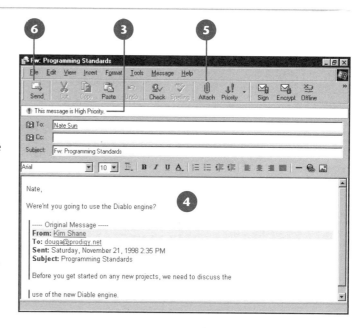

Attaching a File to E-Mail

A powerful feature of e-mail is the ability to share files. You can attach one or more files, such as a picture or a document, to an e-mail message. The recipients of the e-mail message then open the file in the program in which the file was created (if they have the particular application installed on their computer). For example, if you create a budget in Excel, you can attach the spreadsheet to an e-mail message to your boss. If your boss also has Excel, she can open the spreadsheet simply by double-clicking the Excel icon in her e-mail message. Be careful when sending files: make sure that the recipient has the same version of the program.

Attach a File to an E-Mail Message

1. Compose a new message, or open an existing message.

2. Click the Attach button on the toolbar.

3. Select the drive and folder that contains the file you want to attach.

4. Click to select the file.

5. Click Attach. You can attach more than one file to your e-mail message.

6. Click the Send button on the toolbar. Or click the File menu, click Send Later, and then click OK to confirm that the message has been placed in your Outbox folder.

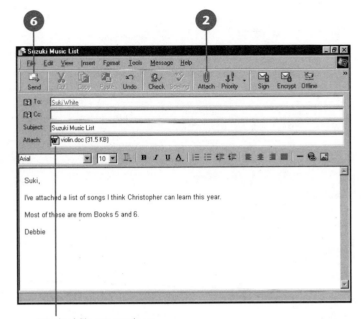

Attached file appears here.

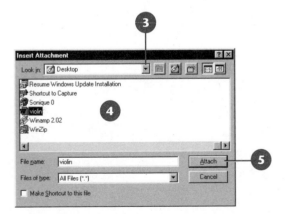

Deleting Your E-Mail

When you delete an e-mail message, Outlook Express simply moves it into the Deleted Items folder. If you want to recover a deleted message, you just have to retrieve it from the Deleted Items folder. To get rid of a message permanently, you need to open the Deleted Items folder, select the message, and click Delete. E-mail messages are also automatically placed in the Sent Items folder every time you send them. You will want to periodically open the Sent Items folder and delete messages so your mail account doesn't get too large. You can also use maintenance options to help you automatically clean up.

TIP

Delete unwanted e-mail messages. *Click a folder icon in the folder list, click the e-mail you want to delete, and then click the Delete button on the toolbar.*

Recover an E-Mail Message from the Deleted Items Folder

1 Click the Deleted Items folder in the folder list to open the folder.

2 Select the e-mail message you want to retrieve.

3 Drag the e-mail message to another folder.

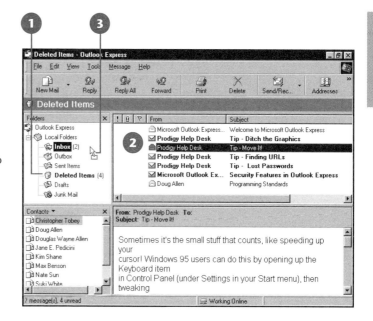

Change E-Mail Maintenance Options

1 Click the Tools menu, and then click Options.

2 Click the Maintenance tab.

3 Click to select the maintenance options you want.

   ◆ Delete messages on exit or after a certain number of days.

   ◆ Compact messages to save space.

4 Click OK.

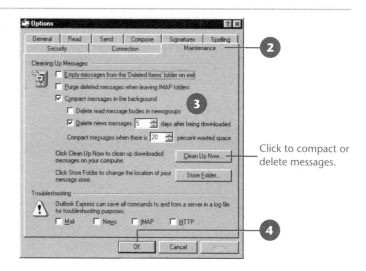

Click to compact or delete messages.

Managing Your E-Mail

One problem that can arise as you receive e-mail is an overabundance of e-mail messages in your Inbox. To help you manage your e-mail messages, Outlook Express lets you create folders for organized storage of your messages. Move messages to folders and subfolders, creating new folders as you need them. Storing messages in other folders and deleting un-wanted messages make it easier to see the new e-mail messages you receive. If you want to store messages on your local hard disk, Out-look Express allows you to save an e-mail message as a file.

TIP

Create folders on the fly.
Select an e-mail message, click the Edit menu, click Move To Folder, click New Folder, enter the name of the new folder, and then click OK.

Create a New Folder

1 Right-click any folder in the folder list, and then click New Folder.

2 Type a name for the new folder.

3 Click the folder in which you want to place the new folder.

◆ Click Local Folders to place the folder in the folder list.

◆ Click one of the other folders in the list to make the new folder a subfolder.

4 Click OK.

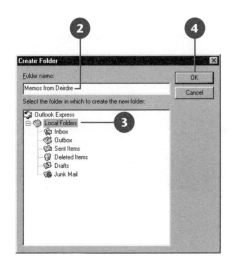

Organize Your E-Mail Messages in Folders

1 Select the e-mail message you want to move. If necessary, hold the Ctrl key and click to select multiple e-mail messages.

2 Drag the e-mail message(s) to the new folder.

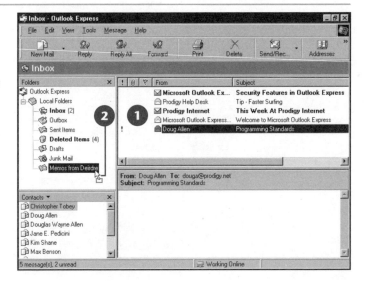

TIP

Save a draft of an e-mail message in the Drafts folder. *A draft is an e-mail message you have not finished yet. Open a new or existing e-mail, click the File menu, and then click Save. Click the Drafts folder in the folder list, and then double-click the e-mail message to view it.*

TIP

Compact a folder to save space. *Click the folder you want to compact in the folder list, click the File menu, point to Folder, and then click Compact.*

SEE ALSO

See "Deleting Your E-Mail" on page 127 for information on working with the Deleted Items folder.

TRY THIS

Use sorting to help manage your e-mail messages. *Click the column headings in a folder where your e-mail messages are stored, such as your Inbox, to sort your messages by recipient, subject, date received, or date sent. You can sort the messages in ascending or descending order.*

Save an E-Mail Message as a File

1 Double-click the e-mail message you want to save.

2 Click the File menu, and then click Save As.

3 Click the Save In drop-down arrow, and then select the drive and folder where you want to store the message.

4 Click the Save As Type drop-down arrow, and then click an available file type.

5 Type a new filename for the e-mail message you are saving.

6 Click Save.

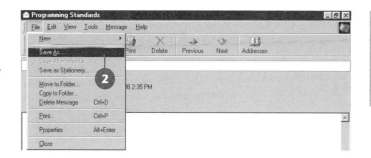

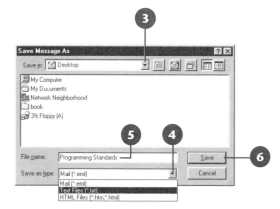

Open a Saved E-Mail Message

1 Use Windows Explorer to locate the saved message file.

2 Double-click the file. If you saved an e-mail message in EML format, Outlook Express starts and displays the message. If you saved a message in TXT format, Notepad opens and displays the message.

Creating E-Mail Stationery

Tired of the typical bland, unexciting look of e-mail? Well, if so, Outlook Express has the answer—Outlook Express stationery. This feature allows you to create e-mail messages with their own colorful background and font styles. You can also customize your messages with a signature or by attaching your business card. A *signature* is any file, text file with your signature, or photo of yourself you choose to use as your signature. Several stationery styles are included with Outlook Express.

TIP

Create a message using other or new stationery.
Click the New Mail button drop-down arrow on the toolbar, and then select the stationery you want to use, or click Select Stationery to select from other choices or create a new one.

Create Stationery Using the Stationery Setup Wizard

1. Click the Tools menu, and then click Options.

2. Click the Compose tab.

3. Click Create New.

4. Click Next to begin the Stationery Setup Wizard.

5. Enter the information for the stationery background picture or color. Click Next to continue.

6. Choose the font, font size, and color. Click Next to continue.

7. Choose the left and top margin. Click Next to continue.

8. Enter a name for your stationery. Click Finish.

9. Click to select the Mail check box to always include stationery with your e-mail messages.

10. Click Select to choose the standard stationery. Click OK to continue.

11. Click OK.

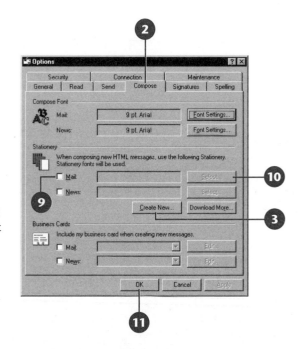

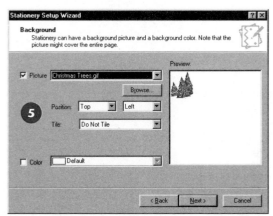

Add your signature to your message quickly. *In an e-mail message, click to place the insertion point where you want the signature, click the Insert menu, and then click Signature to insert your default signature. If you have more than one signature, point to Signature, and then click the signature you want to use for your message.*

Signatures don't have to be just your name. *If you have standard information that you find yourself entering repeatedly in your e-mail messages, create a signature for the information. When composing an e-mail message, you can insert your custom information with the Insert Signature drop-down arrow to display a list of signatures.*

Use a business card instead of a signature. *A business card is your contact information from the Address Book. Click the Tools menu, click Options, click the Compose tab, click to select the Mail check box in the Business Card section, and then click OK.*

Create a Signature

1. Click the Tools menu, and then click Options.

2. Click the Signatures tab.

3. Click New to create a new signature.

4. Type the information for the signature. If available, select the file that contains your signature information.

5. To enter more than one signature, repeat steps 3 and 4.

6. Select the signature you want to use most of the time, and then click Set As Default.

7. If you want, click to select the Add Signatures To All Outgoing Messages check box, or click to select the Don't Add Signatures To Replies And Forwards check box. You can select both options if you want.

8. Click OK.

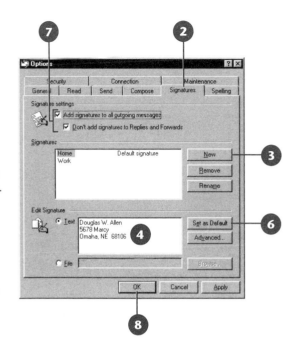

Diverting Incoming E-Mail to Folders

Outlook Express can direct incoming e-mail messages that meet certain criteria that you specify to specific folders. Let's say that you have a friend who loves sending you funny e-mail, but you often don't have time to read it right away. You can set the Inbox Assistant to direct your friend's messages to a folder where the messages are stored until you read them at a later time. You can also prevent junk mail from filling up your Inbox by automatically deleting mail from specific senders.

SEE ALSO

See "Managing Your E-Mail" on page 128 for information on how to create additional custom folders for storing messages.

Set Rules for Incoming E-Mail

1. Click the Tools menu, point to Message Rules, and then click Mail.

   If no rules are set, skip to step 3.

2. Click New to create a new rule or select a rule and click Modify to edit an existing one.

3. Click the appropriate conditions for your rule.

4. Click the appropriate actions for your rule.

5. In the Rule Description box, click a link to enter the underlying information for that condition or action.

6. Specify the criteria for your rule in the selection dialog box that appears, and then click OK.

7. Repeat steps 5 and 6 for each condition and action you have set.

8. Enter a name for this rule.

9. Click OK.

10. Click OK.

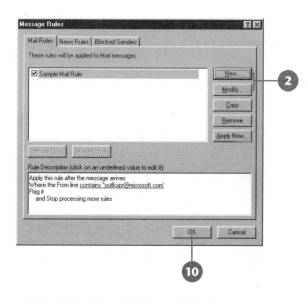

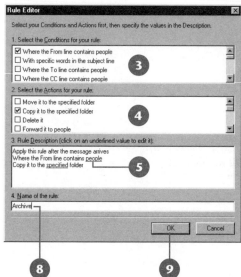

Prioritize your message rules. *If you have two or more message rules that might act on the same incoming message, you may want to prioritize the order of your rules. Click the Tools menu, point to Message Rules, and then click Mail. Click the rule you want to move, and then click the Move Up or Move Down button to change the order.*

Apply rules right now. *You can apply rules that you've just created to messages that you have already received. Click the Tools menu, point to Message Rules, and then click Mail. Click Apply Rules Now. Select the rule(s) you want to apply and the folder that contains the messages. Click Apply Now.*

Change the block senders list. *Click the Tools menu, point to Message Rules, and then click Block Senders List. E-Mail from these senders will not go into any folder, including your Inbox. Click to clear the Mail check box to unblock a sender, or select a sender and click Remove to delete it.*

Block Junk E-Mail from a Sender

1. Select the e-mail you want to block.

2. Click the Message menu, and then click Block Sender.

   The sender is added to your blocked senders list.

3. Click Yes or No to remove all messages from this sender from the current folder.

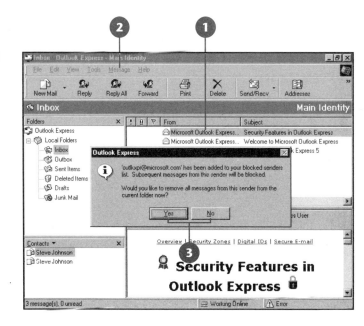

Working with Multiple Accounts

You can set up Outlook Express to receive e-mail from different accounts, or if several people share an e-mail account, you can set up folders for each person, and then route incoming mail messages to each individual's folder. If multiple users use the same computer, Outlook Express can create a separate account for each user, called an *identity*. You can add, modify, delete, and switch identities.

SEE ALSO

See "Setting Up Your Account" on page 117 for information about e-mail accounts.

Add a New E-Mail Account

① Click the Tools menu, and then click Accounts.

② Click the Mail tab.

③ Click Add, and then click Mail.

④ Accept the default display name, or type a new name. Click Next to continue.

⑤ If your e-mail address appears correctly, click Next to continue; otherwise type the correct address.

⑥ Enter the correct information for your e-mail server. Click Next to continue.

⑦ Enter your account name and a password. Click Next to continue.

⑧ Click Finish.

⑨ Click Close to save your new account settings.

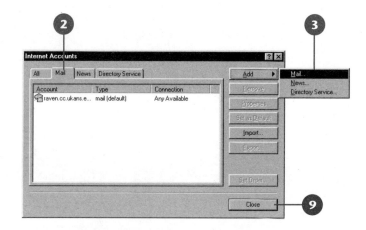

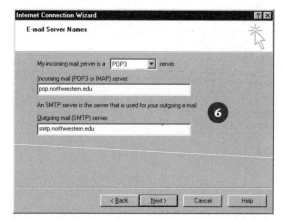

Add a New Identity

1. Click the File menu, point to Identities, and then click Add New Identity.

2. Type an identity name.

3. If you want, click to select the Ask Me For A Password When I Start check box, enter a new password, enter a confirm new password, and then click OK.

4. Click OK.

5. Click No to switch now.

6. Click Close.

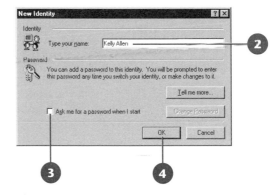

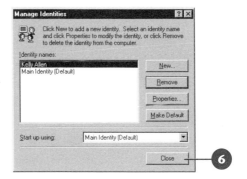

Switch Identities

1. Click the File menu, and then click Switch Identities.

2. Click the name you want to switch to.

3. To add or modify an identity, click Manage Identities.

4. Click OK.

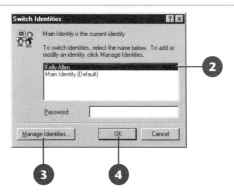

Finding People on the Web

Outlook Express provides seven popular directory service accounts to help you search for people on the Internet. Each directory service accesses different databases on the Internet, which means you have a greater possibility of finding someone if you try multiple services. If you have lots of contact listings, you can also find people in your own Address Book quickly and efficiently, without having to scroll through the entire Address book.

Locate a Person on the Web

1. Click the Edit menu, point to Find, and then click People.

2. Click the Look In drop-down arrow, and select the directory service.

3. Enter the contact's name or e-mail account or both.

4. Click Find Now.

5. If you find the person and you want to keep the information for future use, select the name, and then click Add To Address Book.

6. Click Close.

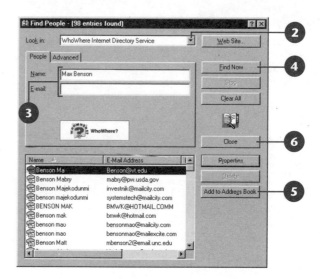

Locate a Contact in Your Address Book

1. Click the Edit menu, point to Find, and then click People.

2. Click the Look In drop-down arrow, and then select Address Book.

3. Type the contact's name, e-mail address, or any other available information.

4. Click Find Now.

5. Click Close.

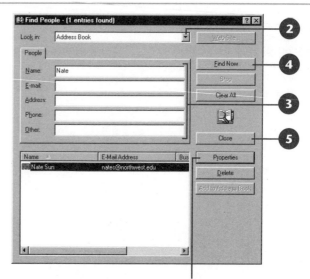

Click to change contact properties.

Importing and Exporting E-Mail Settings

Outlook Express can import the address book, mail messages, and account settings from many of the most popular e-mail programs. You can also export your messages or address book information from Outlook Express to work with other programs.

TIP

Import mail messages from another e-mail program. *Click the File menu, point to Import, and then click Messages. Select the e-mail program, and then follow the wizard instructions to import the e-mail messages.*

TIP

Export messages to Microsoft Outlook or Exchange only. *Click the File menu, point to Export, click Messages, and then click OK.*

Import an Address Book

1. Click the File menu, point to Import, and then click Other Address Book.

2. Click the name of the program that has the addresses.

3. Click Import.

4. Follow the additional instructions.

5. Click OK.

6. Click Close.

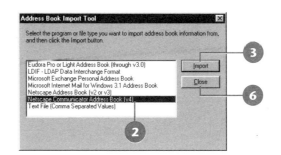

Export your Address Book to a Text File

1. Click the File menu, point to Export, and then click Address Book.

2. Click Text File (Comma Separated Values), and then click Export.

3. Type a filename. Click Next to continue.

4. Select the fields for exporting.

5. Click Finish.

6. Click OK.

7. Click Close.

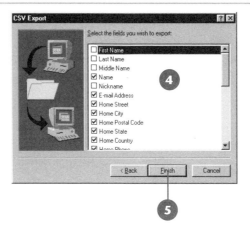

Printing in Outlook Express

You can print your mail messages from any folder at any time using Outlook Express. You can also open the Address Book and print contact information. Printing styles available from the Address Book include Memo, Business Card, and Phone List. The Memo style prints all the information you have for a contact with description titles. The Business Card style prints the contact information without description titles. The Phone List option prints all the phone numbers for a contact.

TRY THIS

Print a list of contacts.
Take a moment to print one of your contact groups using the Phone List option. You'll have a handy printout of the names and phone numbers of the contacts in the group.

Print an E-Mail Message

1 Open the mail message you want to print.

2 Click the File menu, and then click Print.

3 Specify a print range.

4 Specify the number of copies you want to print.

5 Click OK.

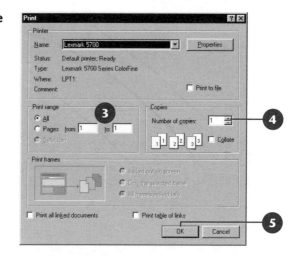

Print Contact Information from the Address Book

1 Open your Address Book.

2 Click the contact whose information you want to print.

3 Click the File menu, and then click Print.

4 Specify a print range.

5 Click the Print Style option you want to use.

6 Specify the number of copies you want to print.

7 Click OK.

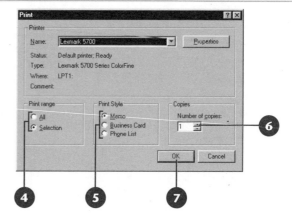

IN THIS SECTION

Starting Outlook Express News

New **Viewing the News Window**

Understanding Newsgroups

New **Configuring the News Reader**

Subscribing to a Newsgroup

Reading the News

New **Finding a Particular Newsgroup or Message**

Posting Messages

New **Reading Messages Offline**

New **Customizing the Outlook Express Window**

New **Changing Outlook Express Message Options**

Getting a Personal Certificate

Exploring Outlook Express News

8

Outlook Express News provides a simple and fun way to participate in ongoing discussions about your hobbies, work, or other topics that interest you. Unlike local organizations, newsgroups enable you to:

◆ Meet people from around the world with similar interests

◆ Get answers to questions you might have on a subject

◆ Share your knowledge and expertise with others

◆ Start a new discussion or participate in an ongoing one

◆ Join a conversation at your leisure—read and reply to messages at your own convenience

Why Newsgroups?

Imagine a conversation with a group of friends about a topic of mutual interest. Now imagine that conversation taking place at two in the morning with people around the world. That's what newsgroups enable you to do. Although joining a newsgroup might seem complicated, if you have exchanged e-mail with others, you already know how to correspond with a newsgroup.

Starting Outlook Express News

Outlook Express News is just a few mouse clicks away, whether you have just started your computer or are working in Internet Explorer. First you need to start Outlook Express from the Start menu or by clicking the Launch Outlook Express button on the Quick Launch toolbar on your Active Desktop. Once you start Outlook Express, you can switch quickly to the News window. If you are Web browsing with Internet Explorer, you can just click a toolbar button to switch directly to Outlook Express News.

SEE ALSO

See "Configuring the News Reader" on page 144 for information on how to set up your news reader for the first time you visit the newsgroups.

Start Outlook Express News from the Quick Launch Toolbar

1 Click the Launch Outlook Express button on the Quick Launch toolbar.

2 If you need to set up an account, click the Set Up A Newsgroup Account link.

3 If you already set up an account, click a news server icon in the folder list, or click the Read News link on the Outlook Express start page.

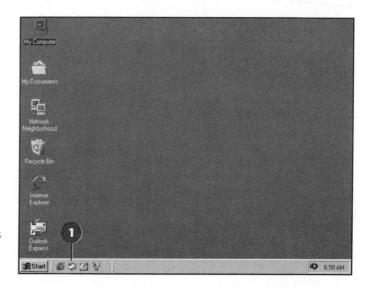

Scroll to see available news servers.

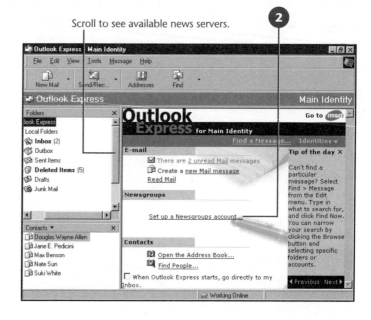

SEE ALSO

See "Starting Outlook Express" on page 116 for information on how to start Outlook Express from the Start menu.

TIP

Set Outlook Express to start when you start your computer. *Right-click the taskbar, click Properties on the shortcut menu, click the Start Menu Programs tab, click Advanced, and then drag the Outlook Express shortcut icon from the Internet Explorer folder to the StartUp folder. Click the Close button in the upper-right corner of the window, and then click OK.*

TIP

Set your default startup connection. *If you use a dial-up connection, you can set Outlook Express to start without prompting you to select a connection option each time. In Outlook Express, click the Tools menu, click Options, click the Connection tab, click one of the option buttons in the When Outlook Express Starts section to select it, and then click OK.*

Start Outlook Express News While Reading Your E-Mail

1. Start Outlook Express, and read your e-mail.

2. Click the name of your news server in the folder list.

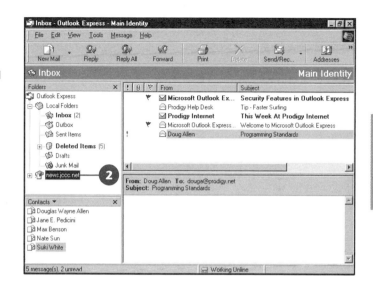

Start Outlook Express News from Internet Explorer

1. Start Internet Explorer.

2. To start the Outlook Express Newsreader while viewing a Web page, click the Mail button on the toolbar, and then click Read News.

Viewing the News Window

Toolbar
The toolbar contains buttons for commands you can use while you read your mail messages.

Menu bar
The menu bar gives you access to all Outlook Express options.

Folder bar
The Folder bar displays the newsgroup currently selected in the folder list.

Folder list
The folder list contains all the folders in Outlook Express. Both e-mail folders and subscribed newsgroups are listed here.

Contacts list
The contacts list displays the names of all the people in your Address Book.

Message list
The message list displays newsgroup messages from the currently selected group in the folder list.

Preview pane
The preview pane displays the contents of the message currently selected in the message list.

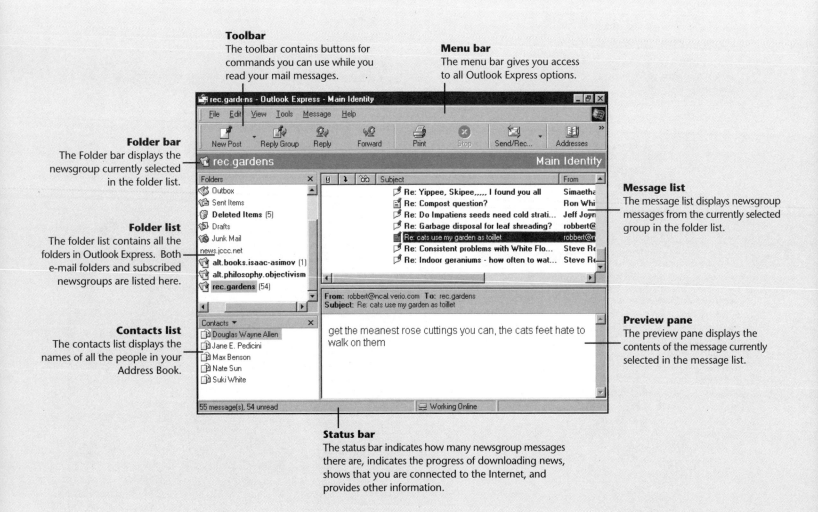

Status bar
The status bar indicates how many newsgroup messages there are, indicates the progress of downloading news, shows that you are connected to the Internet, and provides other information.

Understanding Newsgroups

To help you understand the concept of a newsgroup, consider the following scenarios.

◆ You're working on your 1957 Chevy, and you're having trouble finding a part for the engine. You've tried contacting a couple of garages and mechanics, and you're getting nowhere. Where can you go for help?

◆ You have a presentation next week, and you're want to use a quotation from an Issac Asimov novel. You've tried flipping through the book looking for the right sentence, but it's no use. Is there anyone you can just ask?

◆ Buying the old Victorian house was a dream come true. But now you have constant questions about the best way to renovate and restore the house to its previous glory. How can you find people who have advice to give?

◆ The electronic music of a German composer is your latest fascination, but nobody you know listens to that kind of music. Where can you find other fans to share your thoughts with?

In each case, the answer is probably found in a newsgroup.

Simply, a *newsgroup* is a forum where people from around the world with a common interest can share ideas, ask and answer questions, and comment on and discuss any aspect of a subject.

You can find a newsgroup about almost any topic, from the serious to the lighthearted, from educational to controversial, from business to social. Whatever your interest, there is sure to be a newsgroup where you find others who share your interest.

In many ways, participating in a newsgroup is similar to sending e-mail messages to and receiving replies from a large number of people. But instead of sending messages to hundreds or thousands of people, you simply submit, or *post,* your message on the newsgroup server. Once the message is on a server, interested parties can download it and read it.

In order to participate in a newsgroup, you need a *news reader program,* such as Outlook Express News, which provides you the ability to subscribe to newsgroups, retrieve the latest conversations, read and reply to posted messages, save and print the messages, and so forth.

Outlook Express News helps you *subscribe to* (or, in other words, keep track of) the newsgroups you prefer, organize conversation *threads* (ongoing messages about the same subject), and participate in the discussions. If you know how to create and send e-mail with Outlook Express Mail, you're already familiar with the tools and features you use to compose and post messages to a newsgroup.

8

Configuring the News Reader

Before you can participate in a newsgroup, you must specify a news server. The Internet Connection Wizard walks you though this setup process. This wizard also appears the first time you start Outlook Express Mail or News. To complete the wizard, you'll need the name of the news server you want to use and possibly an account name and password from your Internet service provider (ISP) or system administrator. Unless you plan to install another news reader program to access newsgroups, you should set Outlook Express as your primary news reader so that you use it whenever you link to a newsgroup.

SEE ALSO

See "Choosing Programs to Use with Internet Explorer" on page 91 for information specifying Outlook Express as your news reader for Internet Explorer.

Set up News Using the Internet Connection Wizard

1 On the Outlook Express start page, click the Setup A Newsgroups Account link.

2 Type your name. Click Next to continue.

3 Read the information in each wizard dialog box, and enter the required information. Click Next to continue.

4 In the final wizard dialog box, click Finish.

5 Click Close.

6 Click Yes to download a list of newsgroups available on the news server.

7 Click OK.

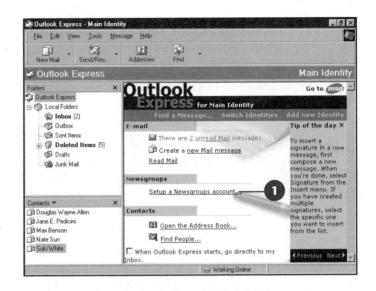

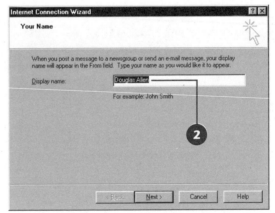

Subscribing to a Newsgroup

Subscribing to a newsgroup places a link to the group in the folder list, providing easy access to the newsgroup. You can subscribe to as many newsgroups as you'd like. If you find that you are no longer interested in a newsgroup, you can unsubscribe from it. You can also view a newsgroup without subscribing to see if you might want to add it to your folder list.

TIP

Newsgroups icon. *When reading news messages in Outlook Express, you can click the News Groups button on the toolbar to list all the newsgroups.*

TIP

Unsubscribe from a newsgroup. *If you no longer want to see a newsgroup in your folder list, right-click the newsgroup name, click Unsubscribe on the shortcut menu, and then click OK.*

View a Newsgroup Without Subscribing

1. Click the Tools menu, and then click Newsgroups.

2. Scroll through the list of available newsgroups.

3. Click a newsgroup you want to view.

4. Click Go To.

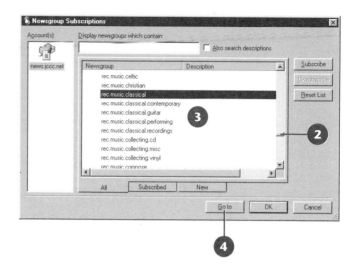

Subscribe to a Newsgroup

1. Click the Tools menu, and then click Newsgroups.

2. Scroll through the list of available newsgroups.

3. Click the newsgroup you want to subscribe to.

4. Click Subscribe.

5. Click Go To to see the posted messages.

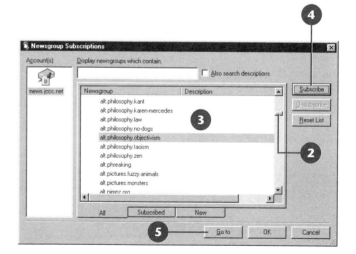

Reading the News

Once you have subscribed to a newsgroup, you will want to view the messages. Click the newsgroup to display its messages, and then click the message you want to read. You can save any message to your hard disk for future reference. Periodically, you should *compact* news folders, which is a process to free up space on your hard disk.

TIP

Posted messages expire after awhile. *If it seems as if you are jumping into the middle of a conversation, it's probably because your news server has deleted older messages to make room for newer ones. Messages last a few days to two weeks before being removed.*

TIP

View only unread messages. *To view only messages you haven't yet read, click the View menu, point to Current View, and then click Hide Read Messages. Those messages you have already read disappear.*

Open and Read News Messages

① Click the newsgroup in the folder list whose message you want to read.

② To sort the messages based on type, click the column button you want to sort by. The column button toggles between sorting the column in ascending and descending order.

Scroll through the list to see the posted messages.

③ To read a message, click its header in the message list.

④ Read the message in the preview pane.

⑤ If you see a link to a Web site, click it to start Internet Explorer and connect to the Web page.

⑥ Click the next message you want to read, or press a keyboard shortcut.

Regular text indicates a read message.

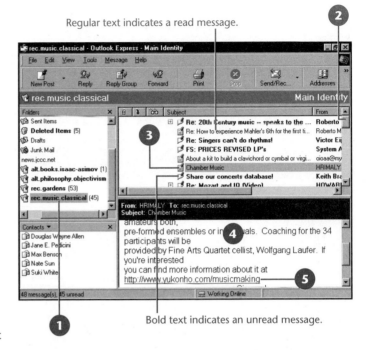

Bold text indicates an unread message.

COLUMN BUTTONS	
Button	**Purpose**
🔖	Indicates the message contains one or more attached documents
👓	Indicates a conversation thread is watched or ignored
⬇	Indicates the message is set for offline viewing

Save a Message

1. Click the message you want to save.

2. Click the File menu, and then click Save As.

3. Click the Save-In drop-down arrow, and then select the drive and folder in which you want to save the message.

4. Enter a new filename.

5. Specify the file type.

6. Click Save.

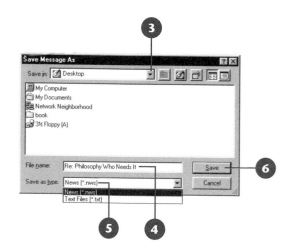

TIP

Conversation threads. *A thread consists of the original message on a particular topic along with any responses that include the original message title preceded by "Re:".*

TIP

Ignore or watch a conversation. *Select the conversation you want to ignore or watch, click the Message menu, and click Ignore Conversation or Watch Conversation.*

TIP

What do those newsgroup names mean? *It's pretty hard to tell what a newsgroup is going to offer just by reading the name. Here are some of the standard newsgroup name categories and what they stand for:*

alt.	*Anything goes*
biz.	*Business and corporate*
comp.	*Computer topics*
gov.	*Federal government*
k12.	*Educational topics*
misc.	*Same as alt.*
rec.	*Recreational*
sci.	*Science topics*
soc.	*Social issues*
talk.	*General discussions*

Clean Up Wasted Space

1. Click the Tools menu, and then click Options.

2. Click the Maintenance tab.

3. Click Clean Up Now.

4. Select the news server.

5. Click to select the check box with the clean up option you want.

   ◆ Empty Deleted Items folder on exit.

   ◆ Compact messages.

   ◆ Delete messages after a certain number of days.

6. Click Close.

7. Click OK.

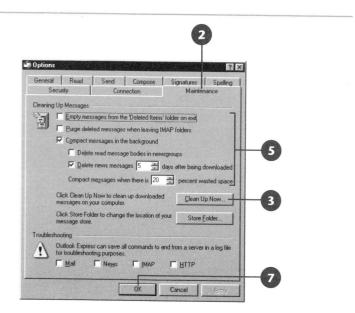

Finding a Particular Newsgroup or Message

When you add a news server account to Outlook Express, it retrieves a list of newsgroups available on that server. Often this list is quite lengthy. Rather than scroll through the entire list looking for a particular topic, you can search the list for that topic. Similarly, you can look for a particular message or thread from all the messages you retrieved from a newsgroup. You can even go to a Web site (such as *www.dejanews.com*) that archives newsgroups and search for posted messages from the last few years.

Search for Specific Types of Newsgroups

1. Click the Newsgroups button on the toolbar.

2. Type the word or phrase for which you want to search.

   As you type, the results appear in the Newsgroup list.

3. Double-click a newsgroup to view its messages.

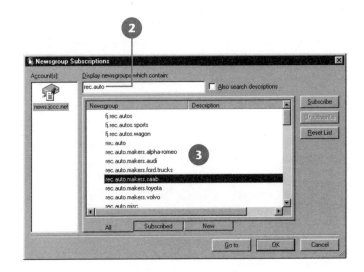

Find a Particular Newsgroup Message

1. Click the Edit menu, point to Find, and then click Message In This Folder.

2. Type the word(s) or phrase you want to locate.

3. If you want, click to select the Search All The Text In Downloaded Messages check box.

4. Click Find Next.

5. Double-click the message you want to read.

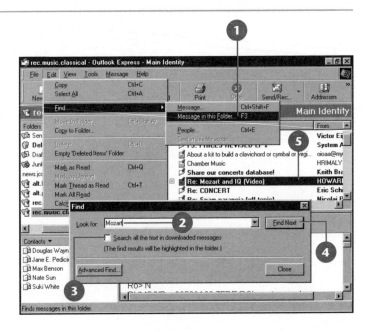

Set Rules for Incoming Newsgroup Messages

1. Click the Tools menu, point to Message Rules, and then click For News.

2. Click New to create a new rule or select a rule and click Modify to edit an existing one.

3. Set your criteria for incoming messages and enter a name for the rule.

4. Click OK.

5. Click OK.

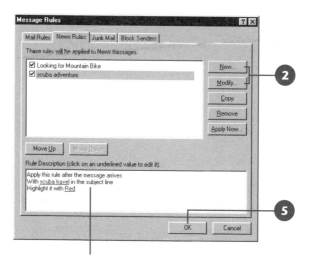

Rule description appears here.

Search a Newsgroup Archive

1. Connect to a Web site containing a newsgroup archive.

   Try connecting to *http://www.dejanews.com.*

2. Enter a keyword to search the archive.

3. Click the Archive drop-down arrow, and then select an archive to search.

4. Click Find and then scroll to view the results.

5. Click a link to read the newsgroup message.

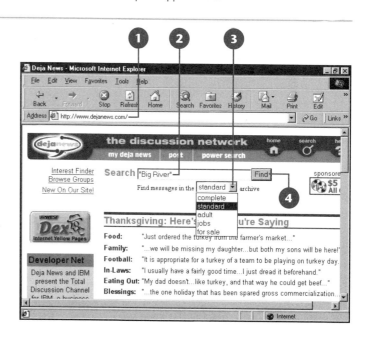

Posting Messages

Part of the fun of newsgroups is that you can participate in an ongoing discussion, respond privately to a message's author, or start a new thread yourself by posting your own message on a topic of interest to you. If you post a message to a newsgroup and then change your mind, you can cancel the message. Keep in mind that if someone has already downloaded the message, canceling the message will not remove it from that person's computer.

Post a New Message

1. Click the newsgroup in the folder list to which you want to post a message

2. Click the New Post button on the toolbar.

3. Type a subject for your message.

4. Type your message.

5. Click the Send button on the toolbar.

6. If necessary, click OK to confirm your message was sent to the news server.

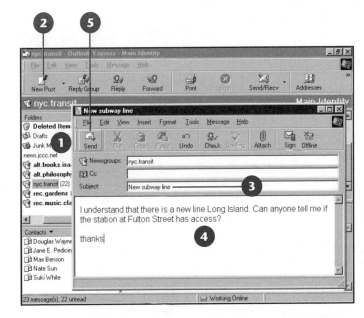

Cancel a Message

1. Select the newsgroup to which you posted the message in the folder list.

2. Select the message you want to cancel. You will need to wait until your message is posted.

3. Click the Message menu, and then click Cancel Message.

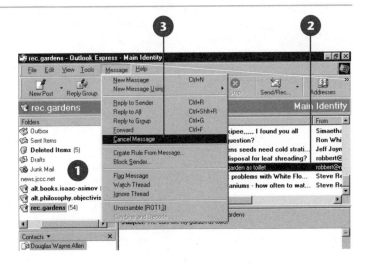

Create stationery for your newsgroup messages. *You can create stationery for your newsgroup messages just as you do for your e-mail messages. Click the Tools menu, click Options, click the Compose tab, click Create New, and then follow the setup wizard to set the options you want, such as changing the font or selecting a stationery, and then click OK.*

Think before you post. *Respond to personal questions posted to a newsgroup directly to the author, not to the entire newsgroup. Remember to click the Reply button.*

Attach a file to a post. *When you compose a message, click the Insert File button on the toolbar to include a picture or document file.*

Post a message with stationery. *Instead of just clicking the New Post button, click the New Post drop-down arrow, and select a stationery for your message.*

Reply to a Message

1 Click the message to which you want to reply.

2 Select the appropriate command.

- ◆ Click the Reply Group button on the toolbar to post your response to the newsgroup.

- ◆ Click the Reply button on the toolbar to send the message's author a private e-mail message.

- ◆ Click the Forward button to send an e-mail message to some other recipient.

3 Type your message, and if you want, delete parts of the original message that are unrelated to your reply.

4 Click the Send button on the toolbar.

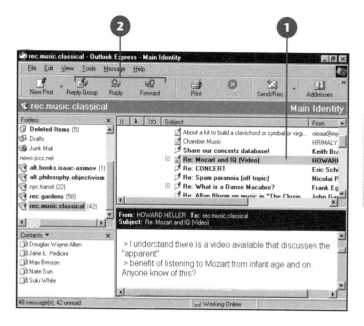

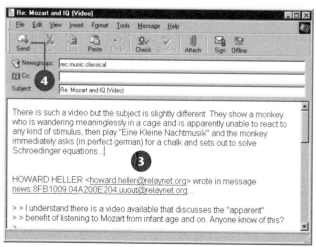

Reading Messages Offline

To keep your phone line free and possibly reduce your Internet connection charges, you can read your newsgroup messages *offline*, while you are disconnected from the Internet. First, when you are online, set Outlook Express to *download* (transfer to your computer) only the *headers* (message topics, authors, and dates) for the various newsgroups to which you are subscribed. Then you can go offline and peruse the headers that have been downloaded. Mark the messages that look interesting, and then go back online to download the messages you marked.

TIP

Work offline. *Before disconnecting from your ISP, make sure you click the File menu, and then click Work Offline.*

Set Outlook Express to Retrieve Only Headers

1. Click the newsgroup server in the folder list.

2. Click the newsgroup you want to view offline.

3. Click the Settings drop-down arrow, and then click Headers Only.

4. If you want, click to select the New Messages Only check box to download new messages along with the headers.

5. Repeat steps 2 through 4 for each newsgroup you want to read offline.

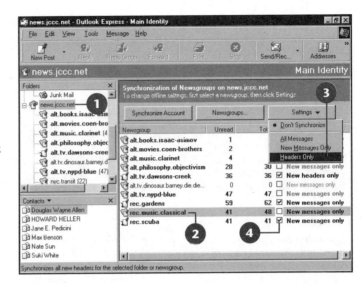

Download Newsgroup Headers

1. If necessary, connect to your ISP.

2. Click the newsgroup server in the folder list.

3. Click Synchronize Account.

   Outlook Express will synchronize with your ISP and download the headers to your computer.

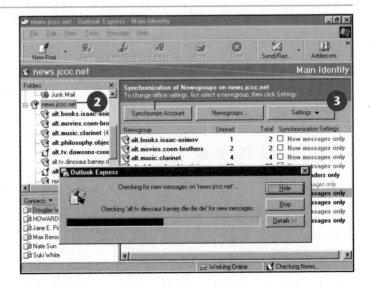

TIP

Subscribe to a newsgroup offline. *While working offline, you can still subscribe to a newsgroup. Click the News Groups button on the toolbar, select a newsgroup you are interested in, and then click the Subscribe button. Click OK. You won't see any messages until you go back online.*

TIP

Read the news online. *If you use a network Internet service provider (ISP) that maintains a constant connection to the Internet, you can read and respond to newsgroup articles online without tying up resources or worrying about your connect time. Go to a newsgroup, read posted messages, and then compose and send your responses without disconnecting.*

SEE ALSO

See "Changing Outlook Express Message Options" on page 156 for more information about changing the number of retrieved message headers.

SEE ALSO

See "Subscribing to a Newsgroup" on page 145 for more information about viewing and joining newsgroups.

Mark Messages Offline for Downloading

1. While offline, right-click the header of a message you want to read.

2. Click Download Message Later.

3. Repeat for each message you want to retrieve.

4. Click the newsgroup server in the folder list.

5. Click Synchronize Account to have Outlook Express dial your ISP and download the messages you marked.

The download icon will appear when you mark an item.

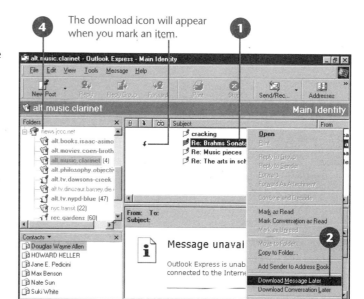

Compose Your Messages and Replies Offline

1. While offline, compose your message or reply as usual.

2. Click the Send button on the toolbar.

3. Click OK to confirm your message will go into the Outbox.

4. Click the newsgroup server in the folder list.

5. Click Synchronize Account to post the messages.

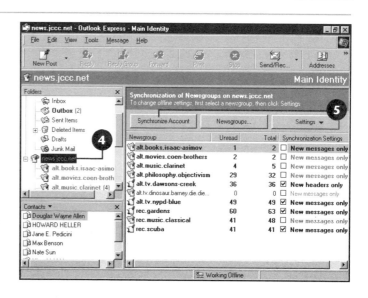

Customizing the Outlook Express Window

As you work in Outlook Express, you'll find that you use some commands very often and others not so frequently. You can customize the toolbar so that it displays only those buttons you find most useful. Similarly, you can add other columns to the message pane or remove any columns that appear by default. In this way, you can tailor Outlook Express to suit your needs and reflect your style of working.

TIP

Restore original toolbar buttons. *If you want to change the toolbar back to its original state, click Reset in the Customize toolbar dialog box.*

TIP

Sort your messages. *Click the View menu, point to Sort By, and then click the sort option you want.*

Customize the Toolbar

1 Right-click the toolbar.

2 Click Customize on the shortcut menu.

3 Click a button you want to add to the toolbar, and then click Add.

4 Click a button you want to remove from the toolbar, and then click Remove.

5 Click Close.

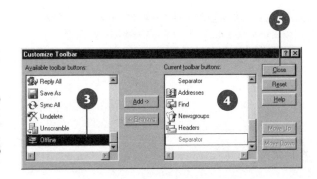

Customize the Columns in the Message List Pane

1 Click the View menu, and then click Columns.

2 Click a column name.

3 Click the Move Up or Move Down button to change the position of the column.

4 Enter a new value for the column width.

5 Click to select or clear the column check box you do or don't want to appear.

6 Click OK.

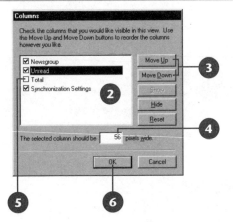

Resize the panes in the Outlook Express window.
Position the mouse pointer between the column headers in any of the panes, and then drag the side of the pane up and down or right and left to resize the various panes.

Maximize your news-reading space. *To make the most possible space for your newsgroup content, turn off all the elements you can. Click the View menu, click Layout. Click to clear all of the options in the Basic section. Now you have a two-pane window with nothing but newsgroup headers and the selected message below.*

Change the current view.
You can change the current view to show all messages, hide read messages, hide read or ignored messages, or customize the current view. Click the View menu, point to Current View, and then click the view you want or click to customize the current view.

Customize the Outlook Window Layout

1 Click the View menu, and then click Layout.

2 Click one or more of the check boxes in the Basic area to show or hide elements of the Outlook Express window.

3 Click an option in the Preview Pane area to customize your preview pane display.

4 Click OK.

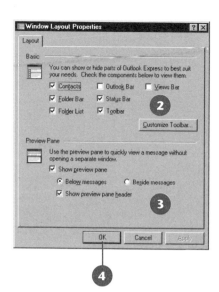

Changing Outlook Express Message Options

Outlook Express offers many options that you can customize to the way you like to work. Based on your preferences, you can change Outlook Express options for reading and sending messages. Depending on the speed of your connection, you may want to download more or fewer headers when connected. Some mail and news programs can only receive messages in a certain format. Some news servers have message size limits and require that you *encode* a message, which compresses and splits a large message into several small ones. Outlook Express can then recombine and decode these messages.

Set the Number of Message Headers to Download

1 Click the Tools menu, and then click Options.

2 Click the Read tab.

3 Click to select the Get Headers At A Time check box.

4 Enter a new value.

5 Click OK.

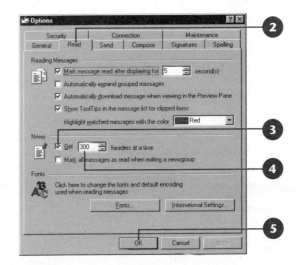

Change Message Sending Options

1 Click the Tools menu, and then click Options.

2 Click the Send tab.

3 Click to select or clear the check boxes with the sending options you want.

◆ Save copy of sent messages

◆ Put people I reply to in my Address Book

◆ Complete e-mail addresses when typing

◆ Include message in reply

4 Click OK.

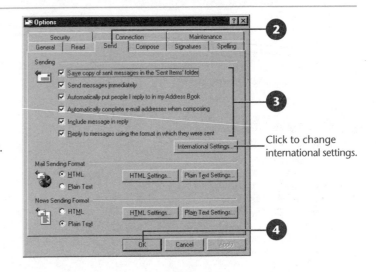

Click to change international settings.

Encode Large Messages

1 Click the Tools menu, and then click Accounts.

2 Click the Mail tab or the News tab.

3 Click the account for which you want to set the message size.

4 Click Properties.

5 Click the Advanced tab.

6 Click to select the Break Apart Messages Larger Than check box.

7 Enter a file size.

8 Click OK.

9 Click Close.

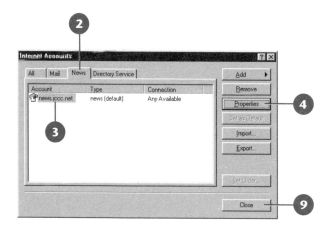

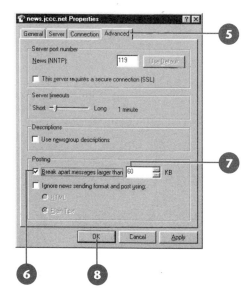

Getting a Personal Certificate

Internet Explorer uses the latest online security so you can securely send information over the Internet. This system prevents anyone from eavesdropping on your communications as you send e-mail, purchase consumer goods, and conduct personal banking over the Internet. The Internet security is provided through encryption and certificates, or Digitial IDs. You can get a Digital ID through a credentials agency such as VeriSign. In Outlook Express, you can encrypt the messages you send and be assured that the e-mail you receive is from a valid source.

SEE ALSO

See "Understanding Security on the Internet" on page 76 for more information about security issues.

Get a Personal Certificate

1. Click the Tools menu and then click Options

2. Click the Security tab.

3. Click Get Digital ID.

   The Microsoft Digital ID Web page is displayed in Internet Explorer.

4. Scroll down, and then click the VeriSign link. If necessary, click OK to acknowledge the Security Alert message.

5. Complete the Digital ID form.

6. Click the Accept button to continue. If necessary, click Yes to accept the Internet warning message.

7. Switch back to Outlook Express, and click OK to close the Options dialog box.

8. Check your Inbox for a digital e-mail confirmation.

9. Open the confirmation e-mail, and then follow the instructions to install your certificate.

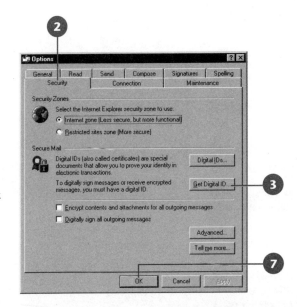

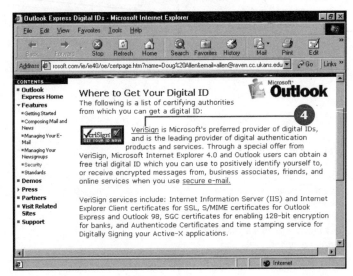

9

Using NetMeeting to Communicate

IN THIS SECTION

Understanding Internet User Location Service

Starting NetMeeting

Viewing the NetMeeting Window

Making and Receiving a Call

Conferencing with People

Using SpeedDial Shortcuts

Communicating with Audio and Video

Exchanging Chat Messages

Using the Whiteboard

Sharing Applications

Sending and Receiving Files

Changing NetMeeting Settings

Chatting for Fun

Changing Your Chat Character

Microsoft NetMeeting takes group communication and conferencing to a whole new level for both business and personal purposes. If you are pleased with the communication capabilities associated with the telephone and electronic mail, you won't believe what NetMeeting can offer. Imagine the following scenarios:

◆ Your boss wants an update on the oil drilling project in Saudi Arabia. With a scheduled NetMeeting, you speak into your computer's microphone and your voice instantly comes out of his speakers across the world.

◆ Mom lives in another city, so once a week you contact her with NetMeeting and your new colorcam. Because you bought her a camera for her computer, it's easy for her to see and hear her grandson singing a song.

◆ You're collaborating with your sister on a new children's book. While you share your illustrations during a NetMeeting call, she marks up the drawing on her computer while you watch on yours.

Understanding Internet User Location Service

What Is ILS?

Microsoft Internet User Location Service, or *ILS*, enables you to find people who are currently connected to an ILS server or Web site on the Internet or an intranet and to communicate with them in real-time.

How Does ILS Work?

An *ILS server* is a computer that keeps track of people who are using NetMeeting. An ILS server compiles a changing database of IP addresses for people who are currently connected to an Internet or an intranet server. An Internet *Protocol,* or *IP, address* is a series of numbers that uniquely identifies a computer on the Internet. No two machines anywhere in the world share the same IP address. When you start NetMeeting and connect to an ILS server, the server registers your IP address, along with your directory information. To place a call, you just select a name from the NetMeeting Directory or from a Web site that contains links to other people's computers. ILS transfers the needed IP addresses between the computers to establish the connection, and then the call is placed.

Unlike your personal Address Book, which stores on your disk or hard drive a database of unchanging information that you enter, the ILS database is stored in RAM and is constantly updated as people connect to and disconnect from the Web site or service.

You can use ILS on the Internet to find and connect to people around the world, or if you are working on an intranet, you can use it to easily locate and contact your colleagues. Contact your system administrator to see if your company supports an ILS server.

Currently selected ILS server

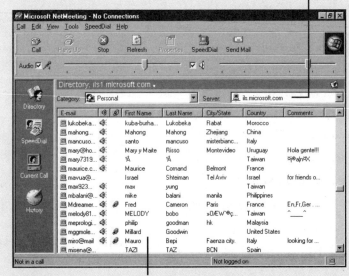

List of users currently connected to the selected server

Who Needs ILS?

You do. Although NetMeeting doesn't need an ILS server to work, ILS makes it easier for NetMeeting users to locate and connect to each other so they can exchange sound, images, and data. Without ILS, you could connect directly to someone if you know that person's IP address, but many people don't know their own IP addresses, and those addresses can change every time they restart their computers on the network.

Where Can You Find ILS?

You can view the ILS directory from within NetMeeting and review a list of people currently connected to that server.

When you start NetMeeting for the first time, a wizard helps you set up your connection to a Microsoft ILS server or one that you supply. When running NetMeeting, you can easily select another ILS directory from a list of servers.

NetMeeting Setup dialog box

Once you are connected, you can use NetMeeting to communicate with Internet *telephony* (a technology that enables you to transmit voice and data between computers), conduct a videoconference, or collaborate on shared applications.

Starting NetMeeting

Like other Windows programs, to start NetMeeting, you use the Start menu. The first time you start NetMeeting, a wizard helps you set up your Directory listing. You will be asked to supply your name, your e-mail address, your city and state, the type of meetings you will conduct, and the ILS directory server you plan to use. This information will appear in the Directory list when you connect to the directory server or the ILS. Other people can use the information to locate you and request a NetMeeting.

SEE ALSO

See "Changing NetMeeting Settings" on page 180 for information on changing Directory list information.

SEE ALSO

See "Understanding Internet User Location Service" on page 160 for information on an ILS.

Start NetMeeting

1. Click the Start button on the taskbar.

2. Point to Programs.

3. Click NetMeeting.

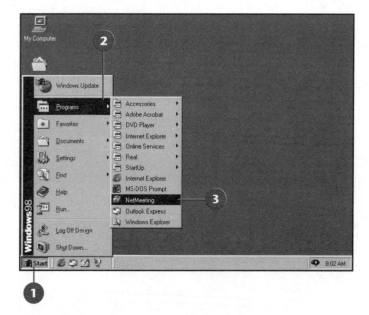

Start NetMeeting for the First Time

1. Click the Start button on the taskbar.

2. Point to Programs.

3. Click NetMeeting.

4. Click Next to continue.

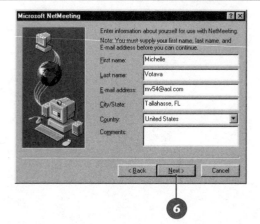

The faster the better.
NetMeeting works best with a fast Internet connection—a 28.8 or faster modem—or a local area network.

Parents beware! *Like many areas of the Internet, there is offensive and sexually explicit language on many of the NetMeeting directory servers. As you scroll through the list of people who are currently connected, you will probably see individuals seeking people to discuss a wide variety of activities. There are no filters for NetMeeting, so you will have to monitor access if you are concerned about your children being exposed to this environment.*

See "Communicating with Audio and Video" on page 170 for more information about setting up NetMeeting.

5 Click the Directory Server drop-down arrow, and then select the directory server you want to use. Click Next to continue.

6 Enter your first name, last name, and e-mail address. Click Next to continue.

7 Select the option button for the way you want your information categorized. Click Next to continue.

8 Click Next to continue.

9 Click the option button to select the speed of your connection. Click Next to continue.

10 Click Next to tune your audio settings.

11 Click Test to check your speaker volume. Click Stop to finish the testing.

12 Slide the volume control if necessary, and test the volume again. Click Next to continue.

13 Read the displayed text into your microphone. The NetMeeting Wizard sets the recording level. Click Next to continue.

14 Click Finish.

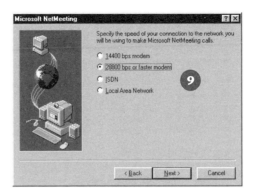

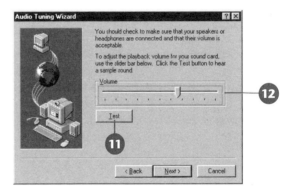

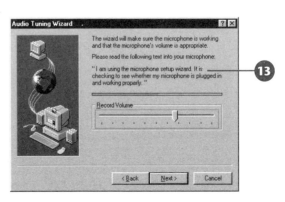

Viewing the NetMeeting Window

NetMeeting

NetMeeting is a great way to communicate with a group of as many as 32 people, even if they are in a different city, state, or country. Depending on your specific needs and your resources, you can converse like on a telephone call, exchange video images, work together on programs, type messages, and even draw on a shared picture or diagram.

To provide you the most flexibility and to meet all of your conferencing needs, the NetMeeting program window is organized by quick buttons for different kinds of tasks. A menu bar and toolbar keep the appropriate tools and commands available at all times.

SpeedDial

The SpeedDial list contains the addresses of people you have previously met and have chosen to add to your SpeedDial list. You can manually add addresses to this list.

Directory

The Directory list shows everyone with whom you can meet at any given moment and the resources they have available—voice, video, or file transfer.

Current Call

The Current Call list provides information about the person with whom you are meeting at that moment. You can send files to others, transmit video and audio with someone, and start the Whiteboard or Chat from here.

History

The History list logs all the calls you have received by the name of the caller, whether you took the call or not, and the time the call came in. This feature is useful for determining how you're spending your time.

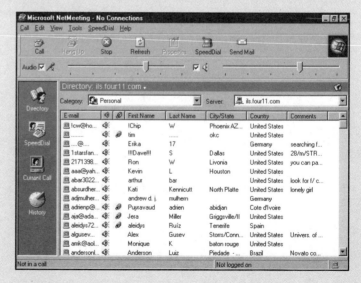

Whiteboard Program

The Whiteboard is a program within NetMeeting that provides a place for all meeting participants to write, draw, or type ideas. It's great for showing agendas, brainstorming solutions, or illustrating concepts.

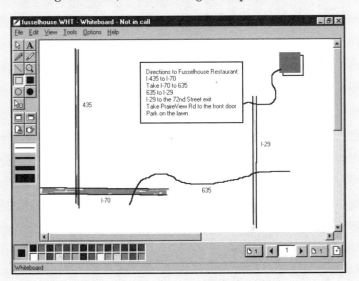

Chat Program

NetMeeting Chat is a program within NetMeeting that provides a place where all meeting participants can type and send messages to the group or to each other privately. This tool makes it easy for everyone to contribute to a meeting.

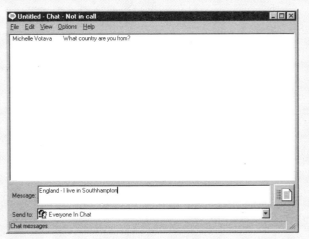

Making and Receiving a Call

NetMeeting makes interacting with people simple. The Directory window lists everyone who is connected to the selected directory server and running NetMeeting. You can call someone on that list or switch to another directory server. In addition, you can call anyone for whom you know the e-mail address, modem phone number, or IP address indicating the exact location of that person's computer. As long as you are logged on to your directory server, you can receive calls from other people. You can decide to answer these calls on a case-by-case basis, or you can automatically accept all calls. No matter who placed the original call, you can disconnect at any time.

Make a Directory Call

1. If necessary, click the Directory icon.

2. Click the Server drop-down arrow, and then select a directory server.

3. Double-click the name of the person you want to call.

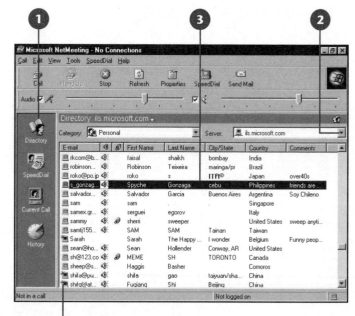

A star burst in the computer icon indicates the person is currently in a call.

Place a Call Manually

1. Click the Call button on the toolbar.

2. Type the e-mail address, IP address, network address, or modem phone number of the person you want to call.

3. Click the Call Using drop-down arrow, and then select the type of connection you want to use.

4. Click Call.

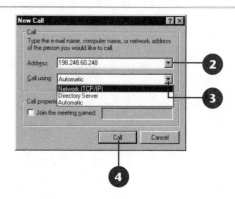

Answer a Call

When you receive a call, a dialog box appears and you will hear ringing similar to a telephone. Choose one of the following options.

◆ Click Accept to take the call.

◆ Click Ignore to not take the call.

Accept All Calls

1. Click the Tools menu, and then click Options.

2. Click the General tab.

3. Click to select the Automatically Accept Incoming Calls check box.

4. Click OK.

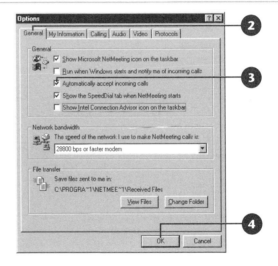

End a Call

1. Click the Hang Up button on the toolbar.

Conferencing with People

With NetMeeting you can meet with more than one person at a time. If you host a meeting, each person who attends calls you at the appointed time. If you want to join a scheduled meeting, you simply call the person who is hosting the meeting. A meeting that is hosted by a third party conferencing service, such as a telephone company or a teleconferencing company, is called a *named meeting*. To join a named meeting, you need to know the name of the meeting as well as that of the *conference bridge*, the server where the meeting is held.

TIP

What happens when you hang up? *When you click the Hang Up button on the toolbar during a call, NetMeeting simply disconnects you. If you are hosting a meeting, you disconnect everyone who called you.*

Host a Meeting

1. Notify all invites of the meeting time via e-mail or a phone call.

2. Click the Call menu, and then click Host Meeting.

3. If necessary, click OK.

4. Wait for participants to call at the scheduled time.

5. Click Accept when each person calls.

Join a Meeting in Progress

1. Click the Call button on the toolbar.

2. Type or click the drop-down arrow and select the address of the person hosting the meeting.

3. Click the Call Using drop-down arrow, and then click the type of connection you want to use to make the call.

4. If necessary, click to select the Join The Meeting Named check box, and then type the meeting name.

5. Click Call.

Click if you don't want to confirm each meeting.

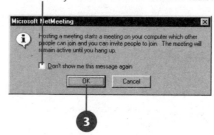

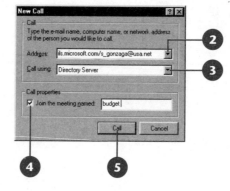

Using SpeedDial Shortcuts

SpeedDial saves the names and computer locations of all the people who accept your calls and whose calls you accept, plus any entries you add manually. It creates a list, located on the SpeedDial tab, that provides a shortcut for contacting these people. If you don't want names added to your SpeedDial list automatically, you must change the SpeedDial settings.

Add People to Your SpeedDial List

1 Select person you want to add to your speed dial list.

2 Click the SpeedDial button on the toolbar.

3 If necessary, modify the caller address.

4 Click the Call Using drop-down arrow, and then select the type of connection you want to use to make the call.

5 Click the Add To SpeedDial List option button.

6 Click OK.

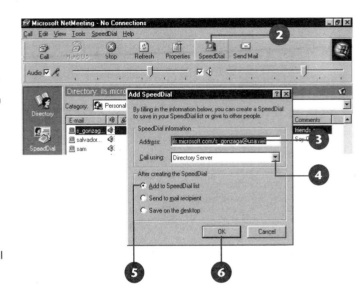

Change Your SpeedDial Settings

1 Click the Tools menu, and then click Options.

2 Click the Calling tab.

3 Click the option button for the Automatically Add SpeedDials option you want.

4 Click to select or clear the check boxes for the SpeedDial Defaults you want.

5 Click OK.

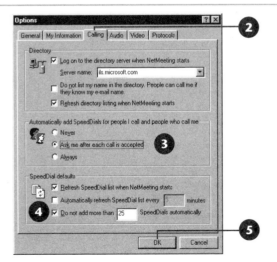

Communi-cating with Audio and Video

The first time you start NetMeeting, the Audio Tuning Wizard will optimize your audio settings to ensure you are heard clearly by having you read aloud. If your audio quality deterio-rates, you might need to retune the audio settings. When you make or receive a call, NetMeeting begins to transmit audio and video, provided your computer has the necessary hardware. You can control when you send or receive video during a call by changing the video options to manual. Each person can send and receive audio and video with only one person at a time in a meeting, although several pairs of people can exchange audio and video at once. You can switch the connec-tion from one person to another at any time during a meeting.

Tune Your Audio

1 Click the Hang Up button on the toolbar to ensure you are disconnected from any NetMeeting calls.

2 Click the Tools menu, and then click Audio Tuning Wizard.

3 Read each of the Audio Tuning Wizard dialog boxes. Click Next to continue.

4 Follow the wizard's instructions, and then click Finish.

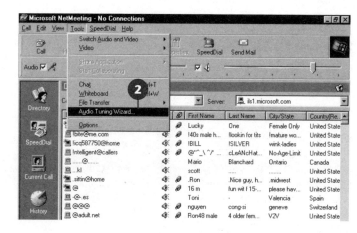

Send and Receive Video Manually

1 Click the Tools menu, and then click Options.

2 Click the Video tab.

3 If necessary, click the Automatically Send Video At The Start Of Each Call check box to deselect it.

4 If necessary, click to clear the Automatically Receive Video At The Start Of Each Call check box.

5 Click OK.

6 To send or receive video during a call, click the Play button.

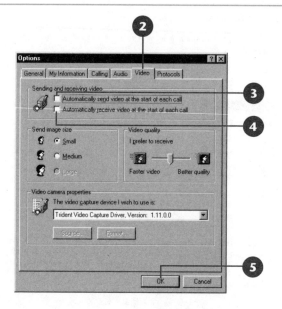

TIP

Preview your own video.
Before you place your call, you can see the video you intend to send or verify that your equipment is working. Click the Current Call icon, and then click the Play button in the My Video window. If you are previewing an image while you place or receive a call, the video will immediately be sent.

TIP

Speaker volume is adjustable. *Drag the Speaker Volume slider on the toolbar to adjust the volume. To mute the speakers, click the Turn On/Off Speaker check box on the toolbar to deselect it. Click the check box again to hear the audio again.*

TIP

Microphone volume is adjustable. *Drag the Microphone Volume slider on the toolbar to adjust the volume. To mute your voice, click to clear the Turn On/Off Microphone check box on the toolbar. Click to select the check box again to resume transmitting your voice.*

Switch Your Connection

1. If necessary, click the Current Call icon.

2. Click the Switch button on the toolbar.

3. Click the person whom you want to talk to and see.

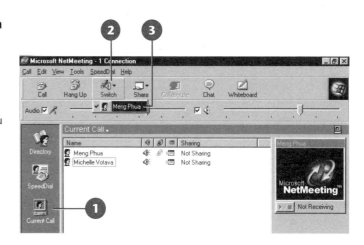

Turn Off Audio or Video

1. If necessary, click the Current Call icon.

2. Right-click the audio icon or the video icon next to the name of the person to whom you want to stop sending audio or video.

3. Click Stop Using Audio And Video.

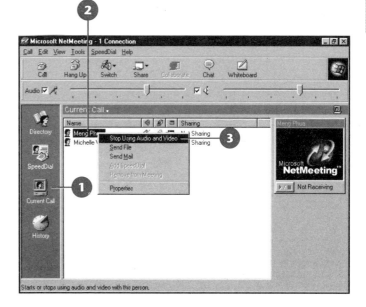

Exchanging Chat Messages

NetMeeting Chat enables all meeting participants to exchange typed messages, which is helpful when more than two people attend a meeting. As soon as one person in the meeting starts Chat, it appears on everyone's screen. Each participant can then type messages to send to the others. Every message appears in the Chat window, identified by the sender's name along with the date and time, if you choose. You can also change how a message will display within the Chat window.

TIP

Whisper to a friend. *You can send a message to just one person in a meeting—called a whisper—by clicking that person's name in the Send To list before pressing Enter.*

Start Chatting

1. If necessary, click the Current Call icon.

2. Click the Chat button on the toolbar.

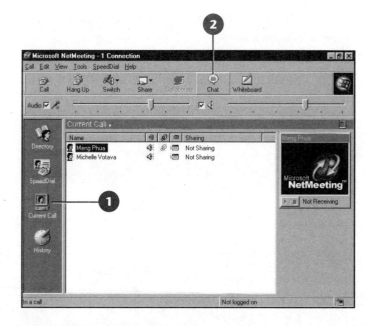

Send a Chat Message

1. Switch to the Chat window.

2. Type your message.

3. Click the Send button or press Enter to send the message.

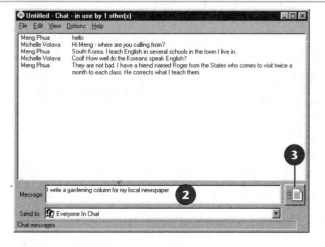

Personalize your chat style. *You can change the font, style, size, and color in which messages are displayed. In the Chat window, click the Options menu, click Font, select the font options and colors you want, and then click OK.*

Store chat files. *You can save and print all the Chat messages from a meeting. In the Chat window, click the File menu, and then click Save, Save As, or Print. Chat files are saved with a .txt (text file) extension; you can open them in Notepad, WordPad, Word, or another program that reads text format files.*

Collaboration and Chat. *If you are collaborating in a meeting and if someone has taken control of the shared application, you will not be able to type in the Chat window.*

See "Sharing Applications" on page 176 for more information about collaborating in a meeting.

Change the Message Display

1. If necessary, switch to the Chat window.

2. Click the Options menu, and then click Chat Format.

3. Click to select or deselect the check boxes to control the information that appears in your Chat messages.

4. Click the option button next to the format in which you want your Chat messages to appear.

5. Click OK.

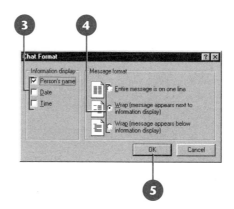

Quit Chatting

1. Click the Close button in the upper-right corner of the Chat window.

2. Click Yes or No to save or not save the current list of messages.

3. If necessary, type a name for the Chat session file.

4. Click Save.

Using the Whiteboard

The Whiteboard is a virtual scratchpad that everyone in a NetMeeting conference can use for jotting down notes and illustrating ideas during a meeting. As soon as one person in the meeting opens the Whiteboard, it appears on everyone's screen. Each participant can then write or draw on the board, and see what others have contributed. The Whiteboard has a variety of tools that you can use to type text, write with a pen, draw lines and shapes, or highlight objects on the board. If a page becomes filled, you can erase unneeded objects from the board, or insert additional pages.

TIP

Quit Whiteboard. *Click the Close button in the upper-right corner of the Whiteboard window, and then click the Save option you want.*

Start and Use the Whiteboard

1. If necessary, click the Current Call icon.

2. Click the Whiteboard button on the toolbar.

3. Click the appropriate tool in the toolbox.

4. Click in the Whiteboard, and then type text or drag the pointer to draw the line or shape you want.

5. If necessary, click the Font Options button to change the font, size, or style of text; to select a new color; or to choose a line weight.

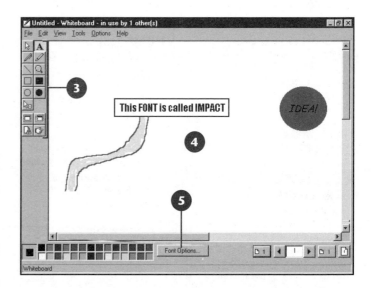

Work with Multiple Pages

◆ To add a page, click the Insert New Page button.

◆ To move to a different page, click the First Page, Previous Page, Next Page, or Last Page button.

◆ To move to a specific page, type page number, and then press Enter.

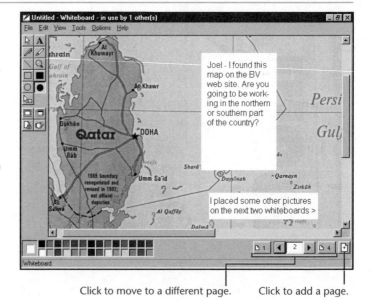

Click to move to a different page.   Click to add a page.

TIP

Erase the current page. *You can completely erase a page on the Whiteboard by moving to the page, pressing Ctrl+Delete, and then clicking OK.*

TIP

Make a point. *During a meeting you can point to any object on the Whiteboard. Click the Remote Pointer On tool in the toolbox, click the Selector tool, and then drag the pointer to the desired location. Click the Remote Pointer On tool again to hide the pointer.*

TIP

Lock the Whiteboard. *You can prevent other meeting participants from changing elements on the Whiteboard by clicking the Lock Contents tool in the toolbox. Click the tool again to allow others access.*

Erase Text or Objects on the Whiteboard

1 Click the Eraser tool in the toolbox.

2 Click the text block or object you want to delete.

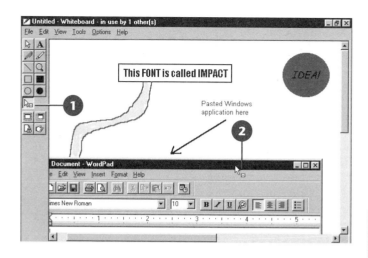

USING WHITEBOARD TOOLS	
Button	**Purpose**
▶	Use the Selector tool to select objects.
A	Use the Text tool to type text.
✏	Use the Pen tool to draw freeform lines with the selected color and line width.
✎	Use the Highlighter tool to draw freeform lines with the selected highlight color and line width.
＼	Use the Line tool to draw straight lines with the selected line width.
🔍	Use the Zoom tool to change the magnification of the Whiteboard.
☐	Use the Unfilled Rectangle tool to draw rectangular shapes with the selected line width.
■	Use the Filled Rectangle tool to draw solid rectangular shapes.
○	Use the Unfilled Ellipse tool to draw elliptical shapes with the selected line width.
●	Use the Filled Ellipse tool to draw solid elliptical shapes.
▣	Use the Select Window tool to select an entire window and paste the contents onto the Whiteboard.
▤	Use the Select Area tool to select an area and paste the contents onto the Whiteboard.

Sharing Applications

During a call, whether with one person or several, you can start and then share any program available on your computer. When you share an application, you are the only person who can work on the file—the others can only watch. You can also *collaborate* with other people to enable them to work in your program as well, although only one person at a time can control the program. Similarly, you can collaborate to work in someone else's application; however, they retain the results of the file you worked on. If you are sharing one of your applications, you can stop sharing it any time you choose.

TIP

Three's company. *Only three people at a time can share an application and collaborate on the work in progress.*

Share an Application

1 During a call, start the application you want to share in the usual way.

2 Click the Current Call icon.

3 Click the Share button on the toolbar, and then click to select the application you want other people to share.

4 If necessary, click OK.

5 Display the application.

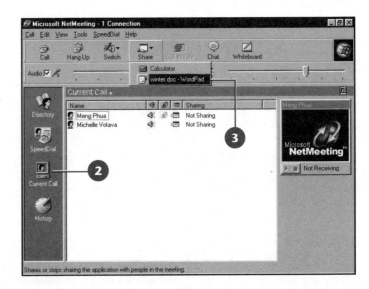

Let Others Work with Your Application

1 During a call, select an application to share.

2 Click the Collaborate button on the toolbar.

3 If necessary, click OK.

4 Display the application window.

5 Tell others who want to work in the application to click the Collaborate button on the toolbar.

6 When you're done, click the Stop Collaborate button on the toolbar, or press Esc.

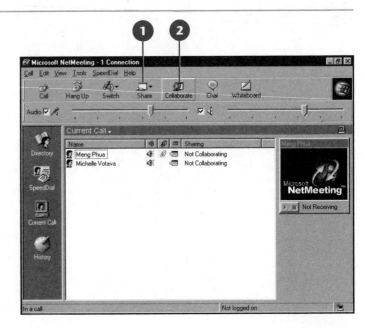

The Clipboard is fair game.
*When you are in a meeting,
whether you are sharing an
application or not, anything
you cut or copy to the Clipboard
can be pasted by all those in the
meeting into applications on
their computers.*

Share your results. *After
collaborating on a file,
distribute the final file to all
participants, or have the person
who shared an application
distribute the final file to all
participants.*

*See "Sending and Receiving
Files" on page 178 for more
information about sending a
file to others.*

Work with Someone Else's Application

1 During a call, wait for someone to share an application.

2 Click the Collaborate button on the toolbar when instructed to do so.

3 Double-click the application window to control the cursor.

4 When you're done collaborating, click the Stop Collaborate button on the toolbar, or press Esc.

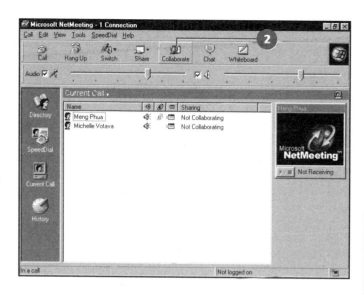

Stop Sharing Your Application

1 If necessary, click the Current Call icon.

2 Click the Share button on the toolbar, and then click the name of the application you no longer want to share.

A shared application has a check mark next to its name.

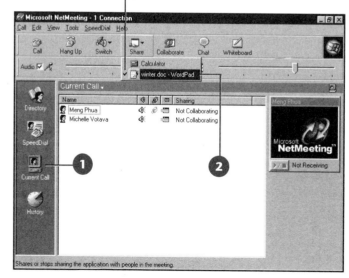

Sending and Receiving Files

During a call, all participants can send or receive files with just a few mouse clicks. Any files you send automatically go to everyone who is participating in the meeting. Likewise, other meeting participants can send files to you during a meeting. You can specify the exact location on your computer to which you want these files automatically sent. With NetMeeting open, you can quickly open any file you have received from someone else during a meeting, whether or not the meeting is still in progress.

TIP

What if you want to send a file to only one person?
Click the Current Call icon, right-click the person's name in the list, click Send File on the shortcut menu, and then double-click the file you want to send.

Send a File

1. During a call, click the Tools menu, point to File Transfer, and then click Send File.

2. Locate the file you want to send.

3. Select the file you want to send.

4. Click Send.

5. Click OK.

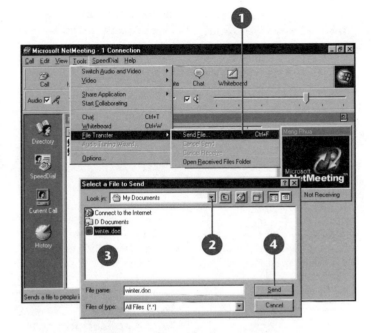

Open a File You Have Received

1. Click the Tools menu, point to File Transfer, and then click Open Received Files Folder.

2. Click the file you want to open.

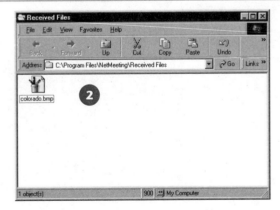

TIP

Keep your files organized.
You should promptly move any files you receive during a meeting to another folder according to your filing system so you can quickly and easily find material later.

TRY THIS

Assign an official note taker. *Assign someone to take notes during a meeting to record items discussed, decisions made, and actions required. Before any participants hang up, have the person taking notes send the file to everyone.*

SEE ALSO

See "Browsing the Web" on page 12 for more information about opening files from your Active Desktop.

SEE ALSO

See "Using the Standard Toolbar" on page 18 for more information about navigating with the toolbar.

Set a Location for Receiving Files

1. Click the Tools menu, and then click Options.

2. Click the General tab.

3. Click Change Folder.

4. Select the folder in which you want to save files you receive.

5. Click OK to confirm the new folder location.

6. Click OK.

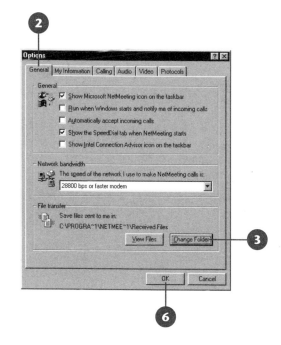

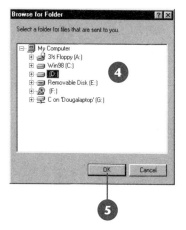

9

Changing NetMeeting Settings

The information you supplied during the NetMeeting setup is listed in the Directory, which others can use to find you and which is visible to those with whom you are meeting. You can easily change or update your directory listing at any time with a new name, address, e-mail address, or other important information. You can also specify that your name not be listed in the directory. You can change whether you connect to the directory server as you start NetMeeting or manually during your session. Finally, you can change your startup ILS server in case you find you are always switching to a different server after you've started NetMeeting.

Change Your Directory Listing

1. Click the Tools menu, and then click Options.

2. Click the My Information tab.

3. If necessary, change your name, e-mail address, or location.

4. Click the option button that describes how you want to categorize your information.

5. Click OK.

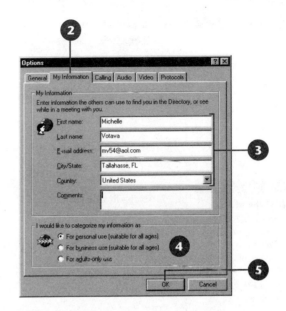

Remove Your Name from the Directory

1. Click the Tools menu, and then click Options.

2. Click the Calling tab.

3. Click to select the Do Not List My Name In The Directory. People Can Call Me If They Know My E-Mail Name check box.

4. Click OK.

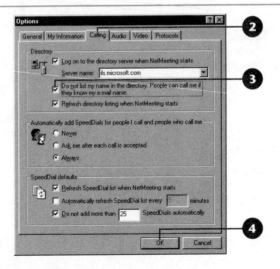

Going unlisted. *You can still receive calls if you are unlisted, but the person who calls you must know your address.*

Log on and off manually. *If you communicate using a modem, you might want to log on and off manually. Click the Call menu, and then click Log On To [Your Directory Server] or Log Off From [Your Directory Server].*

Connect to the Internet at different speeds? *If you use the high-speed network at work and the telephone line at home, you'll want to change your connection speed so NetMeeting operates at the optimum performance. Click the Tools menu, and then click Options. On the General tab, click the Network Bandwidth drop-down arrow whenever you need to change speeds.*

Change Your Startup ILS Server

1 Click the Tools menu, and then click Options.

2 Click the Calling tab.

3 Click to select the Log On To The Directory Server When NetMeeting Starts check box if you want to connect automatically.

4 Click the Server Name drop-down arrow, and then select a directory server.

5 Click OK.

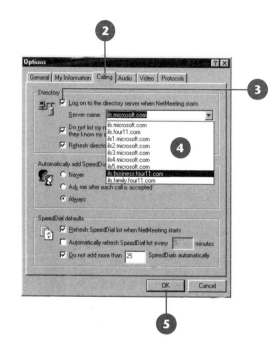

Chatting for Fun

Did you ever want to be a part of a real live comic strip? Now you can! Microsoft Chat is different from the Chat program in NetMeeting. Although both Chat programs enable you to converse with others over the Internet, Microsoft Chat participants appear in a comic strip as characters. You choose what you want to look like, the nickname you want to be called, and enter other information that your fellow chatters can view. When you're ready, enter a chat room to become part of an existing comic strip. To participate, just type out your remarks, choose a facial expression, and then post your image, text, and even sound to the current comic strip panel.

SEE ALSO

See "Getting Updates to Internet Explorer" on page 258 for information on downloading Microsoft Chat.

Start Microsoft Chat and Join a Chat

1. Click the Start button on the taskbar, point to Programs, point to Internet Explorer and then click Microsoft Chat.

2. Click the Server drop-down arrow, and then select a comic server.

3. Click the Go To Chat Room option button, enter the name, and then click OK.

4. If you want to see a list of available chat rooms, click the Show All Available Chat Rooms option button, and then click OK.

5. Click the Personal Info tab.

6. Enter your personal information, and then click OK.

7. Click OK to close the Message of the Day.

8. If you selected the Show All Available Chat Rooms option, double-click the chat room you want to enter.

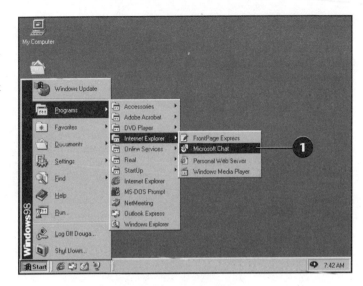

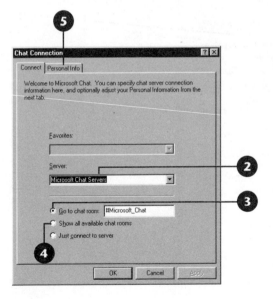

TIP

Gesture as you speak. *The words you type can change the pose and expression of your character. Try starting a sentence with I or you, typing in all capital letters, or using e-mail shorthand such as :-).*

TIP

Record your favorite sayings. *Assign your favorite expressions to a keyboard shortcut so you can quickly send a phrase without having to retype it. Click the View menu, click Options, and then click the Automation tab. In the Macros section, type your saying in the box, select a key combination, name your saying, click Add Macro, and then click OK. During a chat, press the key combination to send this recorded message.*

TRY THIS

Switch between comic strip and just text. *Click the Text View button to switch to all text or click the Comic View button to switch to comic strip view.*

SEE ALSO

See "Changing Your Chat Character" on page 184 for information on changing Microsoft Chat options.

Chat

1. If necessary, click the Connect button on the toolbar to connect to the Comic Chat server.

2. If you want to switch rooms, click the Room menu, click Room List, and then double-click a room.

3. Click a character to include in the frame.

4. Click a facial expression in the emotion palette.

5. Type your remarks.

6. Click one of the chat buttons. For further information, see the Using Chat Tools table.

7. When you're done, click the Close button.

USING CHAT TOOLS	
Button	**Purpose**
🗨	Use the Say tool to insert remarks in a speech bubble.
🗨	Use the Think tool to insert your remarks in a thought bubble.
🗨	Use the Whisper tool to send your remarks to only one character.
⌨	Use the Action tool to insert your nickname and remarks in a box at the top of the panel.
🔊	Use the Sound tool to send a sound clip along with your remarks.

Changing Your Chat Character

With Microsoft Chat, you can choose what your comic strip character looks like and the background of the comic strip. If you want, you can also enter personal information that your fellow chatters can view. Experiment with different characters and backgrounds. Have some fun!

TIP

More panels, please. *To change the number of panels displayed horizontally, click the View menu, click Options, click the Comics View tab, click the Page Layout drop-down arrow, select a new panel width for the comic strip, and then click OK.*

TRY THIS

Save your comic. *Click the File menu, and then click Save to save your Chat session— cartoons and all! After you've saved a Chat session, you can double-click the filename to start Microsoft Chat, and then read your comic.*

Change Your Comic Strip Settings

1. Click the View menu, and then click Options.

2. Click the Personal Info tab.

3. Enter the information you want others in the chat to know about you.

4. Click the Character tab.

5. Click the character you want to be.

6. Click the Background tab.

7. Click a background for the comic strip.

8. Click OK.

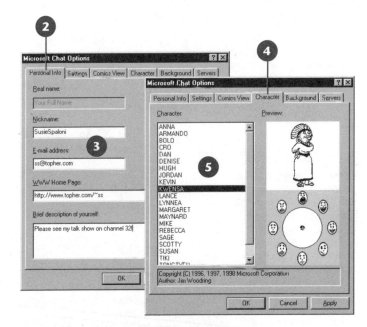

IN THIS SECTION

Starting FrontPage Express

Viewing the FrontPage Express Window and Toolbars

Creating a Web Page Using Templates or Wizards

Inserting and Modifying Text

Inserting and Modifying an Image

Moving and Copying Text and Images

Creating and Editing Hyperlinks

Creating a Bookmark

Setting Up Your Web Page for Printing

Printing Your Web Page

Saving Your Web Page

Opening and Viewing Your Web Page

10

Creating a Web Page with FrontPage Express

Whether you need to create a Web page from scratch or modify an existing one, Microsoft FrontPage Express can help you produce the results you need quickly and easily.

Introducing FrontPage Express

FrontPage Express is a Web page editor that gives you full access to the power of HTML (Hypertext Markup Language) in an easy-to-use interface. With FrontPage Express you can create Web pages from scratch, adding your own text, graphic images, hyperlinks, and other information. You can also use wizards, which provide step-by-step instructions, to create your masterpiece. Once you create your Web page, you can save it and then print it.

FrontPage Express works very much like a word processing program. So if you've used a word processing program before, particularly Microsoft Word, you'll find FrontPage Express easy to learn and use. If you've used Microsoft FrontPage, you already know how to use FrontPage Express. FrontPage Express offers many of the features of the Microsoft FrontPage Editor in a smaller package.

Starting FrontPage Express

You can start FrontPage Express from the Start menu on the taskbar. When FrontPage Express starts, it displays a blank Web page so that you can begin working immediately. You can also start FrontPage Express while surfing the Web. If you see a page that you would like to use as a template for your own page, simply click the Edit button on Internet Explorer's toolbar. A copy of the Web page is downloaded to your computer for you to edit.

SEE ALSO

See "Creating a Web Page Using Templates or Wizards" on page 190 for information about using Web page templates or wizards.

Start FrontPage Express from the Start Menu

1. Click the Start button on the taskbar, and then point to Programs.

2. Point to Internet Explorer (the folder).

3. Click FrontPage Express.

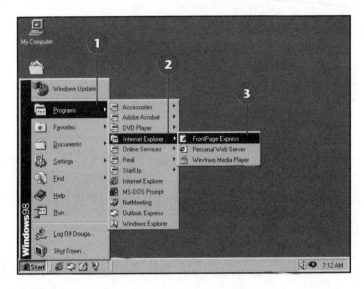

Start FrontPage Express from Internet Explorer

1. Start Internet Explorer and display the Web page you want to edit.

2. Click the Edit drop-down arrow on the toolbar, and then click Edit With Microsoft FrontPage Editor if available.

3. Begin editing the copy of the Web page that has been downloaded.

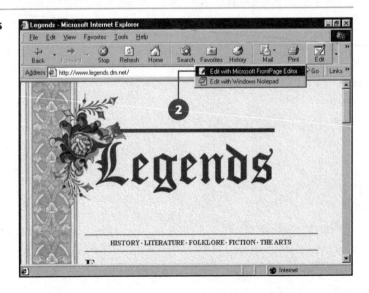

Viewing the FrontPage Express Window

Format toolbar
The Format toolbar contains buttons for the most frequently used font and paragraph formatting commands.

Menu bar
The menu bar gives you access to all the Front Page Express options.

Forms toolbar
The Forms toolbar contains buttons for inserting standard Web page items, such as tables and check boxes.

Standard toolbar
The Standard toolbar contains buttons for the most common commands executed in FrontPage Express.

Mouse pointer
When you are editing a Web page, the mouse pointer appears as an I-beam. The pointer shape changes depending where you are and what you're doing in the FrontPage Express window.

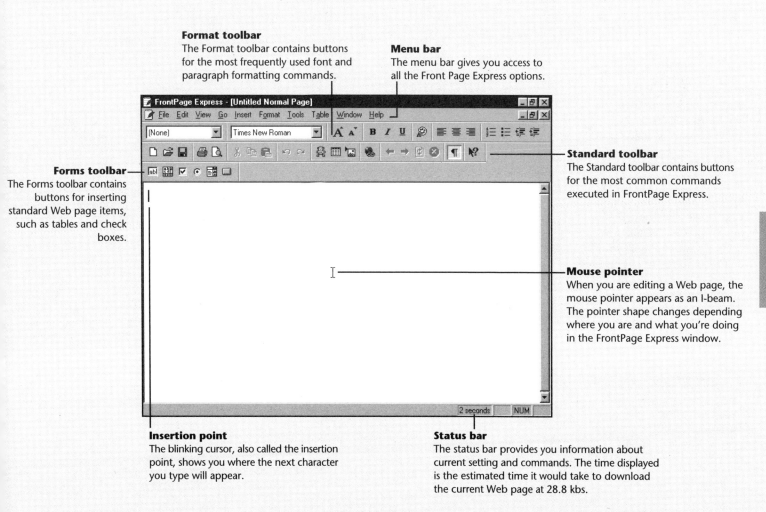

Insertion point
The blinking cursor, also called the insertion point, shows you where the next character you type will appear.

Status bar
The status bar provides you information about current setting and commands. The time displayed is the estimated time it would take to download the current Web page at 28.8 kbs.

10

Viewing the FrontPage Express Toolbars

To work with entire Web pages and individual Web objects, you will often use buttons and boxes located on the three FrontPage Express toolbars: Standard, Format, and Forms. The Standard and Format toolbars contain common features much like those you find in Microsoft Word or Microsoft Excel. The Forms toolbar contains tools you will need to create electronic forms. The tables shown here display and describe all the FrontPage Express toolbar buttons on the three different toolbars.

TIP

Display and hide toolbars.
To display a toolbar, click the View menu, and then click a toolbar without a check mark. To hide a toolbar, click the View menu, and then click a toolbar with a check mark.

STANDARD TOOLBAR

Button	Description
	The New button inserts a blank Web page in the FrontPage Express window.
	The Open button opens an existing Web page.
	The Save button saves the current Web page to a location you specify.
	The Print button opens the Print dialog box in which you specify settings for printing the current Web page.
	The Print Preview button displays the current Web page in the Print Preview window.
	The Cut button or the Copy button removes or copies the current selection from the current Web page and places it on the Clipboard.
	The Paste button inserts the selection from the Clipboard on the current Web page at the position of the insertion point.
	The Undo button or Redo button cancels or restores the effect of your last action.
	The Insert WebBot Component button adds functionality to your Web page, such as a timestamp or search file, without programming.
	The Insert Table button adds a table of the size you specify.
	The Insert Image button opens the Image dialog box from which you select an image to insert on your Web page.
	The Create Or Edit Hyperlink button opens the Create Hyperlink dialog box in which you create or edit a hyperlink.
	The Back button or Forward button returns or takes you to the previous Web page open in FrontPage Express.
	The Refresh button updates the display of the current Web page.
	The Stop button stops loading the current Web page in the FrontPage Express window.
	The Show/Hide button shows or hides special formatting symbols for the current Web page in the FrontPage Express window.
	The Help button opens a Help dialog box with options for finding information about FrontPage Express options and features.

TIP

Don't know what a button does? *Click a toolbar button and then, while you hold down the mouse button, press the F1 key to display information about the button's functionality.*

TRY THIS

Move the Forms toolbar. *Position the mouse pointer over an empty area on the Forms toolbar, and then drag the toolbar to the right of the Standard toolbar. You now have more FrontPage Express window area.*

FORMAT TOOLBAR

Button	Description
Normal ▼	The Change Style button changes the style type of the current text selection.
Times New Roman ▼	The Change Font button changes the font type of the current text selection.
A A	The Increase Text Size button and the Decrease Text Size button change the font size of the current text selection.
B I U	The Bold button, Italic button, and Underline button change the format of the current text selection.
🖉	The Text Color button displays the Color dialog box to let you change the color of the current text selection.
▤ ▤ ▤	The Align Left button, Center button, and Align Right button change the alignment of the current selection.
▤ ▤	The Numbered List button and Bulleted List button change the current text selection to a numbered or bulleted list.
⬅ ➡	The Decrease Indent button and the Increase Indent button move the paragraph text one tab stop to the left or right.

FORMS TOOLBAR

Button	Description
abl	The One-Line Text Box button creates a one-line text box in a Web page.
▦	The Scrolling Text Box button creates a scrolling text box in a Web page.
☑	The Check Box button creates a check box in a Web page.
⦿	The Radio Button button creates a radio option button in a Web page.
▤	The Drop-Down Menu button creates a drop-down menu list in a Web page.
▢	The Push Button button creates a customized button in a Web page.

10

Creating a Web Page Using Templates or Wizards

FrontPage Express provides predesigned templates and Web page wizards that speed up the creation of your Web pages. With the FrontPage Express templates and wizards, you can create a Web page with text and graphics or with forms that users can fill in. Wizards offer you choices in creating a customized Web page, while templates give you an exact copy of the template itself. Specifically, you can create a blank Web page, a personal home page, or a new Web View folder.

SEE ALSO

See "Creating Forms Using Templates and Wizards" on page 230 for more information about using one of the form templates or wizards.

Create a Personal Home Page

1. Click the File menu, and then click New.

2. Click Personal Home Page Wizard.

3. Click OK.

4. Click the check boxes of the major sections you want to include in your home page. Click Next to continue.

5. Type the Web address for your new page.

6. Type a new title for your Web page. Click Next to continue.

   For each major section you selected, a dialog box appears in which you specify the options you want for that section.

7. Read each dialog box and select the options you want to include in your home page. Click Next to continue.

8. When you complete the final wizard dialog box, click Finish.

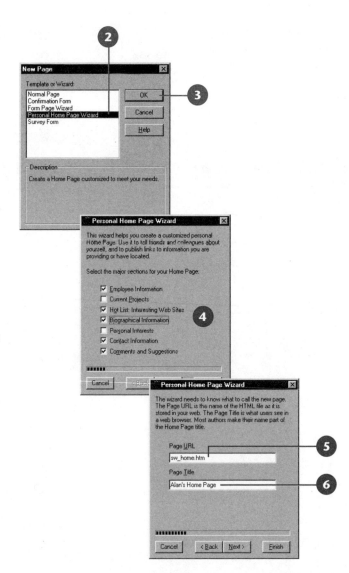

TIP

Create a blank Web page quickly. *Click the New button on the Standard toolbar to create a blank Web page without selecting a template or wizard.*

TIP

Can other people visit my Web page? *Your page is not available until you send it to your Internet service provider (ISP) for publishing on the Web.*

TIP

Close a Web page. *Click the File menu, and then click Close. If necessary, click Yes or No to save the Web page.*

SEE ALSO

See "Saving Your Web Page" on page 204 for more information on saving a Web page using FrontPage Express.

SEE ALSO

See "Publishing Your Web Page" on page 244 for more information about getting your Web page on the World Wide Web.

Create a Blank Web Page

1 Click the File menu, and then click New.

2 Click Normal Page.

3 Click OK.

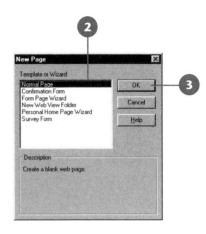

Inserting and Modifying Text

Once you've created a Web page, you can begin filling your page with text. If you've ever worked with Microsoft Word, you'll find this process familiar. To begin typing, you click a location within the Web page to position the insertion point. To modify the text, you select the text you want to change, and then make your changes. If you make a mistake, you can reverse text entry and editing with the Undo command, and then, if necessary, you can restore the action you undid with the Redo command. To replace text throughout your Web page quickly, use the Replace command.

Enter New Text

1 Click to place the insertion point where you want to add new text.

2 Type the new text in the Web page.

3 Press Enter to end one paragraph of text and to begin another paragraph.

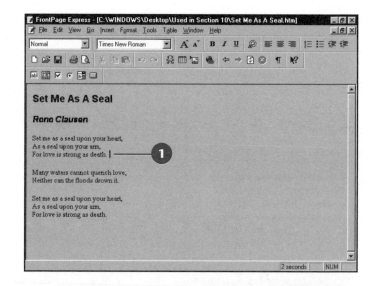

Replace or Delete Existing Text

1 Select the text you want to replace or delete.

2 To replace existing text, type the new text, automatically replacing the selected text.

To delete existing text, press Delete.

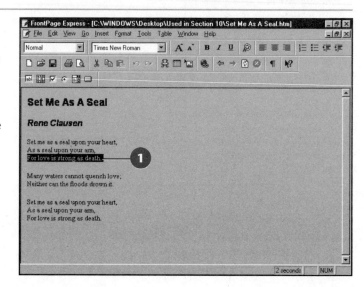

Undo or Redo Edits

◆ Click the Edit menu, and then click Undo to reverse your most recent action.

◆ Click the Edit menu, and then click Redo to restore the last action you reversed.

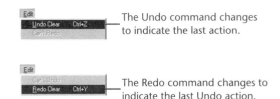

The Undo command changes to indicate the last action.

The Redo command changes to indicate the last Undo action.

Replace Multiple Occurrences of Text

1. Click the Edit menu, and then click Replace.

2. Type the text to replace.

3. Type the text you want to use.

4. If you want, click to select the Match Whole Word Only or the Match Case check box, or both options.

5. Click Find Next to find the next occurrence of the text in the Find What box.

6. Click Replace to replace the selected occurrence of the text with the text in the Replace With box.

7. Click Replace All to replace every occurrence of the text in the Find What box with the text in the Replace With box.

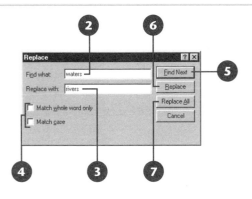

10

Inserting and Modifying an Image

If you know the location of a graphic image or if you want to use clip art supplied by FrontPage Express, you're ready to insert a graphic image in your Web page. Inserting an image is as easy as clicking a button, and once you've inserted a graphic image in a Web page, you can modify its appearance. You can also change its file format type to GIF or JPEG, common Web page graphic file formats for use with other graphics packages.

TIP

What's the difference between JPEG and GIF?
JPEG is best used for photographs because it can reproduce 24-bit files that contain up to 16.7 million colors. GIF is best used for smaller artwork because it can reproduce 8-bit files that contain only 256 colors.

Insert a Graphic Image from a Disk or Web Site

1 Click to place the insertion point where you want to insert your graphic image.

2 Click the Insert Image button on the Standard toolbar.

3 Click the Other Location tab.

4 To select a graphic file from a disk, click Browse, locate and select the file you want, and then click Open.

5 To select a graphic from a Web page, enter the Web site location, and then click OK.

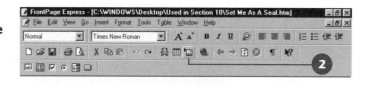

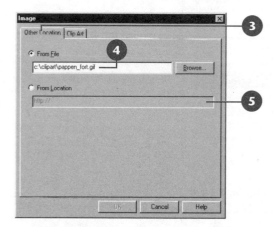

Insert a Graphic Image from Clip Art

1 Click to place the insertion point where you want to insert your graphic image.

2 Click the Insert Image button on the Standard toolbar.

3 Click the Clip Art tab.

4 Click the Category drop-down arrow, and then select a clip art category.

5 Double-click the graphic image you want to insert.

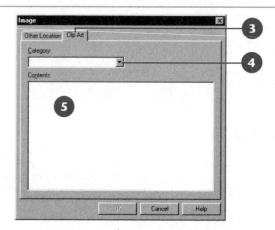

Why change the JPEG quality option? *JPEG reduces the size of an image by compressing similar colors. Increasing the value in the Quality box increases the quality of the image because the image contains more colors.*

See "Moving and Copying Text and Images" on page 196 for information about inserting a graphic image from another application.

Why use the interlaced GIF option? *Interlaced GIF files appear to load one layer at a time, so you can see a representation of the graphic before the entire graphic loads.*

Why use low-resolution graphic images? *You typically create and use low-resolution graphic images because the files are smaller. Users with slow-speed connections to your Web site don't spend a long time waiting for graphic images to load.*

Modify a Graphic Image Appearance

1. Right-click the graphic image, and then click Image Properties on the shortcut menu.

2. Click the Appearance tab.

3. Click the Alignment drop-down arrow, and then select an alignment option.

4. Enter a value greater than zero to add a border.

5. Click OK.

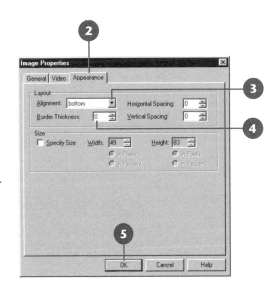

Change a Graphic Image File Format Type

1. Right-click the graphic image, and then click Image Properties on the shortcut menu.

2. Click the General tab.

3. Click the GIF option button or JPEG option button to convert the graphic image to a new type.

4. If you want, select or modify the GIF or JPEG options.

5. Click OK.

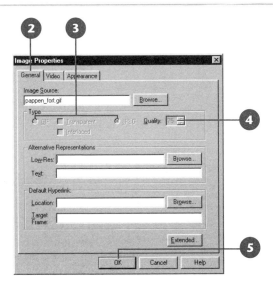

10

Moving and Copying Text and Images

You can move (cut) or copy text and graphic images within a Web page or between Web pages. When you cut or copy, the text or image is stored on the Clipboard, a temporary storage area, until you paste it (or cut or copy a new selection). You can also move or copy selected text or graphic images to a new location without storing it on the Clipboard using a technique called *drag-and-drop* editing.

TIP

Copy text or graphic images between documents. *Right-click the taskbar, and then click Tile Windows Vertically. Click the text or graphic image, press the Ctrl key, and then drag the text or graphic image to the other document window. Release the Ctrl key and the mouse button when the copy is in the correct location.*

Move or Copy and Paste Text or a Graphic Image

1. Select the text or graphic image you want to move or copy.

2. Click the Cut or Copy button on the Standard toolbar.

3. Click where you want to insert the text or graphic image.

4. Click the Paste button on the Standard toolbar.

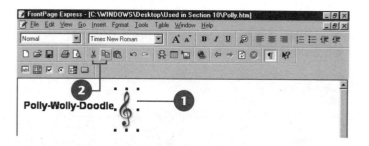

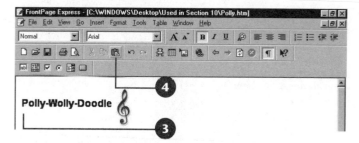

Drag Text or a Graphic Image

1. If you want to drag text or a graphic image between programs or documents, display both programs or document windows.

2. Select the text or graphic image you want to move or copy.

3. To prepare to move the text or graphic image to a new location, position the pointer over the selected text or graphic image, and then press and hold the mouse button.

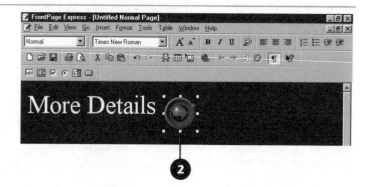

TIP

Selection handles. *When you click an image, small squares appear along the edge of the image. These are called* selection handles.

TIP

Change the width or height of a graphic image. *The middle selection handles on the left and right sides of the graphic image let you resize the width of the image, while the middle selection handles on the top and bottom let you adjust the height of the image.*

TIP

Return a graphic image to its original size. *Right-click a graphic image and click Image Properties on the shortcut menu. Click the Appearance tab, click to clear the Specify Size check box, and then click OK.*

④ To copy the text or graphic image and paste in a new location, press and hold the Ctrl key while dragging the text or image. A plus sign appears in the pointer box.

⑤ Drag the text or image to the new location, and then release the mouse button (and the Ctrl key, if necessary).

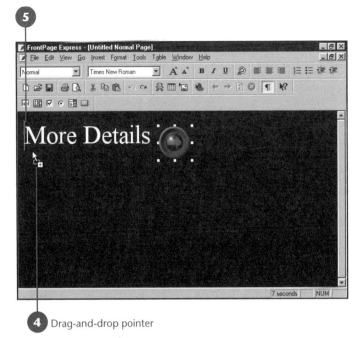

④ Drag-and-drop pointer

Resize a Graphic Image

① Select the graphic image you want to resize.

② Drag a corner selection handle outward to increase or inward to decrease the graphic image's size.

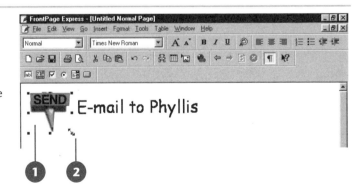

Creating and Editing Hyperlinks

A *hyperlink* is a clickable link to another Web page or a different location on the same Web page. Hyperlinks can be text or a graphic image that represents or describes the information that will be loaded when someone clicks the link. Web browsers usually underline text hyperlinks and display them in a specific color. Image hyperlinks have no such color identifier, but you can tell when the pointer is over a hyperlink because the pointer changes to a pointing hand. By a simple click of a mouse button, you can move from Web page to Web page.

TIP

Remove a hyperlink to a Web page. *Select the hyperlink you want to remove, click the Create Or Edit Hyperlink button on the Standard toolbar, click the tab where the hyperlink is located, click Clear, and then click OK.*

Create or Edit a Hyperlink to an Open Web Page

1. Open the Web page(s) you want to link to.

2. Open the Web page in which you want to place a hyperlink or to edit an existing hyperlink.

3. Select the text or graphic image you want to use as the hyperlink, or select the hyperlink you want to edit.

4. Click the Create Or Edit Hyperlink button on the Standard toolbar.

5. Click the Open Pages tab. The Web pages that are listed are the ones you opened in step 1.

6. Click the Web page you want to link to or edit a link to.

7. Click OK.

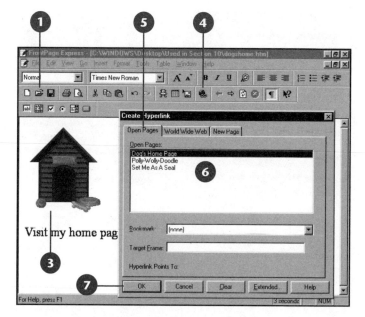

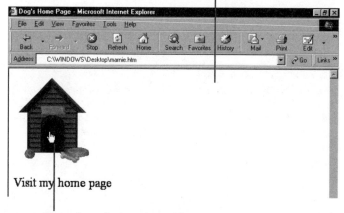

Your Web page viewed in Internet Explorer

The pointer changes shape when you position it over a hyperlink.

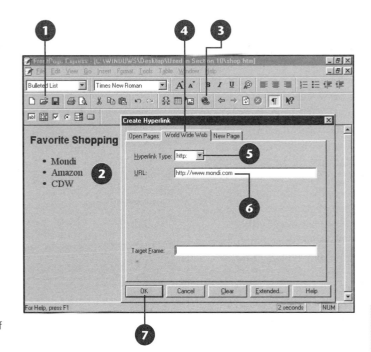

Create hyperlinks that make sense. *Make sure you select the text or graphic that best represents the content you are linking to. For example, if the sentence is "Click here for our product list," it's better to highlight "product list" than "click here."*

Test a text link from within FrontPage Express. *Right-click the text link you want to test, and then click Follow Hyperlink on the shortcut menu. The new location will load in the editor. Click the Back button to go back to your original page. You can't test an image link from within FrontPage Express.*

Create a hyperlink to send e-mail. *Select the text you want to link, click the Create Or Edit Hyperlink button on the Standard toolbar, click the World Wide Web tab, click the Hyperlink Type drop-down arrow, click Mailto:, and then type the destination e-mail address following the protocol in the URL box.*

Create or Edit a Hyperlink to an Internet Address

1. Open the Web page in which you want to place or to edit a hyperlink.

2. Select the text or graphic image you want to create as the link, or select the existing link you want to edit.

3. Click the Create Or Edit Hyperlink button on the Standard toolbar.

4. Click the World Wide Web tab.

5. Click the Hyperlink Type drop-down arrow, and then select the protocol of the Internet resource.

6. Type the hyperlink's URL.

7. Click OK.

Creating a Bookmark

If your Web page is so long that visitors have to scroll to see all of it, then you should consider creating bookmarks for some of the areas of the page. *Bookmarks* refer to specific locations on a long Web page and can work as a navigation tool within a Web page—just as hyperlinks work as navigation tools between Web pages. Simply click a place in your Web page and give that placeholder a name to create a bookmark. After you create a bookmark, you can then create a hyperlink to that bookmark so users can quickly jump to that part of the Web page.

> **TIP**
>
> **You can't move a bookmark.** *To move a bookmark, you need to first remove the existing bookmark, and then add it again.*

Create a Bookmark

1. Open the Web page in which you want to place a bookmark.

2. Select the text where you want to place the bookmark.

3. Click the Edit menu, and then click Bookmark.

4. Type a name for the bookmark.

5. Click OK.

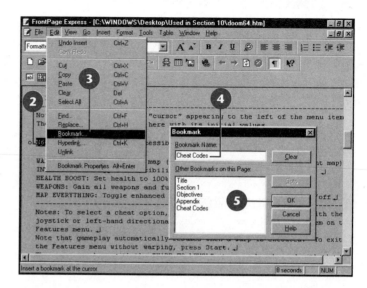

Create a Hyperlink to a Bookmark

1. Open the Web page with a bookmark.

2. Select the text or graphic image you want to use as the hyperlink.

3. Click the Create Or Edit Hyperlink button on the Standard toolbar.

4. Click the Open Pages tab.

5. Click the Bookmark drop-down arrow, and then select the bookmark to link to.

6. Click OK.

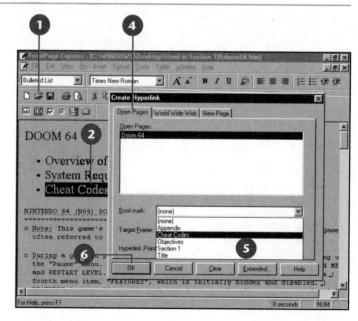

Setting Up Your Web Page for Printing

When you print a Web page, FrontPage Express uses the Print Page Setup dialog box to control the way text and graphics are printed on a page. If you want text to appear at the top or bottom of each printed Web page, you enter the text in the Header or Footer box respectively. You can also use special codes that will print information about the date, time, file information, and so on. To print "Page 1 of 5," "Page 2 of 5," and so on on each page, you can combine text and the codes. The table shown here describes the variable codes. You can also use the Print Page Setup dialog box to change margin settings.

TIP

Print a Web page for a second time quickly. *Click the Print button on the Standard toolbar.*

Set Up Your Web Page for Printing

1 Open the Web page you want to set up.

2 Click the File menu, and then click Page Setup.

3 Type the text or code you want to print at the top of each page. You can combine text and code in the text box.

4 Type the text or code you want to print at the bottom of each page. You can combine text and code in the text box.

5 Specify what size margins you want to use for the printed pages.

6 Click OK.

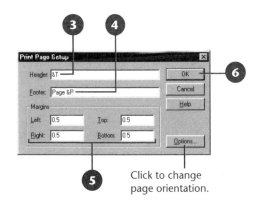

Click to change page orientation.

ENTERING HEADER AND FOOTER CODES	
Code	**Description**
&w	Window title
&u	URL or local path of the current Web page
&d	Date in short format (m/d/y—10/1/01)
&D	Date in long format (month, day, year—October 1, 2001)
&t	Time of day
&T	Time in 24-hour format
&p	Page number
&P	Total number of pages

10

Printing Your Web Page

You should always preview your work before sending it to the printer. A *print preview* is a miniature view of the entire Web page that shows how your document will look when it is printed. Previewing your Web page gives you an opportunity to make changes before you print it.

When you are ready to print your Web page, click the Print button on the Standard toolbar. You can then use the Print dialog box to specify several print options, such as choosing a printer, selecting the number of pages you want to print, and specifying the number of copies.

TIP

Change printer properties.
Click the Properties button in the Print dialog box to change general printer properties for paper size and orientation, graphics, and fonts.

Preview Your Web Page Before Printing It

1. Click the File menu, and then click Print Preview.

2. Click the Next Page or Prev Page button to move through the Web page you want to print.

3. Click the Zoom In or Zoom Out button to magnify or reduce the display size of the Web page you want print.

4. Click the Two Page button to preview two pages side-by-side. Click the One Page button to preview one page.

5. Click the Print button if you decide to print the Web page.

6. When you're done, click the Close button.

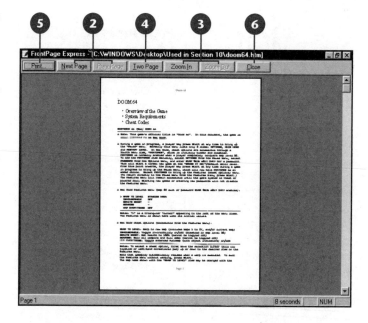

Print button

TIP

A Web page can be more than one page of paper. *A single Web page may actually print on several pieces of paper. That's another reason for previewing your Web page before you print.*

TIP

What if a Print Preview button is grayed out? *Print Preview enables buttons only when they make sense. For example, if there is no previous page, the Prev Page button is not available.*

SEE ALSO

See "Printing a Web Page" on page 66 for information about printing a Web page while viewing it in Internet Explorer.

Print Your Web Page

1 Open the Web page you want to print.

2 Click the Print button on the Standard toolbar.

3 If necessary, click the Name drop-down arrow, and then select the printer you want to use.

4 Indicate how many pages of the Web page you want to print

5 Specify how many copies of the Web page you want to print.

6 Click OK.

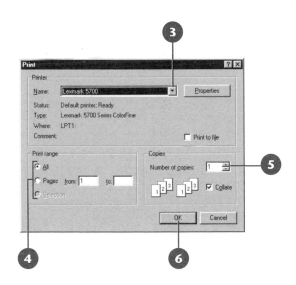

Saving Your Web Page

When you open a new Web page in FrontPage Express, the title bar displays a default title, such as Un-titled. When you save your Web page for the first time, you need to give it a mean-ingful name, which becomes the name in the title bar when people visit your Web page. When FrontPage Express saves a Web page, it saves the Web page's HTML source code. The source code controls what a Web browser, such as Internet Explorer, displays on the screen. FrontPage Express also allows you to save your page in formats other than HTML if your server supports them.

TIP

Save a Web page for the second time quickly. *Click the Save button on the Standard toolbar.*

Save Your Web Page for the First Time to a File

1. Click the Save button on the Standard toolbar.

2. Enter a name for the Web page.

3. Type the filename you want to use for the Web page. You don't need to add the .htm file exten-sion.

4. Click As File.

5. Click the Save In drop-down arrow, and then specify where you want to save the file.

6. Click Save.

7. If necessary, click the Yes, Yes To All, or No button to indicate whether you want the graphic images displayed on the Web page saved with the HTML document.

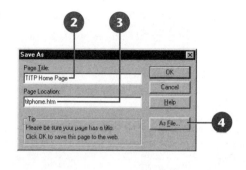

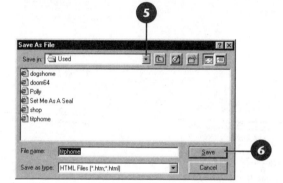

TIP

Use the keyboard shortcut to save. *While working on your Web page in FrontPage Express, save often and quickly by pressing Ctrl+S.*

TIP

Save all open Web pages quickly. *Click the File menu, and then click Save All.*

TIP

Use the Save As command to save a Web page with a different name. *To save your Web page with a different name, so that you have your original Web page and a copy with changes you may want, use the Save As command, replacing the current filename with a new filename. You will then have two files: the original and one with the changes.*

SEE ALSO

See "Publishing Your Web Page" on page 244 for information on saving a Web page to a Web server.

Save a Web Page to a File as a Different Type

1. Click the File menu, and then click Save As.

2. Enter a name for the Web page.

3. Type the filename you want to use for the Web page.

4. Click As File.

5. Click the Save In drop-down arrow, and then select the drive and folder in which you want to save the file.

6. Type a filename.

7. Click the Save As Type drop-down arrow, and then select the file type you want.

8. Click Save.

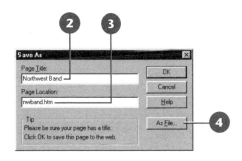

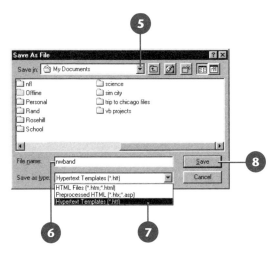

10

Opening Your Web Page

You can open Web pages that you are working on in FrontPage Express from your local hard drive. You can also load Web pages directly from the Internet for editing. FrontPage Express will download the page, including all the text and graphics for you to edit. Besides directly working with Web pages, you can use FrontPage Express to open word processing documents that you can edit and use as Web pages.

SEE ALSO

See "Starting FrontPage Express" on page 186 for information about opening a Web page for editing from Internet Explorer.

SEE ALSO

See "Creating and Editing Hyperlinks" on page 198 for information on how to change text to a hyperlink in your Web page.

Open a Web Page from a File

1. Click the Open button on the Standard toolbar.

2. Click the From File option button, and then click Browse.

3. Click the Look In drop-down arrow, and then select the drive and folder containing the Web page you want to open.

4. Click the Web page you want to open.

5. Click Open.

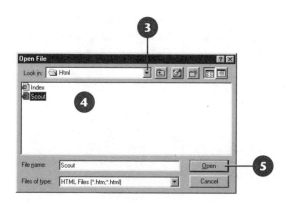

Open a Web Page from an Internet Location

1. Click the Open button on the Standard toolbar.

2. Click the From Location option button.

3. Type the Web address, including the filename of the Web page you want to open.

4. Click OK.

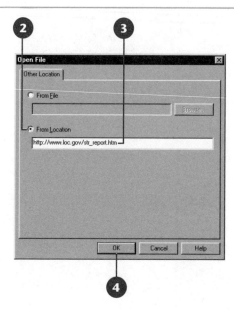

Browse the Web in FrontPage Express. *If the Web page you loaded from the Internet isn't the one you want to edit, you can follow the hyperlinks that are on the page to find the Web page you want. Right-click the underlined text, and then click Follow Hyperlink on the shortcut menu.*

Open a recently used Web page quickly and easily. *If the Web page you want to open is one of the last four Web pages you worked on, it will be listed at the bottom of the File menu in the FrontPage Express window. Just click the File menu, and then click the name of the Web page you want to open.*

Convert a text file to a Web page. *Instead of clicking the HTML option button, click the Text option button, and then click OK. Click the option button for the text paragraph conversion you want, click OK, and then edit the document in FrontPage Express to create a Web page.*

Open a Word Document for Editing as a Web Page

1. Click the Open button on the Standard toolbar.

2. Click the From File option button, and then click the Browse button.

3. Click the Look In drop-down arrow, and then select the drive and folder containing the Word document you want to open.

4. Click the Files of Type drop-down arrow, and then select the file type for the version of Microsoft Word you use.

5. Double-click the file you want to open.

6. Click the HTML option button to specify the editing format.

7. Click OK.

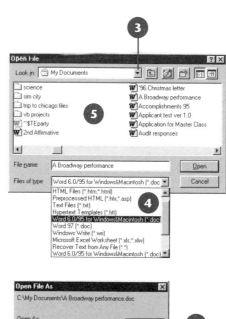

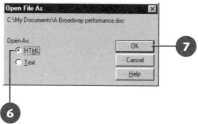

10

Viewing Your Web Page in Internet Explorer

After you finish working on your Web page, you can save it as an HTML file, and then open it in Internet Explorer to see how well your page displays. You can also test the hyperlinks, view the placement of the graphic images, and make certain your Web page looks and reacts the way you want it to.

SEE ALSO

See "Starting FrontPage Express" on page 186 for information about opening a Web page for editing from Internet Explorer.

SEE ALSO

See "Saving Your Web Page" on page 204 for information on how to save a Web page for the first time.

Open a Saved Web Page in Internet Explorer

1. Save your Web page as a file, and then click the Close button to exit FrontPage Express.

2. Start Internet Explorer.

3. Click the File menu, and then click Open.

4. Click Browse.

5. Click the Look In drop-down arrow, and then select the drive and folder containing the Web page you want to open.

6. Double-click the file you want to view in Internet Explorer.

7. Click OK.

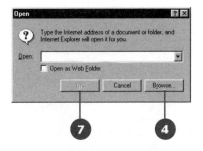

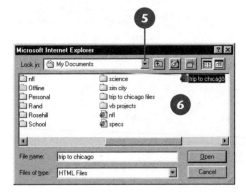

Enhancing Web Pages with FrontPage Express

IN THIS SECTION

Formatting Text

Formatting Paragraphs

Changing Paragraph Styles

Working with Paragraph Lists

Inserting Web Page Elements

Inserting a Video Clip

Changing a Background

Creating a Marquee

Creating and Modifying Tables

Using WebBots

Creating Forms Using Templates or Wizards

Working with Forms

Inserting ActiveX Controls

Inserting Java Applets

Inserting Plug-Ins

Once you've mastered the basics of creating a Web page with Microsoft FrontPage Express, you can try some of the more advanced features. In most cases, there's more than one way to perform tasks such as creating tables or forms. To save you time, this book focuses on the fastest and easiest methods.

Enhancing Your Web Page

After you've created your basic Web page, take a moment to consider how you can enhance its appearance and communicate its message more effectively. For example, you could draw attention to important text and data using a table or clarify the details of a complicated paragraph by creating a list. If you want to get feedback from the people who visit your Web page, you can include forms you create using FrontPage Express wizards. You can also use several FrontPage Express features—among them, WebBots, ActiveX controls, and Java applets—that are designed to help you add extensive functionality to your Web pages in a fast and efficient manner without programming.

Formatting Text

You'll often want to *format*, or change the style, of certain words or phrases to add emphasis to parts of a Web page. Boldface, italics, underline, and other text effects are applied using *toggle buttons*, which means you simply click the same button to turn the effect on or off. For special emphasis, you can combine formats, such as boldface and italics. You can also color and resize text. Formatting makes your Web page more interesting and professional looking.

TIP

Quickly remove formatting. *To remove formatting you've added to text, select the formatted text, click the Format menu, and then click Remove Formatting.*

SEE ALSO

See "Formatting Paragraphs" on page 212 for more information about formatting other text in FrontPage Express.

Boldface, Italicize, or Underline Text

1. Select the text on your Web page you want to format.

2. Click the Bold, Italic, or Underline button on the Format toolbar.

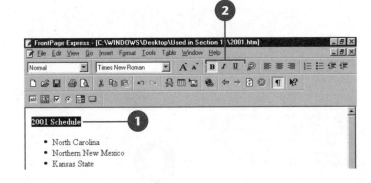

Color Text

1. Select the text on your Web page you want to recolor.

2. Click the Text Color button on the Format toolbar.

3. Click the color you want to use.

4. Click OK.

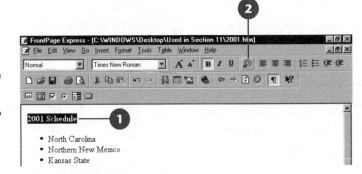

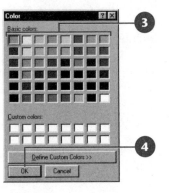

Quickly change a font style. *Select the text for which you want to specify a font, click the Change Font drop-down arrow on the Formatting toolbar, and then select the font you want to use.*

Create a custom color. *Click the Text Color button on the Formatting toolbar, click Define Custom Colors, select a color range in the color spectrum box, drag the color arrow to select a specific color, click Add To Custom Colors, and then click OK.*

See "Inserting and Modifying Text" on page 192 and "Inserting and Modifying an Image" on page 194 for information on adding text and graphics to a Web page that you create.

See "Creating a Web Page Using Templates or Wizards" on page 190 for information about the different ways to create your own Web pages.

Increase or Decrease the Text Size

1 Select the text on your Web page you want to resize.

2 Click the Increase Text Size or Decrease Text Size button on the Format toolbar.

FrontPage Express increases or decreases the font size of the text to the next higher or lower setting.

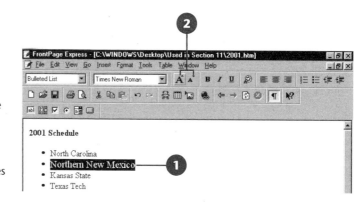

Change Font Attributes and Add Special Styles

1 Select the text on your Web page you want to format.

2 Click the Format menu, and then click Font.

3 Click the Font tab.

4 Select the font, font style, size, effects, and color you want to use.

5 Click the Special Styles tab.

6 Select to select one or more of the special styles check boxes you want to use.

7 Click OK.

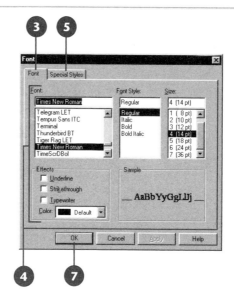

11

Formatting Paragraphs

A *paragraph* is defined as a block of text followed by a carriage return. Pressing the Enter key signals FrontPage Express that the previously entered text is a paragraph. Once you have created your paragraphs, you can format the paragraph alignment and indenting. Alignment moves a selected paragraph to the right margin, left margin, or center of the page. Indenting moves a selected paragraph an indent level to the right or left.

TIP

Quickly select a paragraph. *Double-click just to the left of one of the lines of the paragraph.*

SEE ALSO

See "Formatting Text" on page 210 for information about using boldface, italics, underlines, and colors to enhance your Web page.

Change the Alignment of a Paragraph

1 Select the paragraph in your Web page you want to align.

2 Click one of the following Format toolbar buttons.

- ◆ Align Left to align the paragraph against the left edge of the page

- ◆ Center to center the paragraph horizontally

- ◆ Align Right to align the paragraph against the right edge of the page

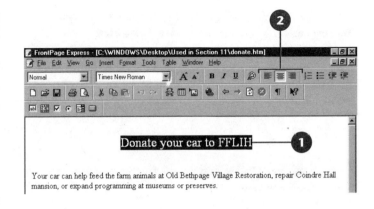

Change the Indent Level of a Paragraph

1 Select the paragraph in your Web page you want to indent.

2 Click one of the following Format toolbar buttons.

- ◆ Decrease Indent to indent the paragraph to the left

- ◆ Increase Indent to indent the paragraph to the right

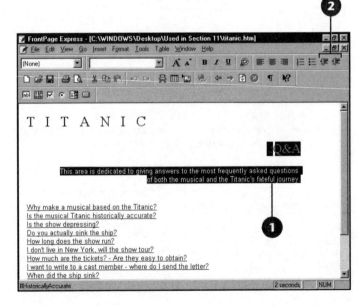

Changing Paragraph Styles

A *style* is a collection of formatting settings you can apply to selected text. Like Microsoft Word, FrontPage Express comes with pre-defined text styles you can use to format your Web page text. To create headings and subheadings on a Web page, you can use one of six built-in styles: Heading 1 through Heading 6. Besides the heading styles, FrontPage Express also includes other built-in styles: Address, Defined Term, Definition, Normal, Bulleted List(s), Numbered List(s), Directory List, and Menu List. Applying these styles to your text throughout your Web page helps to ensure consistency and professionalism.

SEE ALSO

See "Working with Paragraph Lists" on page 214 for more information about creating and formatting lists.

Apply a Heading or Subheading Style

1. Select the text in your Web page you want to use as a heading or subheading.

2. Click the Format menu, and then click Paragraph.

3. Select a heading style you want to use.

4. Click OK.

   FrontPage Express changes the selected text into a heading or subheading.

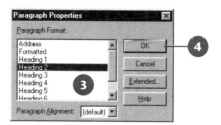

Change a Paragraph Style

1. Select the text in your Web page whose style you want to change.

2. Click the Change Style drop-down arrow on the Format toolbar.

3. Select a style you want to apply.

   FrontPage Express applies the selected paragraph style to the selected text.

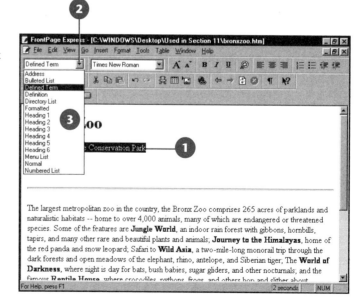

11

Working with Paragraph Lists

The best way to draw attention to a list is to format it with bullets, numbers, or some other special format. You can change the plain list of words to a numerical list or an alphabetical list. If you move, insert, or delete items within a numbered list, FrontPage Express will renumber the list sequence for you. FrontPage Express also provides special lists to create a directory, definition, or menu list.

TIP

Remove numbering from a paragraph list. *Select the numbered list, and then click the Numbered List button on the Formatting toolbar.*

TRY THIS

A list without bullets. *Right-click a list, and then click List Properties. Click the Other tab, click Definition List, and then click OK.*

Create a Numbered List

1. Select the paragraphs in your Web page you want to convert to a numbered list.

2. Click the Numbered List button on the Format toolbar.

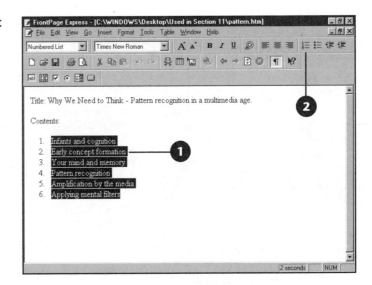

Customize a Numbered List

1. Right-click any item in your list, and then click List Properties on the shortcut menu.

2. Click the sample box you want your numbered list to look like.

3. Specify the number you want to use for the first paragraph.

4. Click OK.

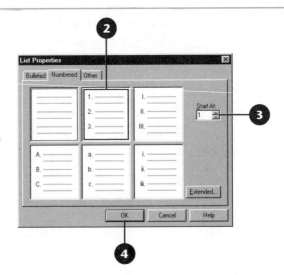

TIP

Remove bulleting from a paragraph list. *Select the bulleted list, and then click the Bulleted List button on the Format toolbar.*

TIP

Quickly change a list format. *Once you have text formatted as a list, you can switch from numbers to bullets or vice versa by clicking anywhere inside the list and clicking the appropriate button on the toolbar. There is no need to select the entire list!*

TRY THIS

Create other special lists. *Select the text you want to convert into a special list, click the Change Style drop-down arrow on the Formatting toolbar, and then select the Directory List, Menu List, or Definition List style.*

SEE ALSO

See "Changing Paragraph Styles" on page 213 for more information about creating other FrontPage Express special lists: Directory List, Definition List, and Menu List.

Create a Bulleted List

1. Select the paragraphs in your Web page you want to convert to a bulleted list.

2. Click the Bulleted List button on the Format toolbar.

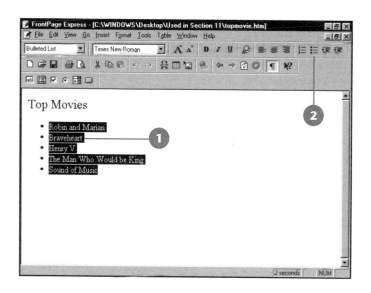

Customize a Bulleted List

1. Right-click any item in your list, and then click List Properties on the shortcut menu.

2. Click the sample box you want your bulleted list to look like.

3. Click OK.

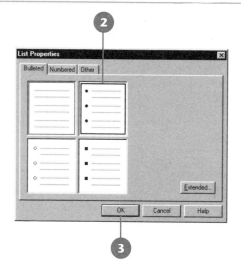

Inserting Web Page Elements

A great way to separate sections, topics, or other elements on a Web page is by adding a horizontal line. You can also add a comment to your Web page that only you see in FrontPage Express. Once you publish the Web page, viewers can't see the comment with their Web browser. If you add a comment, you can't edit the text, but you can copy, move, or delete it.

TIP

Insert a page break. *Click to place the insertion point where you want a page break, click the Insert menu, click Break, click the Normal Line Break option button, and then click OK.*

TIP

Customize a horizontal line. *Right-click the horizontal line, and then click Horizontal Line Properties on the shortcut menu. Specify the width, height, alignment, and color you want to change, and then click OK.*

Insert a Horizontal Line

1 Click to place the insertion point in your Web page where you want to insert a horizontal line.

2 Click the Insert menu, and then click Horizontal Line.

The horizontal line fills the width of your Web page.

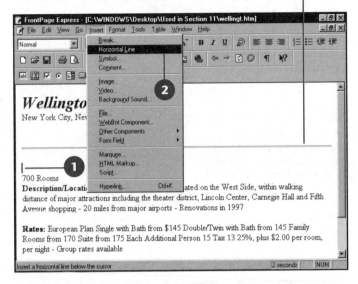

Insert a Comment

1 Click to place the insertion point in your Web page where you want to insert a comment.

2 Click the Insert menu, and then click Comment.

3 Type the comment you want to add to the Web page.

4 Click OK.

The comment text appears in purple to help separate it from the rest of your text.

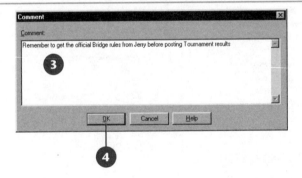

Inserting a Video Clip

A video clip can add a great deal of interest and drama to a Web page. It's easy to insert a video clip in your Web pages and to control when and how a visitor sees the video clip. Before you insert a video clip, remember that video clip files can be very large, which means they can increase the time it takes to retrieve a Web page. To play a video's sound, the visitor's computer must have a sound card and speakers.

TIP

Play a video clip over and over. *On the Video tab of the Image Properties dialog box, click to select the Forever check box in the Repeat section.*

TIP

Show the Play and Stop buttons in a browser. *On the Video tab of the Image Properties dialog box, click to select the Show Controls In Browser check box.*

Insert a Video Clip

1. Click to place the insertion point in your Web page where you want to insert your video clip.

2. Click the Insert menu, and then click Video.

3. If the video clip is located on a disk, enter the path to the file.

4. If the video clip is located at a Web site, click the From Location option button, and then enter the Web address.

5. Click OK.

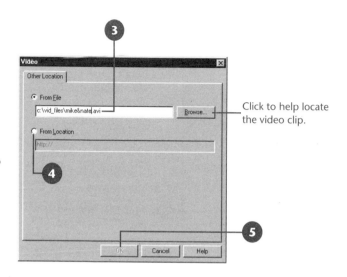

Click to help locate the video clip.

Modify the Way a Video Clip Plays

1. Right-click the video clip, and then click Image Properties on the shortcut menu.

2. Click the Video tab.

3. Specify the number of times you want the video to play.

4. Specify the delay time.

5. Click to select the On File Open or On Mouse Over check box to indicate when to play the video.

6. Click OK.

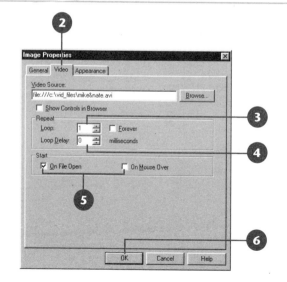

Changing a Background

You can add a background image or sound, or change the background color to dramatically improve the audio and visual appeal of your Web pages. Adding a background image can be effective as long as it does not impair viewing of the text or other images on the Web page. Background images appear titled in your Web page. Assuming your Web page visitor's computer has a sound card and speakers, the background sound plays when the Web page is loaded or refreshed, and it can play a specified number of times or loop continuously.

TIP

Play a background sound more than once. *Click the File menu, click the Page Properties, click the General tab, specify the number of times to play the sound in the Loop box or click to select the Forever check box to play the sound continuously.*

Insert a Background Graphic Image

1. Open the Web page in which you want to insert a background graphic.

2. Click the Format menu, and then click Background.

3. Click to select the Background Image check box.

4. Click Browse.

5. If the file is located on a disk, click the Other Location tab, and then click Browse to locate the file.

6. If you are inserting clip art, click the Clip Art tab, click the Category drop-down menu, and then select a clip art category.

7. Double-click the graphic image or clip art you want to insert.

8. Click OK.

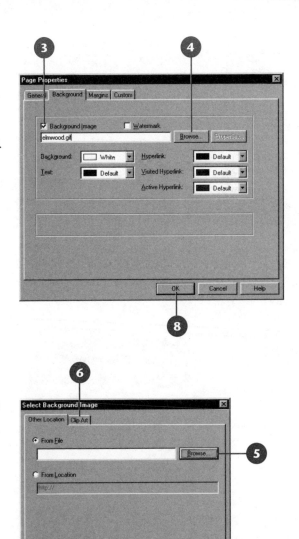

Insert a Background Sound

1. Open the Web page in which you want to insert a background sound.

2. Click the Insert menu, and then click Background Sound.

3. Enter the Web address in the From Location box, or enter the path to the sound file in the From File box. If necessary, click Browse to help locate the file you want.

4. Click OK.

Specify a Background Color

1. Open the Web page whose background color you want to specify.

2. Click the Format menu, and then click Background.

3. Click the Background drop-down arrow, and then select a background color.

4. Click OK.

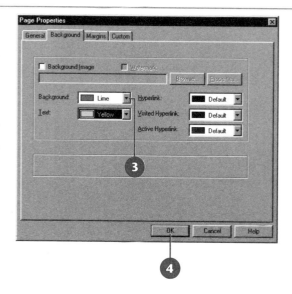

Creating a Marquee

Another way you can add visual interest to your Web pages is by creating a marquee. A *marquee* is a Web element that scrolls your text message across a Web page. Marquees use moving text for emphasis—the same way that some movie theaters use a marquee to tell you what movie is playing and who's starring in it. But as with any other catchy design element, be careful not to overuse it.

TIP

Convert an existing heading to a marquee.
Select the heading text you want to be a marquee, click the Insert menu, click Marquee—the heading text is automatically set as a marquee text—and then click OK.

Create a Marquee

1. Open the Web page in which you want to add a marquee.

2. Click to place the insertion point where you want to insert a marquee, or select the text you want to convert to a marquee.

3. Click the Insert menu, and then click Marquee.

4. Enter the marquee text you want to roll onto and off the Web page.

5. Click OK.

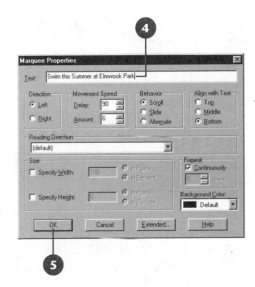

Edit Marquee Text

1. Right-click the marquee, and then click Marquee Properties on the shortcut menu.

2. Edit the marquee text.

3. Click OK.

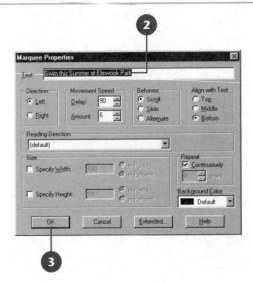

How does marquee behavior work? *Scroll rolls the marquee onto and off the Web page; Slide rolls the marquee onto the Web page and then stops; and Alternate rolls the marquee onto and off the Web page from alternate directions.*

How does marquee movement speed work? *The larger the Movement Speed Amount value, the faster the marquee moves.*

Quickly change marquee width and height. *Click to select the marquee, and then drag one of its selection handles to resize the marquee.*

Delete a marquee quickly. *Click to select the marquee, and then press Delete.*

Change Marquee Properties

1. Right-click the marquee, and then click Marquee Properties on the shortcut menu.

2. Click the Left or Right Direction option button to indicate in which direction the marquee should move.

3. Specify the speed of the marquee.

4. Click a Behavior option button to indicate the kind of marquee you want.

5. Click to select the Specify Width or Specify Height check box, and then set the width or height in pixels or as a percentage of the Web page.

6. Click to select the Continuously check box, or set the number of times you want to repeat the marquee.

7. Click the Background Color drop-down arrow, and then select a marquee background color.

8. Click OK.

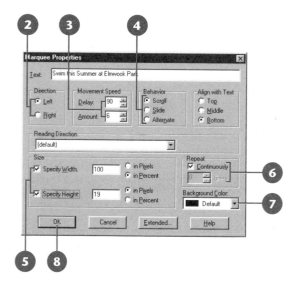

11

Creating Tables

A table organizes information neatly into rows and columns. The intersection of a row and column is called a *cell*. You use cells to hold the table data. Table cells can hold a variety of data: text, numbers, graphic images, and even other tables. You enter the data into cells just as you would type information anywhere else in a Web page, except that the Tab key moves you from one cell to the next. After you create a table or begin to enter data in one, you might want to add more rows or columns to accommodate the data you are entering in the table.

TIP

Quickly insert a table from the toolbar. *Click the Insert Table button on the Standard Toolbar, and then drag the pointer down and to the right to define the size of your table.*

Insert a Table

① Click to place the insertion point in your Web page where you want to insert a table.

② Click the Table menu, and then click Insert Table.

③ Specify the number of rows and columns you want.

④ If you want, specify any of the following layout table options you want.

◆ Column Order defines the behavior of the cursor when you enter text or numbers in the cell.

◆ Alignment defines the placement of text or numbers in the cell.

◆ Border Size defines the thickness of the cell walls.

◆ Cell Padding defines the space between the cell wall and the text or number in that cell.

◆ Cell Spacing defines the space between the cell walls.

⑤ If you want, specify the Table Width in pixels or as a percentage of Web page width.

⑥ Click OK.

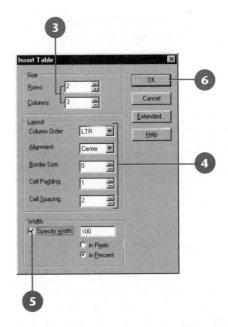

Enter Information in a Cell

1. Click the cell to position the insertion point.

2. Type the text or number you want in the cell.

3. Press Tab to go to the next cell.

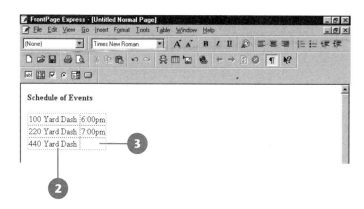

Insert a New Row or Column in a Table

1. Click a cell in the table where you want to insert the new row or column.

2. Click the Table menu, and then click Insert Rows Or Columns.

3. Click the Columns or Rows option button.

4. Specify the number of columns or rows you want to insert.

5. Specify where you want to insert the column (left or right) or row (above or below).

6. Click OK.

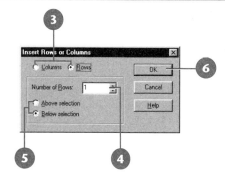

11

Modifying Tables

Once you've created a table and filled it with information, you'll probably want to make changes to the table's appearance. You can change settings for table alignment, border size, cell padding, cell spacing, and overall table width by using the Table Properties command. If your table has borders, you can specify their colors. You can also change the properties for cells, such as the alignment of data within them, their minimum width, the number of rows or columns they span, and their background images or colors.

TIP

Change the width of a table. *Right-click the table, click Table Properties on the shortcut menu, click to select the Specify Width check box, and then specify the table width in pixels or as a percentage of the Web page width.*

Change Table Properties

1. Right-click the table, and then click Table Properties on the shortcut menu.

2. Click the Alignment drop-down arrow, and then select an alignment.

3. Enter a border thickness (in pixels).

4. Enter the amount of space inside the cells (in pixels).

5. Enter the amount of space between the cell border and the cells (in pixels).

6. If you want, click to select the Use Background Image check box, and then select a graphic image file or clip art.

7. Click the Background Color drop-down arrow, and then select a background color.

8. Click the Border, Light Border, or Dark Border drop-down arrow, and then select border colors.

9. Click OK.

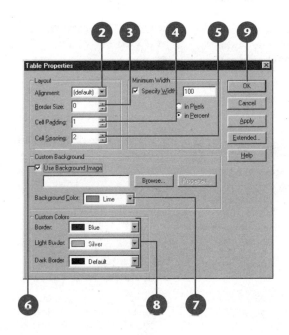

TIP

Combine two or more cells. *Select the two or more adjacent cells that you want to combine together, click the Table menu, and then click Merge Cells.*

TIP

Split a cell into two or more cells. *Select the cell that you want to split, click the Table menu, click Split Cells, click the Split Into Columns or Split Into Rows option button, specify how many columns or rows the selected cell should be split into, and then click OK.*

TIP

Quick select rows and columns. *If you hover the pointer just above a column or just to the left of a row, the pointer changes to a thick arrow. Click to select the entire row or column.*

SEE ALSO

See "Creating Tables" on page 222 for information on inserting columns and rows.

Change Individual Cell Properties

1. Right click the cell, and then click Cell Properties on the shortcut menu.

2. Click the Horizontal or Vertical Alignment drop-down arrow, and then select an alignment.

3. If you want, click to select the Header Cell check box to create a header.

4. Click to select the Specify Width check box, and then enter a cell width in pixels or as a percentage of the Web page width.

5. If you want, click to select the Use Background Image check box, and then specify a graphic file or clip art.

6. Click the Background Color drop-down arrow, and then select a color you want.

7. Click the Border, Light Border, or Dark Border drop-down arrows, and then select custom border colors.

8. Specify how many table rows or columns this cell should span.

9. Click OK.

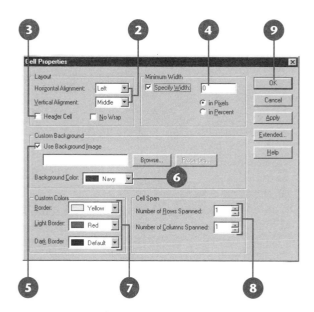

Using WebBots

WebBots help people with little or no background in computer programming add functionality to a Web page. For instance, you can add a WebBot to automatically include the contents of one Web page in another, update the date and time a page is changed, or create a search page. Keep in mind that in order for WebBots to work properly, the server hosting the Web page must have the FrontPage Server Extensions installed. These extensions are automatically installed with the Microsoft Personal Web Server.

TIP

How does the Include WebBot work? *The Include WebBot places the "included" Web page on the Web page you are editing. Create a single page with your contact information, and "include" it on all the pages of your Web site. If your phone number changes, fix the one on the "included" page, and all the pages will be correct the next time they are loaded.*

Insert the Include WebBot

1. Open the Web page in which you want to place the Include WebBot.

2. Click the Insert WebBot Component button on the Standard toolbar.

3. Click Include.

4. Click OK.

5. Type the Internet address, Uniform Resource Locator (URL), for the Web page you want to include.

6. Click OK.

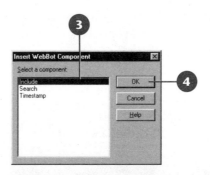

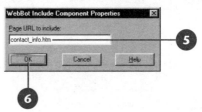

Change the Properties of the Include WebBot

1. Right-click the Include WebBot, and then click WebBot Component Properties on the shortcut menu.

2. Edit or replace the Web page.

3. Click OK.

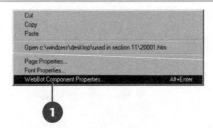

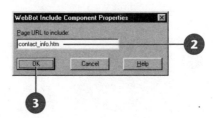

TIP

Delete a WebBot. *Click the WebBot to select it, click the Edit menu, and then click Clear.*

TIP

Change properties of the Timestamp WebBot. *Right-click the Timestamp WebBot, click WebBot Component Properties on the shortcut menu, change the WebBot Display, Date Format, and Time Format options, and then click OK.*

SEE ALSO

See "Setting Up a Personal Web Server" on page 246 for information about FrontPage Server Extensions.

SEE ALSO

See "Using Interactive WebBots" on page 228 for information about the Search WebBot component.

Insert a Timestamp WebBot

1. Open the Web page in which you want to place the Timestamp WebBot.

2. Click the Insert WebBot Component button on the Standard toolbar.

3. Click Timestamp.

4. Click OK.

5. Select one of the Display option buttons to indicate which date you want to display.

6. Click the Date Format drop-down arrow, and then select a date format.

7. Click the Time Format drop-down arrow, and then select a time format.

8. Click OK.

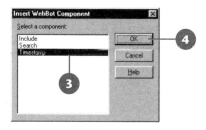

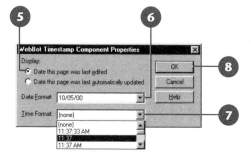

11

Using Interactive WebBots

FrontPage Express allows you to insert interactive WebBots that provide visitors with the opportunity to interact with your Web page. The Search WebBot, for example, lets you offer visitors the ability to perform quick searches for matching words or phrases in the text of your longer Web pages. For WebBots to work properly, the server hosting the Web page must have the FrontPage Server Extensions installed.

TIP

How to use the Word List To Search field? *You can use the word "All" in the Word List To Search field to search all the pages of the Web site. You can also enter the directory name of a Web site to specify that the Search WebBot should search only that directory.*

Insert a Search WebBot Field

1 Open the Web page in which you want to place the Search WebBot.

2 Click the Insert WebBot Component button on the Standard toolbar.

3 Click Search.

4 Click OK.

5 If you want, type a new search label for input.

6 Specify the width (in characters) for the search label.

7 If you want, change the label for the Start Search button.

8 If you want, change the label for the Clear button.

9 Specify how and for what you want the Search WebBot to search.

10 Click OK.

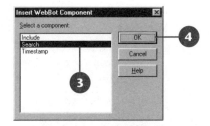

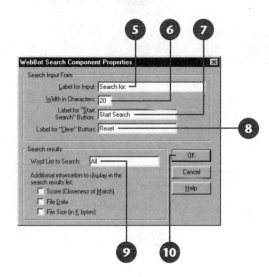

SEE ALSO

See "Using WebBots" on page 226 for more information about using other WebBot components.

SEE ALSO

See "Setting Up a Personal Web Server" on page 246 for information about FrontPage Server Extensions.

TIP

Find the closest match during a search. *Right-click the Search WebBot, click WebBot Component Properties on the shortcut menu, click to select the Score check box to return a list of found documents and the scores that show the closeness of the match, and then click OK.*

Change the Properties of the Search WebBot

1. Right-click the Search WebBot area of your Web page, and then click WebBot Component Properties on the shortcut menu.

2. If you want, change the search label for input.

3. Specify the width (in characters) for the search label.

4. If you want, change the label of the Search For button.

5. If you want, change the label of the Clear button.

6. Specify how and for what you want the Search WebBot to search.

7. Click OK.

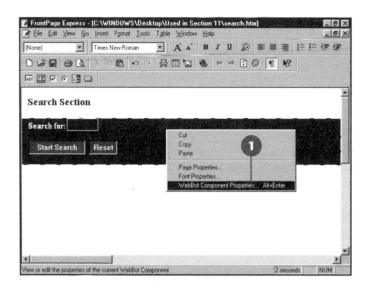

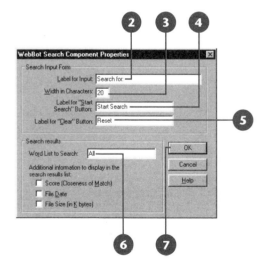

11

Creating Forms Using Templates or Wizards

Forms let you collect information from your Web page visitors. Web forms contain these basic elements: questions or requests for information, fields in which visitors type information, Submit and Reset buttons, and form properties associated with the WebBots that control what happens to the visitor's input. The Form Page Wizard speeds up the creation of a form, and the form templates provide predesigned layouts for certain types of forms. The wizard not only creates a form for you but also inserts the proper WebBots into the properties of the form.

SEE ALSO

See "Working with Forms" on page 232 for information about changing form properties.

Create a Form Using the Form Page Wizard

1. Click the File menu, and then click New.

2. Click Form Page Wizard, and then click OK. Click Next to continue.

3. Type the filename in the Page URL box, and type the title in the Page Title box. Click Next to continue.

4. Click Add, and then select the type of information you want to collect with this form. Click Next to continue.

5. Select the appropriate option to identify the items to collect. Click Next to continue.

6. Select the appropriate options to describe how your questions should be presented. Click Next to continue.

7. If necessary, select the appropriate output option button and check boxes to describe how the information you collect should be handled.

8. Click Finish.

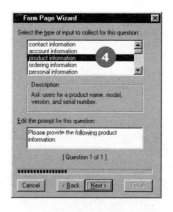

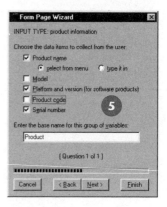

TIP

When to use a confirmation form. *Use a confirmation form to acknowledge a Web visitor's input. On the Web page where you are gathering information, right-click the Submit button, and then click Form Properties on the shortcut menu. Click the Settings button, click the Confirm tab, and then enter the name of your confirmation form.*

TIP

Where are survey form results stored? *A survey form utilizes the Save Results WebBot to save the survey results. To review the settings, right-click the survey form, click Form Properties on the shortcut menu, click the Settings button, and then click the Results tab. When you are done, click OK.*

TIP

What happens to a form when it is submitted? *When a user submits a form, a form handle (WebBot) on the Web server processes the information in the form.*

SEE ALSO

See "Saving Your Web Page" on page 204 for information about saving your Web page for the first time.

Create a New Confirmation Form

1. Click the File menu, and then click New.

2. Click Confirmation Form.

3. Click OK.

4. Select and modify the sample text in the form.

5. Click the Save button on the Standard toolbar.

6. Click the As File button, specify a filename for the form and a location in which to store the file, and then click Save.

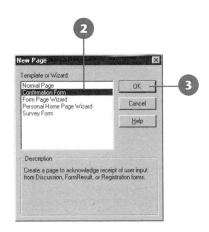

Create a New Survey Form

1. Click the File menu, and then click New.

2. Click Survey Form.

3. Click OK.

4. Select and modify the sample text in the form.

5. Click the Save button on the Standard toolbar.

6. Click the As File button, specify a filename for the survey form and a location in which to store the file, and then click Save.

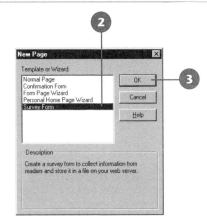

11

Working with Forms

Fields are the building blocks of forms. FrontPage Express provides a variety of form fields that you can use to create a new form or modify one that already exists. You can insert a text box, scrolling text box, check box, radio button, push button, drop-down menu, or image field in your Web page form. Form fields can be inserted right next to text or graphics on your Web page. Once a field is inserted on the Web page, you can set or change the properties of how that field behaves on your form.

TIP

Quickly insert a form field using the toolbar. *If necessary, click the View menu, and click Forms Toolbar to display the Forms toolbar. Click the form field button to insert that field on your Web page.*

Insert a Form Field

1. Open the Web page in which you want to add a form field.

2. Click the Insert menu, point to Form Field, and then click the form field to use.

3. If you want, click to reposition the insertion point where you want the title of the form field to appear.

4. Type the title for the form field.

Text box   Radio button   Check box

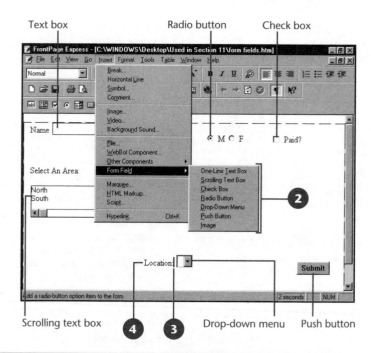

Scrolling text box   4   3   Drop-down menu   Push button

Change the Properties of a Form

1. Right-click the form area (inside the dotted rectangle), and then click Form Properties.

2. Click the Form Handler drop-down arrow, and then select a form handler.

3. Type a new name for the form.

4. Click Settings. Your Settings dialog box might be different.

3   2   4

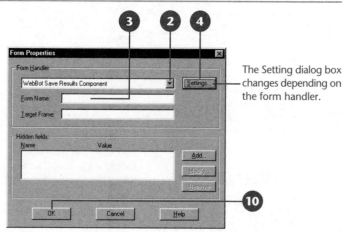

The Setting dialog box changes depending on the form handler.

What is a forms handler?
A forms handler is simply a program that runs on a Web server. The form handler program runs whenever someone submits a form to it. Most form handlers are WebBots. Ask your Internet service provider (ISP) for more information and to see what form handlers are available for you to use.

Add a choice to a drop-down menu. *Right-click the Drop-Down Menu field, click Form Field Properties on the shortcut menu, click Add, type the name of the first item in the drop-down menu in the Choice box, click to select the Initial State option button, and then click OK. Using the Height box, change the number of drop-down menu choices shown, and then click OK.*

⑤ Click the Results tab.

⑥ Type the name of the file where the results of the form input will be stored.

⑦ Click the File Format drop-down arrow, and then select a file format.

⑧ Click to select the Additional Information To Save check boxes you want.

⑨ Click OK, and then click OK again.

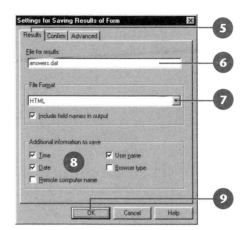

Change the Properties of a Form Field

① Right-click the form field, and then click Form Field Properties. Your Properties dialog box might be different.

② If you want, type a new name for the field.

③ If necessary, click Add, and then fill in boxes appropriate to the form field.

④ Click Modify or Remove to change or delete a form field option.

⑤ Click the form field option, and then click the Move Up or Move Down button to change the position.

⑥ Click OK.

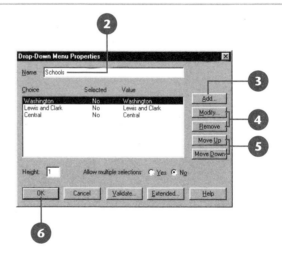

Inserting ActiveX Controls

ActiveX controls are software components that add functionality to your Web page that you can't create using standard HTML. Examples of ActiveX controls include a label control that can display text in different sizes and at different angles, a timer control that can generate timed events, a stock ticker control that can display stock information, and an animation control that can display animations. ActiveX controls are created using programming languages. You can also insert a PowerPoint slide show animation into your Web page as an ActiveX control.

TIP

More information on ActiveX controls. *Check out Microsoft's ActiveX Web site at* **http://www.microsoft.com /activex.**

Insert an ActiveX Control

1. Open the Web page in which you want to insert an ActiveX control.

2. Click the Insert menu, point to Other Components, and then click ActiveX Control.

3. Click the Pick A Control drop-down arrow, and then select the ActiveX control you want to insert.

4. To change the ActiveX control properties, click Properties.

5. Type a name for the ActiveX control when it's used along with a script.

6. Specify in pixels how you want the ActiveX control to be placed on the Web page.

7. For Web browsers that don't support ActiveX controls, enter the text you want to display instead.

8. Specify a network location that the Web browser can search for the ActiveX control.

9. Click OK.

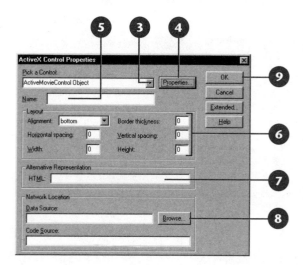

TIP

View a PowerPoint animation. *To view a PowerPoint animation on a Web page, you must have the PowerPoint Animation Player installed on your computer. You can download it from Microsoft's PowerPoint Web site at **www.microsoft.com /powerpoint/**. Or Internet Explorer will ask you if you would like it installed when you first load a Web page with a PowerPoint presentation.*

SEE ALSO

See "Using ActiveX Controls" on page 102 and "Controlling ActiveX and Java Content" on page 104 for information about using ActiveX controls in Internet Explorer.

Insert a PowerPoint Presentation

1 Open the Web page in which you want to insert the PowerPoint presentation.

2 Click the Insert menu, point to Other Components, and then click PowerPoint Animation.

3 Click Browse.

4 Click Browse again, and then double-click the PowerPoint presentation file you want to use.

5 Click the ActiveX Control option button.

6 Click OK.

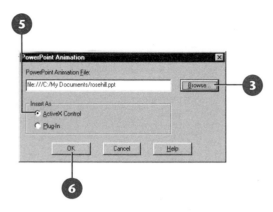

Inserting Java Applets

Java applets are created in a programming language called Java. Like ActiveX controls, Java applets add dynamic functionality to your Web page. You can find thousands of Java applets on the Web. Examples include scrolling banners and stock tickers, and many more. Your Web browser needs to support Java if you want to see or interact with a Java applet that's running on a Web page. Internet Explorer has extensive Java support.

TIP

Check out Java applets.
You'll find ratings of hundreds of popular Java applets at **http://www.jars.com**. *Make sure you download the CLASS file if you want the applet to run from your Web server.*

TIP

Where to get applet parameter information.
You need the documentation that came with the Java applet to determine the names and values for the applet.

Insert a Java Applet

1 Open the Web page in which you want to insert a Java applet.

2 Click the Insert menu, point to Other Components, and then click Java Applet.

3 Type the name of the applet source. Source files for Java applets typically have a .CLASS file extension.

4 If necessary, type the URL of the applet.

5 Type a warning message for Web browsers without Java support.

6 Click Add.

7 Type the name of the applet parameter you want to set.

8 Enter the parameter value in the Value box.

9 Click OK.

10 Specify the width and height sizes (in pixels) for the Java applet.

11 Specify the layout spacing (in pixels), and select an alignment.

12 Click OK.

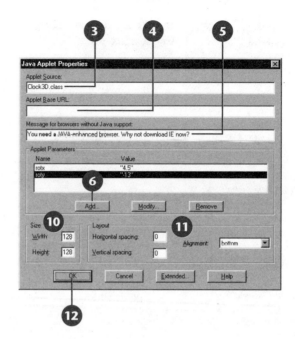

Inserting Plug-Ins

A plug-in is an accessory program that extends Netscape's capabilities. Many Web authors have added elements to their Web sites through the use of Netscape Plug-Ins. Internet Explorer users aren't left out from viewing these elements. If you switched to Internet Explorer from Netscape, you might want to continue using the plug-ins you downloaded and installed. Be sure to test your plug-in from Internet Explorer to verify that it performs as you expected.

TIP

Quickly adjust the size of a plug-in. *Select the plug-in on the Web page, and then drag its border controls with the mouse pointer.*

SEE ALSO

See "Understanding Add-Ons, Plug-Ins, and Viewers" on page 94 for information about plug-ins.

Insert a Plug-In

1. Open the Web page in which you want to insert the plug-in.

2. Click the Insert menu, point to Other Components, and then click Plug-In.

3. Click Browse.

4. Click Browse again, and then double-click the plug-in file you want to use.

5. Type a warning message for Web browsers without plug-in support.

6. Specify the width and height (in pixels) for the plug-in.

7. Click the Alignment drop-down arrow, and then select a layout alignment.

8. Specify the layout border thickness and the horizontal and vertical spacing values (in pixels).

9. Click OK.

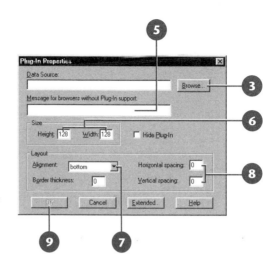

11

IN THIS SECTION

Getting Support and Tools for Web Page Developers

Getting Online Support

Using the Internet Explorer Logo

Publishing Your Web Page

New **Setting Up a Personal Web Server**

New **Understanding Office Server Extensions and Web Discussions**

New **Having and Joining a Web Discussion**

Installing Internet Explorer from the Web

Administering to Internet Explorer Users

Uninstalling Internet Explorer

Getting Updates to Internet Explorer

Working with Internet Explorer Tools

Microsoft Internet Explorer has many tools that make it easy for you to publish your Web pages, get the latest version of Internet Explorer, manage Internet Explorer installations, and receive online software support, as well as gain easy access to free software. The Web Publishing Wizard, which is part of the standard Internet Explorer installation, automates the process of publishing your Web pages to the World Wide Web or a personal Web server. You can even use the Internet Explorer logo in your Web page. Download the latest version of Internet Explorer from the World Wide Web and update the programs in the Internet Explorer suite with the Product Updates program. If you are a software administrator at your company, you can use Internet Explorer's Administrator Kit to help you manage Internet Explorer installations to many users.

Because the Internet changes every day, Microsoft helps you keep up to date with software programs and tools—available on the Microsoft Web site. These resources are easy to access and free of charge. If you have questions or need help, Microsoft also provides online software support.

Getting Support and Tools for Web Page Developers

The Microsoft Web site includes online help for Web page developers. For general information about developing Web pages, visit the Site Builder Network (SBN) Workshop Web site. The SBN Workshop Web site includes links to many other useful pages—such as the authoring, design, programming, server, and gallery pages—plus news about new development tools for Internet Explorer. The Tools & Samples Gallery provides Web page developers with images, sounds, sample style sheets, and other useful Web tools. The Developer Training Web page offers online chatting with other Web developers as well as information on courses you can take to upgrade your development skills.

Visit the Site Builder Network Workshop Web Site

1. Start Internet Explorer and connect to *http:// www.microsoft.com/ workshop.*

2. Read the Web page for details about the SBN Workshop Web site.

3. Click any of the Site Builder Network topic links.

4. Click any of the Web development topic links.

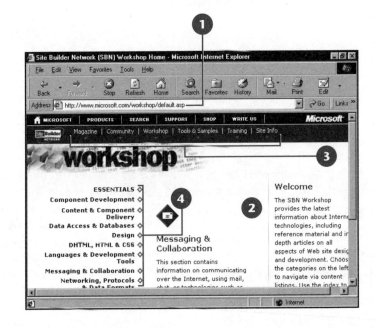

TRY THIS

Check out other support Web sites for Web page developers. *Connect to the following online technical support Web sites:*
http://www.techweb.com
http://www.webreference.com
http://www.quadzilla.com

SEE ALSO

See "Inserting ActiveX Controls" on page 234 and "Inserting Java Applets" on page 236 for information about ActiveX and Java.

SEE ALSO

See "Creating a Web Page Using Templates or Wizards" on page 190 for more information on creating your own Web pages.

SEE ALSO

See "Getting Online Support" on page 242 for information on how to find answers to your technical questions from Microsoft's Support Web site.

Visit the Site Builder Workshop Gallery

1. Start Internet Explorer and connect to *http://www.microsoft.com/gallery.*

2. Click an available link to read about a specific topic.

Visit the Site Builder Network Training Site

1. Start Internet Explorer and connect to *http://www.microsoft.com/devtraining.*

2. Click an available link to find out more about online training.

12

Getting Online Support

Microsoft has developed a knowledge database of information for all of its products. This *Knowledge Base* is the same tool that Microsoft's support engineers use. By using specific keywords and a couple of search techniques, you should find the solution to most of your problems in the Knowledge Base. If you want online support for Internet Explorer, you can connect to the Internet Explorer Support Home Page to find the information you're looking for.

TIP

Save Knowledge Base information in a file. *Find the information you want to save in the Knowledge Base, click the File menu, click Save As, click the Save As Type drop-down arrow, select Text File, and then click Save.*

Get Online Support

1. In the Internet Explorer window, click the Help menu, and then click Online Support.

2. If necessary, verify your online profile to continue.

3. Click the My Search Is About drop-down arrow, and then select the Microsoft application you want help with.

4. Click the option button for your search parameters.

5. Enter the keywords related to your problem, or type the question you want answered.

6. Click Find.

7. Click a link on the search results page that contains the information you want to find.

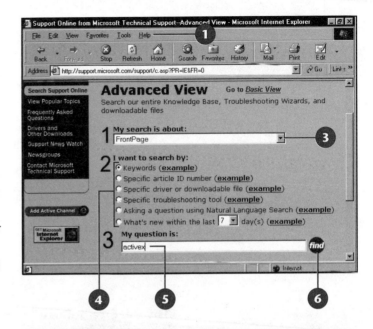

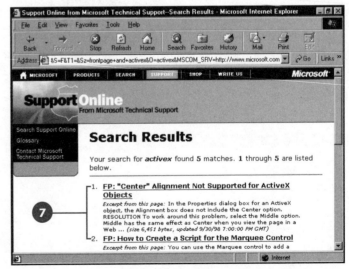

Using the Internet Explorer Logo in Your Web Page

If you're using some of the new features provided by FrontPage Express on your Web page, you may want to encourage visitors to download Internet Explorer so they can easily take advantage of these innovations. Microsoft allows the use of their Get Microsoft Internet Explorer logo on your Web page if you follow some simple rules. Once you have copied the logo to your computer, you can add it to one of your Web pages, and create a link back to Microsoft's Internet Explorer Download Web Site.

SEE ALSO

See "Inserting and Modifying an Image" on page 194 for information on how to add graphic images to your Web page.

Visit the Internet Explorer Logo Program Web Page

1. Start Internet Explorer and connect to *http://msdn.microsoft.com/osig/ie/usage.asp.*

2. Read the Web page for details about using the Get Internet Explorer logo on your Web page.

3. Right-click the Get Microsoft Internet Explorer Window, and then click Save Picture As.

4. Select a folder on your local drive where you want to download the logo, and then click Save to continue.

5. Open your Web page for editing in FrontPage Express.

6. Insert the Get Microsoft Internet Explorer logo into your Web page.

7. Click the logo image, click the Create Or Edit Hyperlink button on the toolbar to create a link to *http://www.microsoft.com/windows/ie/download,* and then click OK.

8. Save your Web page.

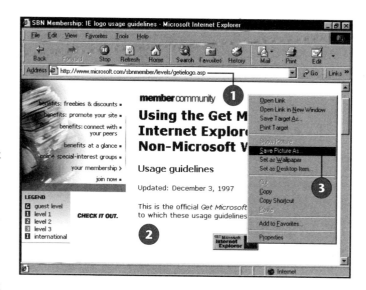

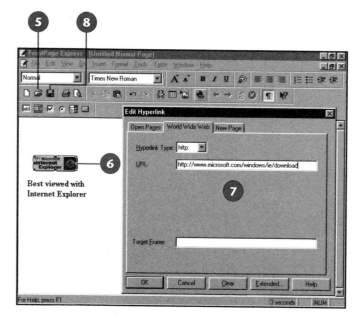

12

Publishing Your Web Page

Once you finish creating a Web page, you publish it to a Web server so that people can visit your page. When you *publish* a Web page, you move the Web page and graphic images to a Web server. As part of the standard installation of Internet Explorer, a Web Publishing Wizard is included to help you publish your Web page to a Web server. You can start the Web Publishing Wizard from the Start menu or from FrontPage Express. The wizard automates the process of copying files from your computer to the Web server—just follow the step-by-step instructions, and the wizard does the rest.

SEE ALSO

See "Setting Up a Personal Web Server" on page 246 for information on publishing a Web page to the Microsoft Personal Web Server (PWS).

Publish a Web Page to the World Wide Web

1. Click the Start button on the taskbar, point to Programs, point to Accessories, and then point to Internet tools.

2. Click Web Publishing Wizard. Click Next to continue.

3. Click Browse Folders or Browse Files, and then select the folder or file you want to publish.

4. Click Next to continue.

5. Type or select a name to describe your Web server. Click Next to continue.

6. Type the Web address or URL for your Web site where the page(s) will be published.

7. Type the name of the folder or directory where the files are being copied from. Click Next to continue.

8. Enter your user name and password for your Web server. Click OK when you're done.

9. Click Finish.

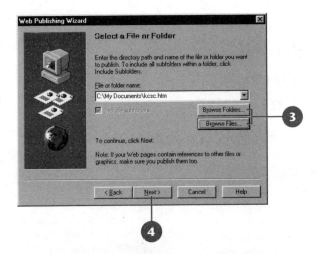

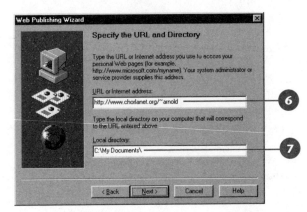

TIP

Trouble publishing your files? *If you have trouble publishing your files to an HTTP Web site, the Web Publishing Wizard asks you for another location. The best choice is an FTP (File Transfer Protocol) Web site. Select the FTP protocol option, and enter the FTP server name. Call your Internet service provider (ISP) for the FTP server name.*

TIP

What is a Web server? *On the World Wide Web, the Web server is the computer that runs the program that responds to HTTP requests by providing Web pages. These computers may be at your ISP's site or somewhere in your company.*

TIP

If you don't know, call your service provider. *If you don't know what to type or select as you step through the Web Publishing Wizard, call your ISP for the information you need.*

Publish a Web Page from FrontPage Express

1. Start FrontPage Express and open the Web page you want to publish.

2. Click the File menu, and then click Save As.

3. Enter a name for the Web page.

4. Type the Internet address and filename that you want for your Web page.

5. Click OK.

6. If necessary, click Yes To All to publish the graphic images associated with the Web page.

7. Click Next to continue.

8. Enter your user name and password.

9. Click OK to publish the files to your Web server.

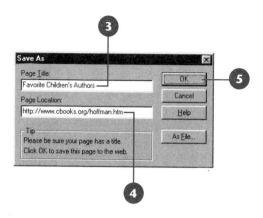

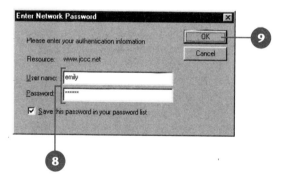

12

Setting Up a Personal Web Server

Microsoft Personal Web Server (PWS) turns any computer running Windows 95 or 98 into a Web server, enabling easy publication of Web pages to the Internet or a corporate intranet. PWS simplifies the sharing of information via Web pages. It is designed for small-scale usage—just a few visitors at a time should visit a Web site that is being served by a PWS. Once you've downloaded and installed the PWS, it will start automatically. You may want to run the Personal Web Manager to stop the server or change PWS settings.

TIP

Install PWS from the Windows 98 CD. *Using Windows Explorer, open the Add-Ons folder on your Windows 98 CD. There you will find a folder named PWS. Open that folder and click Setup to install PWS.*

Download and Set Up a Personal Web Server

1. Create a folder in which to store the downloaded files.

2. Start Internet Explorer and connect to *http://www.microsoft.com/ie/pws/*.

3. Scroll to the bottom of the page and click the Download link, and then click the Download button.

4. Read the Web page, and then follow the download instructions. You may need to register with Microsoft and fill out a short survey to continue.

5. Click OK to download the Personal Web Server setup files into your new folder.

6. Start Windows Explorer, and then double-click the Personal Web Server install file in your new folder.

7. Read the Personal Web Server Setup Wizard dialog boxes, and follow the instructions.

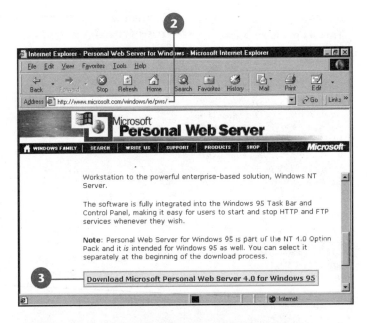

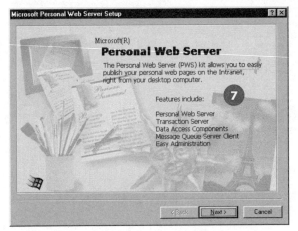

Start or Stop the Personal Web Server

1 Click the Start button on the taskbar, point to Programs, point to Personal Web Server, and then click Personal Web Manager.

2 Click Close to close the Tip Of The Day if necessary.

3 Click Main.

4 Click Stop to make your personal Web site unavailable.

5 Click Start to make your PWS available.

6 Click the Close button.

Take the Personal Web Server Tour

1 Click the Start button on the taskbar, point to Programs, point to Personal Web Server, and then click Personal Web Manager.

2 Click Close to close the Tip Of The Day if necessary.

3 Click Tour.

4 Read the tour screens, clicking the double-arrow buttons to move between screens.

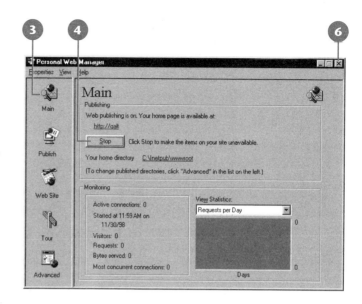

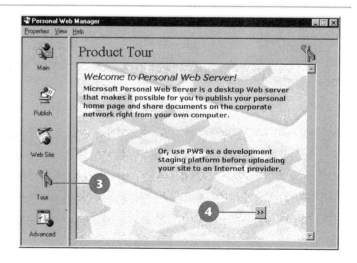

Understanding Office Server Extensions

Microsoft Office 2000 uses *Office Server Extensions* to provide a bridge between current Web technologies and the fuctionality needed to make the Web a friendly place to work with people and information. Office Server Extensions are a set of features that makes it easy to work with Office files and collaborate on the Web. Office Server Extensions allow you to publish and view Web documents directly from a Web server—a computer on the Internet that stores Web pages—with Office programs or Internet Explorer; to perform Web discussions and exchange information on documents located on the Web server; and to receive notification when a document on a Web server has been changed.

Office Server Extensions are a superset of Microsoft FrontPage extensions and other technologies that reside on a Windows NT–based Web server to provide additional publishing, collaboration, and document management capabilities. Office Server Extensions do not replace existing Web server technologies. Rather, the extensions in Office are designed to enhance your experience with Office in a Web-based environment.

Office Server Extensions are included with Office 2000 Premium edition. To set up your computer with Office Server Extensions, you need a computer with Windows NT Workstation 4.0 or later running Personal Web Server 4.0 or later, or Windows NT Server 4.0 or later running Internet Information Server 4.0 or later. With the Server Extensions Configuration Wizard, you can set up and configure an existing Web server to use the Office Server Extensions.

Web File Management

Office Server Extensions make publishing and sharing documents on Web servers as easy as working with documents on file servers. Office enables you to create folders, view properties, and perform file drag-and-drop operations on Web servers just as you would on normal file servers. In Internet Explorer, Office Server Extensions enable on-the-fly display of Web directory listings, files, and HTML views of Web folders.

Understanding Web Discussions

With the Office Server Extensions installed on a Web server, you can have online discussions in Web page (HTML) files and Office 2000 documents. A *Web discussion* is an online, interactive conversation that takes place within the Web page or document (also called "in-line") or that occurs as a general discussion about the Web page or Office document, which is stored in the discussion pane at the bottom of the page. A Web discussion can only occur or be added through Internet Explorer or an Office document. Using the Discussions toolbar at the bottom of the window, you can insert new comments, edit and reply to existing comments, subscribe to a particular document, and view or hide the Discussions window.

Web Subscription and Web Notification

Collaboration on the Web is much simpler with Web Subscription and Web Notification features. Office gives users an opportunity to "subscribe" to particular documents on a Web server and to be automatically "notified" by e-mail when the status of selected documents changes. You can choose to be notified when a document changes, is created, or is deleted. You can be notified immediately, once per day, or even weekly to prevent undue amounts of e-mail in cases where a document changed several times in a short period. To subscribe to a Web document, click the Subscribe button on the Discussions toolbar.

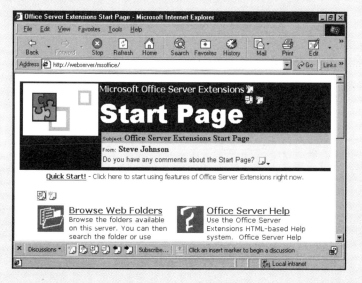

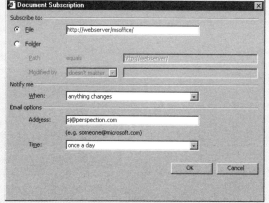

12

Having a Web Discussion

A Web discussion allows multiple users to discuss specific documents. The discussions are stored separately from their document counterparts and are merged later when you view the results. The documents can be on the Internet, an intranet, or on a network. The advantage to a Web discussion is that the context of your online collaboration is preserved in a file that can be viewed at a later date.

SEE ALSO

See "Understanding Web Discussions" on page 249 for information on what's needed to have a Web discussion.

Select a Web Discussion Server

1. Click the Discuss button on the Standard toolbar.

   If you are selecting a discussion server for the first time, skip to Step 4.

2. On the Discussions toolbar, click the Discussions button, and then click Discussion Options.

3. Click Add.

4. Type the name of a discussion server provided by your administrator.

   The discussion server needs to have Office Server Extensions to hold a Web discussion.

5. If your administrator has set up security by using the Secure Sockets Layer (SSL) message protocol, click to select the Secure Connection Required (SSL) check box.

6. Type a name you want to use for the Web discussion server.

7. Click OK.

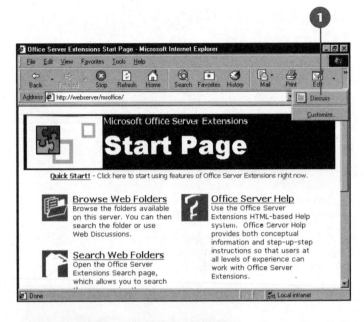

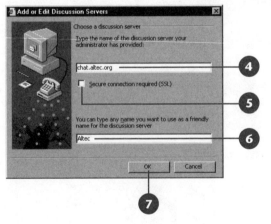

TIP

Hide the Discussion pane.
During a discussion, click the Show/Hide Discussion Pane button on the Discussion toolbar to show or hide the Discussion pane.

TIP

Expand and collapse all discussion remarks. *During a discussion, click the Expand All Discussions button or Collapse All Discussion button on the Discussions toolbar.*

TIP

Print discussion remarks.
Start a discussion, click the Discussions button on the Discussions toolbar, click Print Discussions, and then select the print options you want.

SEE ALSO

See "Joining a Web Discussion" on page 252 for information on replying to and filtering out discussion remarks.

Start and Close a Web Discussion

1. Open the Web page for which you want to start a discussion.

2. Click Discuss on the Standard toolbar.

3. Start an in-line discussion or a discussion in the discussion pane.

   ◆ To start an in-line discussion, click the Insert Discussion In The Document button on the Discussions toolbar, and then click one of the Insert Discussion In The Document icons on the Web page.

   ◆ To start a discussion in the discussion pane, click the Insert About The Document button on the Discussions toolbar.

4. Type the subject of the discussion.

5. Type your comments.

6. Click OK.

7. When you're done, click the Close button on the Discussion toolbar.

Click to enter discussion text.

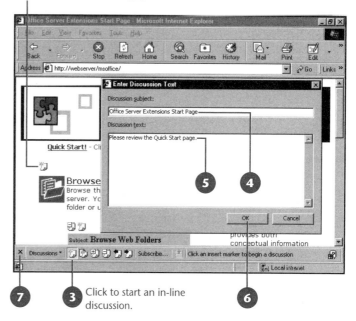

3 Click to start an in-line discussion.

Discussion pane

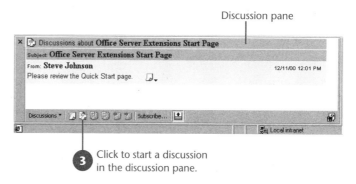

3 Click to start a discussion in the discussion pane.

12

Joining a Web Discussion

Once you have joined a Web discussion, you can reply to discussion remarks or add remarks of your own. You can also filter the discussion remarks in a Web page so that you read only discussions inserted by a particular person or within a certain time frame.

SEE ALSO

See "Having a Web Discussion" on page 250 for information on what's needed to have a Web discussions.

TIP

Delete a discussion remark. *During a discussion, click the Show A Menu Of Actions button for the remark you want to delete, and then click Delete. Click Yes to confirm the deletion.*

Reply to a Web Discussion Remark

① Open the Web page that contains the discussion you want to join.

② Click Discuss on the Standard toolbar.

③ Click the Show A Menu Of Actions button, and then click Reply.

④ Type your reply.

⑤ Click OK.

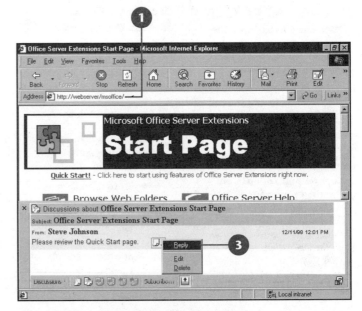

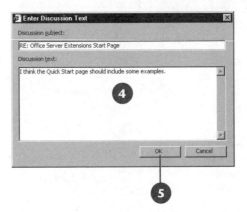

Filter Out Discussion Remarks

1. Open the Web page that contains the discussion you want to join.

2. Click Discuss on the Standard toolbar.

3. Click Discussions on the Discussion toolbar, and then click Filter Discussions.

4. Click the Created By drop-down arrow, and then select whose remarks you want to see.

5. Click the Creation Time drop-down arrow, and then select the time frame you want.

6. Click OK.

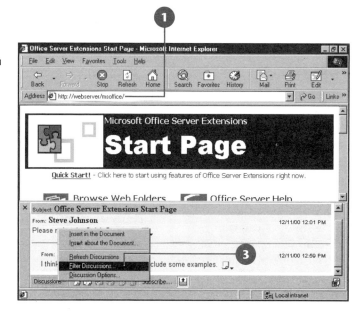

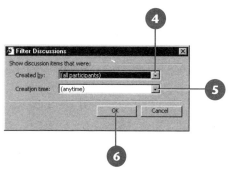

Installing Internet Explorer from the Web

If you aren't running the latest version of Internet Explorer yet, you can get it from the World Wide Web. You begin by downloading the setup program—a small file you can receive quickly. When you run the setup program, you will connect to a Microsoft download site, pick your options for installation, and then install the program directly from the Web.

TIP

Can I get the latest version of Internet Explorer on CD? *Internet Explorer is available from Microsoft on CD. See the Internet Explorer Web site for more details. Internet Explorer is also part of the Microsoft Office 2000 suite and can be installed from that CD.*

Download the Internet Explorer Setup Program from the Web

1. Start Internet Explorer and connect to *http:// www.microsoft.com/ie/ download/.*

2. Click to select an operating system.

3. Click the Internet Explorer 5 And Internet Tools link.

   Click Yes or No to determine what components are installed on your computer.

4. Click to select the Internet Explorer 5 And Internet Tools check box.

5. Click Download, read the instructions, and then click Start Download.

6. Follow the installation instructions to complete the setup.

Copy the setup file to another computer. *Once you have downloaded the setup program to your computer, you can copy it to another computer. Run the setup program on that computer to install Internet Explorer from the Web.*

Download Internet Explorer now and install later. *One of the options available to when you run the setup program is to download the program to disk instead of installing from the Internet. Once you have downloaded the entire Internet Explorer suite to your hard drive, you can run the setup program again to install the software.*

Repair corrupted or removed Internet Explorer files. *Click the Help menu, click Repair, and then click Yes. Upon completion, click Yes to restart your computer.*

Install Internet Explorer

1. Click the Start button on the taskbar, and then click Run.

2. Type the path to the Internet Explorer setup program. If necessary, click Browse to find the setup program on your hard drive.

3. Click OK.

4. Click the I Accept The Agreement option button. Click Next to continue.

5. Select the installation option.

6. Click Next to continue.

7. Select an Internet location to continue the setup over the Internet. Click Next to continue.

8. Use the default installation folder location, or enter a new location. Click Next to continue.

9. If you are upgrading new items, click the Upgrade Only New Items option button, and then click OK.

10. Click OK.

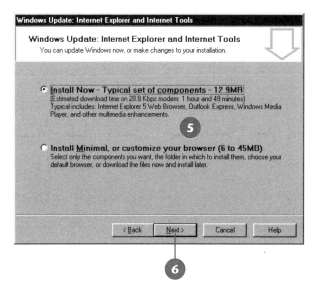

12

Administering to Internet Explorer Users

The Internet Explorer Administration Kit (IEAK) includes all the tools your business needs to deploy Microsoft Internet Explorer company wide. The IEAK lets you customize Internet Explorer to best meet your needs, including putting your own company logo on the software. With the IEAK, you can install and manage Internet Explorer from a central network location without having to set up individual computers one at a time.

TIP

The IEAK runs from Windows NT. *Microsoft has designed the IEAK to be administrated from a Windows NT server. You will need to have administrator access on Windows NT to manage installations of Internet Explorer.*

Download and Set Up the IEAK

1. Create a folder in which to store the downloaded files.

2. Start Internet Explorer and connect to *http:// ieak.microsoft.com*.

3. Read the Web page, and then follow the instructions to sign up for the kit.

4. Download the Internet Explorer Administration Kit setup files into your new folder.

5. Type **C:** in the Address bar, press Enter, and then double-click the setup file in your new folder.

6. Read the Internet Explorer Administration Kit Setup Wizard dialog boxes, and follow the instructions carefully.

Uninstalling Internet Explorer

Internet Explorer is just as easy to uninstall as is it to install. You may want to remove individual components or the entire installation of Internet Explorer in order to save space or because you want to install an upgrade on a clean system.

TIP

Add a component to Internet Explorer. *Follow the steps for uninstalling, but in step 6 click the Add A Component option button, click OK, select the component you want, and then click OK.*

TIP

Repair your Internet Explorer installation. *Follow the steps for uninstalling, but in step 6 click the Repair Internet Explorer option button, and then click OK.*

Uninstall Internet Explorer and Its Components

1. Click the Start button on the taskbar, point to Settings, and click Control Panel.

2. Double-click the Add/Remove Programs icon in the Control Panel.

3. Click the Install/Uninstall tab.

4. Click Microsoft Internet Explorer 5 And Internet Tools.

5. Click Add/Remove.

6. Click Advanced.

7. Click to select the check boxes for the components you want to remove along with Internet Explorer.

8. Click OK.

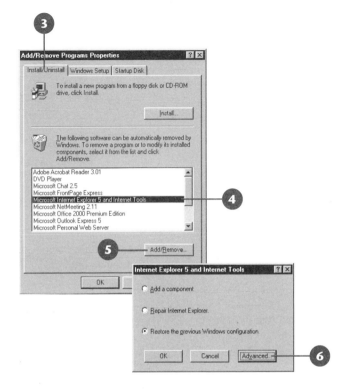

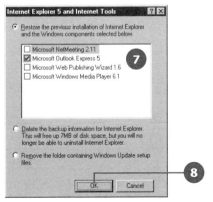

12

Getting Updates to Internet Explorer

Microsoft makes it easy to update Internet Explorer software. All you have to do is start the Product Updates program located on the Internet Explorer Help menu, and the program does the rest, updating Internet Explorer and its related programs. Besides updating the Internet Explorer software you already have installed, you can install other Internet Explorer components from the Microsoft Web site. Internet Explorer's Active Setup program analyzes your computer to determine what is currently installed and makes it easy to add components.

Get Updates or Add Components to Internet Explorer

1. Click the Start button on the taskbar, point to Settings, and click Control Panel.

2. Double-click the Add/Remove Programs icon in the Control Panel.

3. Click Microsoft Internet Explorer 5.

4. Click Add/Remove.

5. Click the Add A Component option button.

6. Click OK.

7. Click to select the check boxes for the components you want to install.

8. Click Next to continue.

9. Click Yes to install the components from the Internet.

10. Select a site for downloading.

11. Click Next to download and install the components.

12. Click Finish.

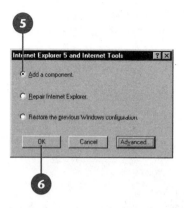

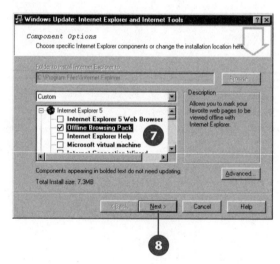

Index

SPECIAL CHARACTERS

\ (backslash), vs. slash, 15
/ (slash), vs. backslash, 15
"400 Bad Request" error
    message, 50
"401 Unauthorized User" error
    message, 50
"403 Forbidden Page" error
    message, 50
"404 File Not Found" error
    message, 50
"502 Service Overloaded" error
    message, 50
"503 Service Unavailable" error
    message, 50

Accessibility dialog box, 63
Acrobat PDF viewer
    installing, 97
    viewing PDF documents, 99
Acrobat PDF Web site
    addresses, 99
actions
    redoing edits, 193
    undoing, 19, 193
Active Channels, 7
Active Desktop, 21

accessing Web sites from, 22
adding a Web
    background, 25
adding a Web screen
    saver, 25
adding channels to, 43
adding Web items to, 24
customizing, 24–25
hiding, 22
hiding Web items on, 22
illustrated, 21
shortcuts, 73
showing, 22, 23
showing Web items on, 22
active frames, printing, 18,
    66, 67
Active Setup program (Internet
    Explorer), 258
ActiveX controls, 101, 102, 234
    examples, 234
    information Web site,
        illustrated, 101
    inserting in Web pages, 234
    PowerPoint animations, 234,
        235
    PowerPoint file format
        required, 235
    security options, 104
    using, 102
Add a New Address dialog box,
    81, 82
Add Favorite dialog box, 34, 40

Add Language dialog box, 84
add-ons (add-on programs), 94,
    98–99
    choosing, 91
    finding, 95
    installing, 96–97
Add or Edit Discussion Servers
    dialog box, 250
Add/Remove Programs Proper-
    ties dialog box, 257
Address bar (Internet Explorer
    window), 11, 14
    adding to the taskbar, 71
    browsing hard disks
        (local), 14
    browsing Web pages, 12
    finding information on the
        Internet, 33
Address bar drop-down arrow,
    illustrated, 12
Address Book (Windows), 6
    adding contacts to, 120, 121
    creating contact groups, 121
    exporting, 137
    finding contacts, 136
    importing other address
        books, 137
    printing contact information,
        138
    sorting, 121
    updating contact informa-
        tion, 120

Address Book Import Tool dialog box, 137
address book programs, choosing, 91
addresses. *See* Internet addresses; IP addresses; personal information; Web site addresses
administering Internet Explorer on networks, 256
Administration Kit. *See* Internet Explorer Administration Kit (IEAK)
Advanced tab (Internet Options dialog box), 66, 88, 90, 103
Align Left button (Format toolbar, FrontPage Express window), 189
Align Right button (Format toolbar, FrontPage Express window), 189
aligning paragraphs, 212
AltaVista (search engine), 30
animation controls (ActiveX), 234
animations
  playing, 112
  See also PowerPoint animations
answering calls, 167
applets. *See* Java applets (programs)
applications. *See* programs
Apply button (in dialog boxes), 20
articles. *See* news messages
attaching files to mail messages, 123, 125, 126
attachments, forwarding mail messages as, 125
audio
  broadcasting, 110, 111

microphone volume, 171
speaker volume, 171
streaming, 98, 110
tuning settings, 170
turning off, 171
See also sounds
Audio Tuning Wizard, 163, 170
authority certificates (for doing business on the Internet), 76–77
AutoComplete
  entering Internet addresses, 12, 13
  turning off, 13
AutoCorrect, 13
AutoDetect Offline, 37, 39
AutoSearch, 32, 33

Back button (Standard toolbar, Internet Explorer window), 18, 19
Back list, jumping to locations from, 16
background colors, specifying, 86, 87, 219
background images, 25
  adding to tables/table cells, 224
  adding to the Active Desktop, 25
  copying, 58, 59
  inserting, 218
  renaming, 59
  saving, 58, 59
  specifying colors, 86, 87, 219
Background Sound dialog box, 219
background sounds
  inserting and deleting, 219
  playing, 218

Background tab (Display Properties dialog box), 25
backslash (\), vs. slash, 15
"Bad Request" error message, 50
bitmap files, saving graphic images as, 57
blank Web pages, creating, 191
blocking mail messages, 133
Block Sender dialog box, 133
Bold button (Format toolbar, FrontPage Express window), 189
boldfacing text, 210
Bookmark dialog box, 200
bookmarks, 200
  creating, 200
  creating hyperlinks to, 200
  importing, 46
  removing, 200
broadcasting audio/video, 110, 111
Browse for Folder dialog box, 35, 179
Browser pane (Internet Explorer window), 11
browsers. *See* Web browsers
browsing
  hard disks (local), 14–15
  text-only surfing, 88
  the Web, 12–13, 207
Bulleted List button (Format toolbar, FrontPage Express window), 189
bulleted lists
  creating and customizing, 215
  removing bulleting from, 215
business cards, 131
  printing, 138
business information, storing, 81
buttons

dialog box option buttons, 20
See also Quick Launch toolbar buttons; toolbar buttons

calling programs, choosing, 91
Calling tab (Options dialog box), 169, 180, 181
calls
  accepting all, 167
  answering, 167
  canceling, 167
  do not disturb option, 167
  vs. e-mail, 167
  hanging up, 167, 168
  placing, 160, 166, 167
  resource lists, 164
  See also meetings (conference calls)
Cancel button (in dialog boxes), 20
canceling calls, 167
captions (in Web page tables), inserting, 223
CDs. *See* disks
Cell Properties dialog box, 225
cells (in Web page tables), 222
  aligning cell contents, 224
  combining, 225
  creating headers for, 225
  deleting information in, 223
  entering information in, 223
  modifying, 225
  moving from cell to cell, 222
  spacing, 224
  splitting, 225
Center button (Format toolbar, FrontPage Express window), 189

certificates (for doing business on the Internet), 76–77
Change Font button (Format toolbar, FrontPage Express window), 189
Change Style button (Format toolbar, FrontPage Express window), 189
Channel bar (Active Desktop), 21
adding channels to, 43
viewing, 43
Channel Guide (Microsoft), visiting, 43
channel properties dialog boxes, 44
channels, 29, 30
adding, 42–43
preview pages, 42
updating, 44
viewing favorites, 43
channel screen savers, 24
creating, 25
characters (in comic strip chats)
changing, 184
drawing, 183
character sets, language, adding, 84, 85
Chat (NetMeeting), 165, 172–73
exiting, 173
starting, 172
Chat Connection dialog box, 182
chat messages
customizing, 173
formatting, 173
sending, 172
storing, 173
chat rooms, entering, 182
chatting, 172–73
collaboration and, 173
as comic strip characters, 182–84
chat tools, 183

Chat window, 172
Check Box button (Forms toolbar, FrontPage Express window), 189
check boxes
in dialog boxes, 20
inserting in Web page forms, 232
check mark (by a menu item), show Active Desktop indicator, 22
clickable links, 17
clicking
enabling single-clicking, 22
See also right-clicking
Clip Art, inserting graphic images in Web pages from, 194
Clipboard (Windows)
access to in meetings, 177
copying graphic images to, 19, 56, 196
copying text to, 19, 31, 57, 60, 196
Close button (Internet Explorer window), closing Internet Explorer, 28
closing
Internet Explorer, 28
See also exiting
collaboration (sharing applications), 176–77
and chatting, 173
maximum participants, 176
stopping, 177
on the Web, 249
Color dialog box, 210
colors
background colors, 86, 87, 219
custom colors, 211
hyperlink colors, 219
specifying, 86, 87, 210, 211, 219

text colors, 86, 87, 210, 211, 219
Colors dialog box, 87
columns (in Web page tables)
deleting, 223
inserting, 223
selecting, 225
Columns dialog box, 154
comic strip chats, 182–84
changing characters, 184
entering nicknames, 182
gesturing while speaking, 183
increasing panels for, 184
joining, 182
recording sayings, 183
sending recorded sayings, 183
settings, 184
Comment dialog box, 216
comments, inserting, 216
Compose tab (Options dialog box), 130
composing
mail messages, 122–23
news messages, 153
computers
configuring for proxy servers, 9
starting Outlook Express at startup, 141
conference bridge, 168
conference calls. See meetings
configuring
computers, for proxy servers, 9
Internet Explorer, on corporate systems, 9
confirmation forms (for Web page visitors), creating, 231
Connect dialog box, 182
connecting to the Internet, 8–9
getting information on, 8

password requirement, 10
Connection Wizard, 6
connecting to the Internet, 8
launching, 9
See also Internet Connection Wizard
contact groups, 120
creating, 121
contact properties dialog boxes, 120, 121
contacts, 120
adding, 120, 121
choosing from several with the same first name, 123
Outlook Express start page links, 118
printing contact information, 138
See also Address Book (Windows)
Contacts list (News window), 142
Content Advisor, 77
installing, 80
rating Web sites, 80
Content tab (Internet Options dialog box), 80, 81
conversation threads (of news messages), 143, 147
converting, text files to Web pages, 207
Copy button (Standard toolbar, Internet Explorer window), 19
copying
background images, 58, 59
graphic images, 19, 56, 60, 196
text, 19, 31, 57, 60, 196
copyrights, violating, 57
corporate systems, configuring Internet Explorer, 9

Credit Card Password dialog box, 83
CSV Export dialog box, 137
Ctrl+drag, copying text/graphic images between documents, 196
Ctrl+F, displaying the Find dialog box, 31
Current Call list (NetMeeting window), 164
Customize Toolbar dialog box, 154
customizing
    the Active Desktop, 24–25
    bulleted lists, 215
    chat messages, 173
    folders, 15
    horizontal lines, 216
    Internet Explorer, 69–91
    the Internet Explorer window, 74–75
    the MSN Home Page, 70
    the News window, 154–55
    numbered lists, 214
    the Outlook Express toolbar (News window), 154, 155
    the Preview pane (News window), 155
    search options, 33
    toolbars, 75
Cut button (Standard toolbar, Internet Explorer window), 19
cutting
    graphic images, 196–97
    text, 19, 196–197

Decrease Indent button (Format toolbar, FrontPage Express window), 189

Decrease Text Size button (Format toolbar, FrontPage Express window), 189
Delete button (Standard toolbar, Internet Explorer window), 19
Deleted Items folder, retrieving deleted messages, 127
deleting
    background sounds, 219
    files/folders, 19
    mail messages, 127
    marquees, 221
    news messages, 147
    text, 192
    Web page table cell information, 223
    Web page table columns/rows, 223
desktop. See Active Desktop
desktop patterns (wallpaper), creating, 59
desktop shortcuts, creating, 73
Developer Training Web page (SBN Workshop Web site), 240
dialing calls, 167
dialog boxes
    displaying, 20
    elements, 20
    getting help on, 27
    selecting options in, 20
directories. See folders (local hard disk directories); Internet directories
Directory list (NetMeeting window), 164
    changing your listing, 180
    going unlisted, 181
    removing your listing, 180
    setting up your listing, 162–63

directory servers. See ILS servers
directory services (for Web addresses), changing, 136
Discuss button (Standard toolbar, Internet Explorer window), 18
Discussion pane, hiding, 251
discussions. See Web discussions
Discussions toolbar, 249
disks
    inserting graphic images from, 194
    playing sounds and videos from, 107
Display Properties dialog box
    Background tab, 25
    Screen Save tab, 25
    Web tab, 22
documents
    copying text/graphic images between, 197
    moving to previous/next, 19
    name/address displays, 11
    navigating, 16, 19
    refreshing (reloading), 17
    viewing PDF documents, 99
download sites, 52
Download tab, Web site properties dialog boxes, 44
downloading FTP site files, 54–55
downloading Web site files, 50, 51, 52–53
    free software, 48, 53
    media clips, 61
    news message headers, 152, 156
    off-peak hours for, 50, 53
    Personal Web Server, 246
    stopping, 53
    style sheets, 63
    virus precautions for, 51
drag and drop

adding favorites, 37
attaching files to mail messages, 126
moving text/graphic images, 196–97
organizing favorites, 35
drawing characters in comic strip chats, 183
drawing tools, Whiteboard tools, 175
drives. See hard disks (local)
drop-down lists. See drop-down menus (lists)
Drop-Down Menu button (Forms toolbar, FrontPage Express window), 189
drop-down menus (lists)
    adding choices to, 233
    in dialog boxes, 20
    inserting in Web page forms, 232

e-mail. See mail messages
e-mail accounts
    adding, 134
    adding/changing/switching identities, 135
    multiple, 134
    setting up, 117
e-mail programs
    choosing, 91
    See also Outlook Express
e-mail protocols, 117
Edit button (Standard toolbar, Internet Explorer window), 18
editing
    hyperlinks, 198–99
    Office Web pages, 64, 65
    text, 192, 193

encoding large messages, 157
Enter Discussion Text dialog
    box, 252
Enter Network Password dialog
    box, 245
entering
    Internet addresses, 12, 13
    nicknames (for chats), 182
    symbols, 193
    text, 192
    See also inserting
erasing Whiteboard elements,
    175
error messages, 50
exiting
    Chat (NetMeeting), 173
    Internet Explorer, 28
    Whiteboard (NetMeeting),
        174
Explorer bar (Internet Explorer
    window), 11
    finding Web pages, 18
    listing available channels, 18
exporting
    the Address Book, 137
    mail messages, 137
external programs, choosing, 91

favorites, 30
    accessing, 18, 22, 72, 73
    adding, 34, 37
    deleting, 35
    importing, 46
    organizing, 34, 35, 109
    renaming, 35
    synchronizing, 40, 41
    viewing, 35, 36, 37
    viewing offline, 40–41
    See also Favorites list

Favorites button (Standard
    toolbar, Internet Explorer
    window), 18
Favorites folder, 30
Favorites list, 29
    adding channels, 42
    adding drives, 36, 37
    adding folders, 36, 37
    adding files, 36, 37
    adding Web sites, 34
    adding Web sites to the Links
        toolbar from, 73
    scrolling, 37
    viewing, 36, 37
File Download dialog box, 53,
    96, 254
file formats (for graphic image
    files), 56, 194
    changing, 195
file formats (for Web pages),
    saving Web pages in
    different, 205
"File Not Found" error
    message, 50
file repository sites, and
    viruses, 51
files
    adding to the Favorites list,
        36, 37
    adding to the Start menu, 23
    attaching to mail messages,
        123, 125, 126
    browsing local hard disk
        files, 14–15
    deleting, 19
    downloading. *See* download-
        ing FTP site files;
        downloading Web site
        files
    inserting text files in Web
        pages, 193
    moving on the Start
        menu, 23

opening, 14, 36, 178
opening Web pages from,
    206
organizing, 179
receiving during meetings,
    178, 179
saving mail messages as, 129
sending during meetings,
    178, 179
temporary Internet files,
    88, 89
viewing, 37
See also folders (local hard
    disk directories); text
    files
File Transfer Protocol sites. *See*
    FTP sites
Filled Ellipse tool (Whiteboard),
    175
Filled Rectangle tool
    (Whiteboard), 175
Filter Discussions dialog box,
    253
filtering news messages, 149
Find A Contact link (Outlook
    Express start page), 118
Find dialog box
    copying text into, 31
    displaying, 31
finding
    add-ons, 95
    Address Book contacts, 136
    ILS (Internet User Locator
        Service), 161
    Internet addresses, 136,
        160–61
    newsgroups, 148, 149
    news messages, 148
    people on the Internet, 136,
        160–161
    plug-ins, 95
    text, 31, 228–29
    viewers, 95

Web information, 18, 29–48
Web sites, 18, 29, 32–33, 38
    See also Web site addresses
Find People dialog box, 136
Folder bar (News window), 142
Folder list (News window), 142
Folder list (Outlook Express
    window), 119
Folder options dialog box, 15
folders (at FTP sites), 55
folders (local hard disk
    directories)
    adding to the Favorites
        list, 36
    browsing, 14–15
    creating for downloading, 53
    customizing, 15
    deleting, 19
    displaying, 14
    displaying the next level
        up, 19
    display options, 15
    Favorites folder, 30
    History folder, 38, 39
    sorting directory lists, 15
    See also Outlook Express
        folders
Font dialog box, 211
fonts
    changing, 86, 211
    resizing, 86, 211
Fonts dialog box, 86
footers
    entering, 201
    print variable codes, 67, 201
"Forbidden Access or Access
    Denied or Connection
    Refused by Host" error
    message, 50
"Forbidden Page" error
    message, 50
form fields, 232
    changing properties, 233
    inserting, 232

Form Page Wizard, creating
forms, 230–31
Form Properties dialog box, 233
form templates, creating forms
from, 230
formatting
chat messages, 173
paragraphs, 212–15
text, 210–11
Format toolbar (FrontPage
Express window), 187
buttons, 189
forms, 230–233
changing properties, 232–33
confirmation forms, 231
creating, 230–31
elements, 230
inserting fields in, 232
submitting, 231
survey forms, 231
forms handlers, 233
Forms toolbar (FrontPage
Express window), 187
buttons, 189
inserting form fields, 232
moving aside, 189
For Netscape Users (Microsoft
Web page), 27, 47
Forward button (Standard
toolbar, Internet Explorer
window), 18, 19
forwarding mail messages, 125
Forward list, jumping to
locations from, 16
frames, 67
printing, 18, 66, 67
free software, downloading,
48, 53
FrontPage Express (Microsoft),
6, 185–237
browsing the Web, 207
creating Web pages, 185–208
enhancing Web pages,
209–37

high-end features, 209
publishing Web pages, 245
starting, 18, 186
toolbars, 187
FrontPage Express window
features, illustrated, 187
toolbars, 187
FrontPage Server Extensions,
226, 247
and Office Server Extensions,
248
testing, 247
FTP sites
downloading files from,
54–55
folders, 55
private site login syntax, 55
public site file access
directory, 55
publishing Web pages to, 245
Full Screen mode (Internet
Explorer window),
turning on/off, 74

games
playing over the Internet,
113
trying before buying, 53
Web sites, 113
General tab (Internet Options
dialog box), 38, 39, 62,
63, 84, 85, 89
General tab (Options dialog
box), 179
GIF files, 56
interlaced option, 195
opening, 56
saving as bitmaps, 57
vs. JPEG files, 194
graphic images

changing file formats, 194,
195
copying, 56, 60, 196
creating desktop patterns
from, 59
inserting, 194
low-resolution, 195
measuring, 57
modifying, 194, 195
moving, 196–97
opening saved, 56, 59
resizing, 197
saving, 56, 57
selecting, 196
storage format, 68
style sheets and, 62
watermark images, 219
See also background images
graphics programs (for opening
graphics), 56

handles. See selection handles
hanging up (ending/canceling
calls), 167, 168
hard disks (local)
browsing, 14–15, 36
increasing temporary file
space, 88, 89
refreshing (reloading), 16
sorting drive lists, 15
See also folders (local hard
disk directories)
headers
entering, 201
print variable codes, 67, 201
headers (news messages),
downloading, 152, 156
headings, converting into
marquees, 220
heading/subheading styles,
applying, 213

help, 26–27
on dialog boxes, 27
for Netscape users, 27, 47
online support, 242
on playing NetShow
content, 111
on toolbar buttons, 189
on VRML, 112
Help Contents, getting help
from, 26, 47
Help Index, getting help from,
26–27, 47
help topics
displaying, 26
printing, 26
Highlighter tool (Whiteboard),
175
History button (Standard
toolbar, Internet Explorer
window), 18
History list
changing the view, 38
clearing, 39
closing, 39
deleting entries from, 39
searching for entries, 39
specifying retention time, 39
viewing, 38
History list (NetMeeting
window), 164
Home button (Standard toolbar,
Internet Explorer
window), 18
home information, storing, 81
home pages
changing, 17
creating, 190
default page, 70
going to, 17
horizontal lines
customizing, 216
inserting, 216
hosting meetings, 168
HotBot (search engine), 30

HTML source code (for Web pages), 204
hyperlinks (on Web pages), 198
  changing colors, 87, 219
  clickable, 17
  creating, 198–99, 200
  editing, 198–99
  identifying, 198
  moving from link to link, 17
  offline availability, 41
  removing, 198
  sending mail messages with, 199
  testing, 199
  underlining, 87
  See also links (to Web pages)

icons, mail message flags, 123, 124
IEAK. *See* Internet Explorer Administration Kit
ILS (Internet User Locator Service), 160–61
  finding, 161
ILS database, 160
ILS directories, 161
ILS servers (directory servers), 160
  connection speeds, 181
  logging on/off, 181
Image dialog box, 194
Image Properties dialog box, 195, 217
images. *See* background images; graphic images
IMAP e-mail protocol, 117
Import/Export Wizard, 46
importing
  address books, 137
  bookmarks and favorites, 46

mail messages, 137
Include WebBot, 226
  inserting in Web pages, 226
  modifying, 226
Increase Indent button (Format toolbar, FrontPage Express window), 189
Increase Text Size button (Format toolbar, FrontPage Express window), 189
Insert Attachment dialog box, 126
Insert Rows Or Columns dialog box, 223
Insert Table dialog box, 222
Insert WebBot Component dialog box, 226, 227, 228
inserting
  background images, 218
  background sounds, 219
  comments, 216
  form fields, 232
  graphic images, 194
  horizontal lines, 216
  the Internet Explorer logo, 243
  Java applets, 236
  page breaks, 216
  plug-ins, 237
  PowerPoint animations, 235
  symbols, 193
  text files, 193
  video clips, 217
insertion point (FrontPage Express window), 187
installing
  add-ons/plug-ins/viewers, 96–97
  Internet Explorer, from the Web, 254
interlaced GIF files, 195
Internet

connecting to, 8–9
directory services, 136
finding information on, 32–33
getting up-to-date information from, 30
opening Web pages from, 206
playing games over, 113
playing sounds and videos from, 98, 106, 110–11
shopping on, 76–77, 82–83
See also Web; and specific Web topics
Internet accounts, setting up, 117
Internet Accounts dialog box, 134, 144, 157
Internet addresses, 13
  creating/editing hyperlinks to, 199
  entering, 12, 13
  finding, 136, 160–61
  selecting, 13
  See also URLs; Web site addresses
Internet calls programs, choosing, 91
Internet connection charges, reducing, 152–53
Internet Connection Wizard
  adding mail accounts, 134
  setting up mail accounts, 117
  specifying news servers, 144
  See also Connection Wizard
Internet directories, 30
  accessing, 32
Internet Explorer
  Active Setup program, 258
  adding components to, 257
  administering on networks, 256
  advanced options, 90
  availability on CD, 254

basics, 5–28
closing, 28
configuring, on corporate systems, 9
Content Advisor, 77
customizing, 69–91
development tools, 240
download time, 255
finding information with, 29–48
getting help on, 26–27
handling information with, 49–68
improving system performance, 88–89
installing additional components, 96–97
installing from the Web, 254–55
multimedia options, 93–113
online support, 242
program suite, 6, 239
repairing installations, 257
search features, 29
security features, 76–77
starting, 10
starting FrontPage Express from, 186
starting Outlook Express News from, 141
switching from Netscape to, 237
Tour (Microsoft Web page), 26, 27, 47
uninstalling, 257
updating, 258
viewing Web pages in, 208
Internet Explorer Administration Kit (IEAK), 239
  downloading and setting up, 256
Internet Explorer logo, using in Web pages, 243

Internet Explorer Logo Program
Web page, 243
Internet Explorer setup program
downloading from the Web,
254
making copies, 255
Internet Explorer Suite, 6
updating, 239, 258
See also Active Channels;
Active Desktop;
FrontPage Express;
Internet Explorer;
NetMeeting; NetShow;
Outlook Express
Internet Explorer window
customizing, 74–75
features, illustrated, 11
Internet Options dialog box
Advanced tab, 66, 88, 90,
103
Content tab, 80, 81
General tab, 38, 39, 62, 63,
84, 85, 89
Programs tab, 91
Security tab, 78, 79, 104, 105
Video tab, 170
Internet security, 76–77
Internet service providers (ISPs),
network, 153
Internet telephony, 161
Internet User Locator Service.
See ILS
IP addresses, 160, 166
ISPs (Internet service providers),
network, 153
Italic button (Format toolbar,
FrontPage Express
window), 189
italicizing text, 210
Items To Synchronize dialog
box, 41, 44, 45

Java (Web browser programming language), 100, 101
and ActiveX, 101
information Web site,
illustrated, 100
JIT compiler, 103
security options, 104, 105
See also Java applets (programs)
Java Applet Properties dialog
box, 236
Java applets (programs), 100,
103, 236
getting information on, 236
inserting in Web pages, 236
ratings Web site addresses,
236
running, 103
security options, 104, 105
Javascript, 100–101
JIT (Just-In-Time) Java compiler,
103
joining meetings, 168
JPEG files
opening, 56
quality option, 195
saving as bitmaps, 57
saving graphic images as, 56
vs. GIF files, 194
jumping to recently visited
locations, 16
junk mail, blocking from sender,
133
Just-In-Time compiler. *See* JIT
(Just-In-Time) Java
compiler

keyboard shortcuts. *See* shortcut
keys

Knowledge Base (Microsoft
products)
accessing, 242
saving information, 242

label controls (ActiveX), 234
Language Preference dialog box,
84, 85
languages. *See* languages of Web
pages; programming
languages
languages of Web pages
adding character sets, 84, 85
deleting, 85
display support, 84
prioritizing, 85
LANs (local area networks)
connecting to, 9
synchronizing offline pages
on, 45
laptops, synchronizing offline
pages on, 45
Launch Internet Explorer
Browser button (Quick
Launch toolbar), 10
Launch Outlook Express button
(Quick Launch toolbar),
starting Outlook Express
News, 140
Line tool (Whiteboard), 175
links. *See* hyperlinks (on Web
pages); links (to Web
pages); shortcuts
links (to Web pages)
adding to the Links bar, 73
clickable, 17
Links toolbar buttons, 11
moving from link to link, 17
See also hyperlinks (on Web
pages)

Links bar (Internet Explorer
window), 11, 72–73
adding/deleting buttons to/
from, 72, 73
adding to the taskbar, 71
creating desktop shortcuts
from, 73
displaying as a separate
bar, 72
rearranging items on, 73
resizing, 17
Links bar buttons, renaming, 73
List Properties dialog box, 214,
215
Local Area Network (LAN)
Settings dialog box, 9
local area networks. *See* LANs
locking the Whiteboard, 175
low-resolution graphic images,
195
Lycos (search engine), 30

macro virus checking, in Word
and Excel, 51
mail accounts, multiple, 134
Mail button (Standard toolbar,
Internet Explorer
window), 18
mail message icons (flags), 123,
124
mail messages
adding business cards to, 131
adding signatures to, 131
attaching files to, 123, 125,
126
attaching Web pages to, 123
blocking, 133
composing, 122–23
deleting, 127

mail messages, *continued*
  diverting incoming
     messages, 132
  encoding large messages, 157
  exporting, 137
  forwarding, 125
  importing from other
     programs, 137
  maintenance options, 127
  Message list, 119
  organizing, 128
  printing, 138
  reading, 124
  replying to, 124–25
  retrieving, 124, 125
  retrieving deleted messages,
     127
  saving, 129
  saving drafts, 129
  sending, 122–23, 199
  size limitations, 157
  sorting, 129
  stationery, 130
  storage options, 157
  and viruses, 51
  vs. telephone calls, 167
Mail option (Outlook Express
    start page), 118
mail servers, starting, 18
Maintenance tab (Options
    dialog box), 127
Manage Identities dialog box,
    135
Marquee Properties dialog box,
    221
marquees
  changing properties, 221
  converting headings into,
    220
  creating, 220
  deleting, 221
  editing text, 220
  movement, 221

media clips
  downloading, 61
  organizing favorites, 109
Media Player (Windows), 7, 106,
    107-8
  play streaming audio/video,
    106, 110–11
meetings (conference calls)
  chatting, 172–73, 182–84
  hosting/joining, 168
  illustrating points, 174–75
  note takers, 179
  receiving files during, 178,
    179
  sending files during, 178,
    179
  switching connections, 171
  whispering to individuals,
    172, 183
  See also collaboration
    (sharing applications)
memos, printing, 138
Menu bar (FrontPage Express
    window), 187
Menu bar (Internet Explorer
    window), 11
  hiding, 18
Menu bar (News window), 142
Menu bar (Outlook Express
    window), 119
menus, adding drop-down
    menu choices, 233
Message list (Outlook Express
    window), 119
Message List pane (Outlook
    Express window),
    customizing columns,
    154
Message Rules dialog box, 133,
    149
messages. *See* chat messages;
    mail messages; news
    messages

microphone volume, adjusting,
    171
Microsoft Chat Options dialog
    box, 184
Microsoft FrontPage Express. *See*
    FrontPage Express
    (Microsoft)
Microsoft Gallery, downloading
    media clips from, 61
Microsoft Home Page,
    customizing, 70
Microsoft Internet Explorer 5.
    See Internet Explorer
Microsoft Internet Explorer 5 At a
    Glance, 1–3
  approach, 1–2
  goals, 4
  overview, 2–4
Microsoft Internet Explorer
    Setup dialog box, 257
Microsoft Knowledge Base. *See*
    Knowledge Base
    (Microsoft)
Microsoft NetMeeting. *See*
    NetMeeting (Microsoft)
Microsoft NetMeeting dialog
    box, 162, 163, 168
Microsoft Netshow. *See* NetShow
    (Microsoft)
Microsoft on the Web, getting
    information from, 47
Microsoft Profile Assistant,
    storing personal
    information, 81
Microsoft VRML, 112
Microsoft Wallet. *See* Wallet
    (Microsoft)
Microsoft Web pages, listed, 47
Microsoft Web site, 239, 240
  add-on pages, 95
  downloading files from, 48,
    53, 61, 63
  downloading language
    character sets, 84

  downloading media clips
    from, 61
  downloading style sheets
    from, 63
  getting help on Internet
    Explorer, 26
  product support, 242
  viewer pages, 95
  See also Site Builder Network
    Workshop Web site
Microsoft Word. *See* Word
    (Microsoft)
mouse pointer
  fist with pointed finger, 17
  FrontPage Express window,
    187
moving
  files, on the Start menu, 23
  graphic images, 196–97
  text, 19, 196–97
moving back/forward in
    documents/Web
    pages, 16
MSN Home Page,
    customizing, 70
multimedia options, 93–113
  turning off, 88, 109
  See also ActiveX controls;
    add-ons (add-on
    programs); Java (Web
    browser programming
    language); sounds;
    video; viewers
My Computer icon, browsing
    hard disks (local), 14–15
My Information tab (Options
    dialog box), 180

named meetings, joining, 168
names, storing personal
    names, 81

navigating
  in dialog boxes, 20
  documents, 16, 19
  Web pages, 16, 17, 18
NetMeeting (Microsoft), 6,
    159–84
  Internet connection speed
    and, 163
  placing calls, 160
  starting, 160, 162–163
  uses, 161
NetMeeting Chat. *See* Chat
    (NetMeeting)
NetMeeting Directory. *See*
    Directory list (NetMeeting
    window)
NetMeeting Setup dialog box,
    161
NetMeeting Whiteboard. *See*
    Whiteboard (NetMeeting)
NetMeeting window, organiza-
    tion, 164
Netscape, switching to Internet
    Explorer from, 237
Netscape users, getting help on
    Internet Explorer, 27, 47
NetShow (Microsoft), 6, 110–11
NetShow content, playing,
    110–11, 111
networks, administering
    Internet Explorer on, 256
New Call dialog box, 166, 168
New Identity dialog box, 135
New Page dialog box, 190, 191,
    231
news message command keys,
    146
news messages, 143
  canceling, 150
  command keys, 146
  composing, 153
  deleting, 147
  determining the format, 157

downloading headers only,
    152, 156
downloading without
    pictures, 157
encoding large messages, 157
expiration of, 146
filtering, 149
finding, 148
marking offline for
    downloading, 153
naming, 150
posting, 150–51
reading, 146, 152, 153
replying to, 151, 153
saving, 147
size limitations, 157
stationery, 151
storage options, 157
threads, 143, 146
viewing, 142
viewing unread messages,
    147
news reader programs, 143
news readers, specifying, 91, 144
news servers, specifying, 144
News window
  customizing, 154–55
  features, illustrated, 142
Newsgroup Subscriptions dialog
    box, 148
newsgroups, 139, 143
  finding, 148, 149
  listing, 145
  name categories, 147
  Outlook Express start page
    links, 118
  searching archives, 149
  subscribing to, 145
  unsubscribing from, 145
  viewing, 145
  See also news messages
Newsgroups dialog box, 145
nicknames (for chats), entering,
    182

note takers (at meetings), tasks,
    179
notepad. *See* Whiteboard
    (NetMeeting)
Numbered List button (Format
    toolbar, FrontPage
    Express window), 189
numbered lists, creating and
    customizing, 214

Office 2000 (Microsoft)
    extensions. *See* Office
    Server Extensions (OSE)
Office documents, style sheets
    from, 63
Office programs, changing
    language settings, 85
Office Server Extensions (OSE),
    248
Office Web pages, editing and
    updating, 64, 65
Offline Favorite Wizard, 40, 42
offline pages
  managing, 44
  synchronizing, 45
offline working, 40–41, 152–53
OK button (in dialog boxes), 20
One-Line Text Box button
    (Forms toolbar, FrontPage
    Express window), 189
online support, getting, 242
Open Address Book link
    (Outlook Express start
    page), 118
Open command (File menu),
    browsing Web pages, 12
Open dialog box, 111
Open File As dialog box, 206,
    207
Open File dialog box, 206, 207

opening
  files, 14, 36, 178
  mail messages, 124
  news messages, 146
  saved graphic images, 56, 59
  Web pages, 13, 38, 206–7
  Word documents for editing
    as Web pages, 207
option buttons (radio buttons)
  in dialog boxes, 20
  inserting in Web page forms,
    232
options, determining
    functionality, 90
Options dialog box
  Calling tab, 169, 180, 181
  General tab, 179
  My Information tab, 180
  Read tab, 156
Organize Favorites dialog
    box, 35
organizing
  favorites, 34, 35, 109
  files, 179
  mail messages, 128
  See also sorting
OSE (Office Server Extensions),
    248
Outlook Express (Microsoft), 6
  message handling options,
    156–157
  starting, 18, 116, 140, 141
  See also Outlook Express
    Mail; Outlook Express
    News
Outlook Express folders
  compacting, 129
  creating, 128
  Deleted Items folder, 127
  diverting mail messages to,
    132
Outlook Express Mail, 115–38
  adding mail accounts, 134

Outlook Express Mail,
   continued
   choosing, 91
   starting, 18, 116
   stationery, 130
   See also mail messages;
     Outlook Express folders
Outlook Express News, 139–58
   starting, 140–41
   stationery, 151
   See also news messages
Outlook Express News window.
   See News window
Outlook Express start page, 118
   adding contacts from, 121
   icon, 119
Outlook Express toolbar (News
   window), 142
   customizing, 154, 155
   restoring the original
     buttons, 154
Outlook Express toolbar
   (Outlook Express
   window), 119
Outlook Express window
   customizing, 154–55
   features, illustrated, 119

page breaks, inserting in Web
   pages, 216
"The page cannot be displayed"
   error message, 50
"The page cannot be found"
   error message, 50
page orientation (of Web pages),
   changing, 201
Page Properties dialog box, 218,
   219
page setup (of Web pages),
   specifying for printing,
   66, 67, 201, 203

Page Setup dialog box, 66
paragraph lists
   bulleted lists, 215
   changing, 215
   numbered lists, 214
   removing numbering from,
     214
   special, 215
Paragraph Properties dialog box,
   213
paragraph styles, changing, 213
paragraphs
   aligning, 212
   changing styles, 213
   creating, 212
   formatting, 212–15
   numbered/bulleted lists,
     214–15
   selecting, 212
passwords
   for connecting to the
     Internet, 10
   for credit cards, 83
   for mail accounts, 134
   for viewing screened-out
     content, 77, 80
Paste button (Standard toolbar,
   Internet Explorer
   window), 19
payment methods
   adding to Wallet, 82–83
Payment Options dialog box, 83
PDF documents, viewing, 99
PDF viewers, 97
   See also Acrobat PDF viewer
Pen tool (Whiteboard), 175
people, finding Internet
   addresses, 136, 161
performance, improving system
   performance, 88–89
personal certificates (for doing
   business on the
   Internet), 76

getting, 158
Personal Home Page Wizard,
   190
personal information
   adding addresses to
     Wallet, 82
   NetMeeting Directory
     listings, 162–63, 180
   storing, 81
Personal Web Server (Microsoft),
   6, 246–47
   accessing settings, 247
   downloading, 246
   starting/stopping, 247
Personal Web Server Properties
   dialog box, 247
Personal Web Server tour, 247
personalizing. *See* customizing
phone calls. *See* calls
phone lists, printing, 138
photographs. *See* graphic images
pictures. *See* graphic images
playing
   animations (VRML), 112
   sounds, 98, 106–107,
     110–11, 218
   video clips, 217
   videos, 98, 106–107, 110–11
Plug-In Properties dialog box,
   237
plug-ins (plug-in programs), 94,
   237
   finding, 95
   inserting in Web pages, 237
   installing, 97
   resizing, 237
   See also add-ons (add-on
     programs)
pointer. *See* mouse pointer
POP e-mail protocol, 117
posting news messages, 150–51
   thinking before, 151
PowerPoint Animation dialog
   box, 235

PowerPoint animations, 234
   inserting in Web pages, 235
   viewing, 235
previewing
   video, 171
   Web pages, 202
preview pages, of channels, 42
Preview pane (News window),
   142
   customizing, 155
Preview pane (Outlook Express
   window), 119
Print All Linked Documents
   option (Print dialog
   box), 67
Print button (Standard toolbar,
   Internet Explorer
   window), 18
Print dialog box, 67, 138, 203
printing
   business cards, 138
   contact information, 138
   help topics, 26
   mail messages, 138
   memos, 138
   phone lists, 138
   See also printing Web pages
printing Web pages, 202–3
   active frames, 18, 66, 67
   current page, 18, 67
   footer print variable codes,
     67, 201
   header print variable codes,
     67, 201
   previewing, 202
   setup options, 66, 67, 201,
     203
printer properties, changing,
   202
print options (for Web pages),
   setting, 66, 67, 201, 203
Print Page Setup dialog box, 201

Print Preview button (Standard toolbar, FrontPage Express window), 188, 203
print previews (of Web pages), 202
private FTP sites
    downloading files, 54, 55
    login syntax, 55
Product Updates program, updating the Internet Explorer Suite, 239, 258
Profile Assistant (Microsoft), storing personal information, 81
programming languages
    VRML (Virtual Reality Modeling Language), 112
    See also Java (Web browser programming language)
programs
    adding to the Start menu, 23
    applets (Java programs), 100
    applications utilizing ActiveX, 101
    Chat program, 165
    external, choosing, 91
    form handlers, 233
    graphics programs, 56
    Internet Explorer Suite, 6
    running. *See* running programs
    sharing. *See* collaboration (sharing applications)
    Whiteboard program, 165
    See also ActiveX controls; add-ons (add-on programs); software; viewers
Programs tab (Internet Options dialog box), 91

Properties button (Standard toolbar, Internet Explorer window), 19
proxy servers, 8
    configuring computers for, 9
public FTP sites
    downloading files, 54, 55
    file access directory, 55
publisher certificates (for doing business on the Internet), 77
publishing Web pages, 244–45
Push Button button (Forms toolbar, FrontPage Express window), 189
push buttons, inserting in Web page forms, 232
PWS. *See* Personal Web Server (Microsoft)

Quick Launch toolbar (taskbar)
    adding to the screen, 116
    starting Internet Explorer, 10
    starting Outlook Express, 116
Quick Launch toolbar buttons, 10, 116

R

Radio Button button (Forms toolbar, FrontPage Express window), 189
radio buttons. *See* option buttons
rating Web sites, 80
    RSAC system, 77
Read News link (Outlook Express start page), 118
Read tab (Options dialog box), 156

reading mail messages, 124
    starting Outlook Express while, 141
reading news messages, 146, 152, 153
reading offline, 40–41, 152
RealAudio Web site addresses, 99
RealPlayer add-on
    illustrated, 98
    installing, 96
    play streaming audio/video, 98
receiving files during meetings, 178, 179
recorded sayings (in chats), sending, 183
Recreational Software Advisory Council (RSAC) rating system, 77
Redo button (Standard toolbar, FrontPage Express window), 188
redoing edits, 193
Refresh button (Standard toolbar, Internet Explorer window), 18
Refresh button (Standard toolbar, FrontPage Express window), 188
refreshing (reloading)
    documents/disks, 17
    Web pages, 16, 17, 18
Repair (Microsoft Web page), 47
Replace dialog box, 193
replacing text, 192, 193
replying
    to mail messages, 124–25
    to news messages, 151, 153
"The request to the host has taken longer than expected" error message, 50

resizing
    fonts, 86, 211
    graphic images, 197
    the Links bar, 17
    plug-ins, 237
Restricted sites dialog box, 79
Restricted Sites zone, adding/removing Web sites to/from, 79
retrieving mail messages, 124, 125
    deleted messages, 127
right-clicking
    adding toolbars to the status bar, 75
    changing table width, 224
    creating wallpaper, 59
    deleting History list entries, 39
    finding the closest matches, 229
    forwarding mail messages, 125
    listing toolbars, 74
    measuring graphic images, 57
    sending files to individuals during meetings, 178, 179
    showing/hiding toolbars, 116
    testing hyperlinks, 199
    viewing favorites, 35, 36, 37
rows (in Web page tables)
    deleting, 223
    inserting, 223
    selecting, 225
RSAC (Recreational Software Advisory Council) rating system, 77
Rule Editor dialog box, 132
rules for incoming messages
    prioritizing, 133
    setting, 132

Run dialog box, 255
running programs, 14
    Java applets, 103
    setup programs (for add-ons/
        viewers), 96

S

Save As dialog box, 52, 204, 205,
    245
Save As File dialog box, 204, 205
Save button (Standard toolbar,
    FrontPage Express
    window), 188
Save Message As dialog box, 147
Save Picture dialog box, 57, 59
Save Web Page dialog box, 62
saving
    background images, 58, 59
    graphic images, 56, 57
    mail messages, 129
    news messages, 147
    text, 68
    Web pages, 65, 68, 204–05
sayings (in chats), recording/
    sending, 183
SBN Workshop Web site
    (Microsoft), 240
Schedule tab, Web site proper-
    ties dialog boxs, 44
schedules, synchronizing offline
    pages, 45
scheduling programs,
    choosing, 91
screen
    cutting/copying from, 19
    showing the full screen, 18
    See also Internet Explorer
        window
screen savers. See channel screen
    savers
Screen Save tab (Display
    Properties dialog box), 25

screening out content, 77, 80
Scrolling Text Box button
    (Forms toolbar, FrontPage
    Express window), 189
Scrolling Text Box Properties
    dialog box, 232
Search button (Standard toolbar,
    Internet Explorer
    window), 18
    finding information on the
        Internet, 32–33
search directories. See Internet
    directories
search engines, 30
    accessing, 32
search features, 29
search options, customizing, 33
Search WebBot
    finding the closest matches,
        229
    inserting in Web pages, 228
    modifying, 229
searching. See finding
security levels, setting, 78, 79
security on the Internet, 76–77
    creating security zones,
        78–79
    rating Web sites, 80
Security Settings dialog box,
    104, 105
Security tab (Internet Options
    dialog box), 78, 79, 104,
    105
security zones, 76, 78–79
    adding/removing sites to/
        from the Restricted
        Sites zone, 79
    controlling ActiveX controls/
        Java applets, 104–05
    selecting, 78
    setting levels, 78, 79
Select Background Image dialog
    box, 218
selecting

columns/rows, 225
    graphic images, 196
    paragraphs, 212
    text, 193
selection handles, 197
    resizing graphic images, 197
Selector tool (Whiteboard), 175
Send Feedback (Microsoft Web
    page), 47
Send tab (Options dialog box),
    157
sending
    chat messages, 170
    files (during meetings), 178,
        179
    mail messages, 122–23, 199
    recorded sayings, 183
    Web pages, 123
“Server busy” error message, 50
“The server does not have a DNS
    entry” error message, 50
“Service Overloaded” error
    message, 50
“Service Unavailable” error
    message, 50
Settings for Saving Results of
    Form dialog box, 233
setup programs (for add-ons/
    viewers), running, 96
ScreenTips, for Web sites, 33
sharing programs. See
    collaboration (sharing
    applications)
shopping on the Internet, 76–
    77, 82–83
    certificates, 76–77
shortcut keys
    for links to Web pages, 73
    for navigating Web pages, 17
shortcuts
    creating, 73
    See also hyperlinks (on Web
        pages); links (to Web
        pages); shortcut keys

Show Desktop button (Quick
    Launch toolbar), 22
Show/Hide button (Standard
    toolbar, FrontPage
    Express window), 188
signatures (for mail messages),
    130
    adding, 131
    creating, 131
Signatures tab (Options dialog
    box), 131
single-clicking, enabling, 23
Site Builder Network Workshop
    Web site, 240
slash (/), vs. backslash, 15
slider (in dialog boxes), 20
software
    collection site addresses, 95
    downloading free software,
        48, 53
    virus checking software, 51
    See also programs
sorting
    the Address Book, 121
    drive/directory lists, 15
    mail messages, 129
sounds
    adding to chat comic strip
        characters, 183
    background sounds, 218
    changing properties, 108
    playing, 98, 106–07, 110–11,
        218
    Web site addresses, 107
    See also audio
speaker volume, adjusting, 171
speaking in comic strip chats,
    183
SpeedDial list (NetMeeting
    window), 164
    adding people to, 169
spin boxes, in dialog boxes, 20

Standard toolbar (Internet Explorer window), 11, 18–19
  document buttons, 19
  Web buttons, 18
Standard toolbar (FrontPage Express window), 187, 188
  buttons, 188
Start button (taskbar), adding files/programs to the Start menu, 23
starting
  Chat (NetMeeting), 172
  FrontPage Express, 18, 186
  Internet Explorer, 10
  mail servers, 18
  NetMeeting, 160, 162–63
  Outlook Express, 18, 116, 140, 141
  Outlook Express News, 140–41
  Personal Web Server, 247
  Web discussions, 251
  Web editors, 18
  Whiteboard (NetMeeting), 174
Start menu
  accessing Web sites, 23
  adding files/programs to, 23
  moving files on, 23
  starting FrontPage Express, 186
  starting Internet Explorer, 10
  starting Outlook Express, 116
start page, jumping to, 18
startup, starting Outlook Express at, 141
startup connection, setting a default, 141
stationery
  for news messages, 151
  for Outlook Express Mail messages, 130

Stationery Setup Wizard, 130
status bar (FrontPage Express window), 187
status bar (Internet Explorer window), 11
  adding toolbars to, 75
  hiding/showing, 75
status bar (News window), 142
stock ticker controls (ActiveX), 234
Stop button (Standard toolbar, Internet Explorer window), 18
Stop button (Standard toolbar, FrontPage Express window), 188
storing
  chat messages, 173
  messages, 156
streaming audio/video, 98, 110–11
style sheets (for Web pages), 62–63
  creating, 62
  displaying Web pages with, 62, 63
  downloading Microsoft style sheets, 63
  and graphic images, 62
subscribing to newsgroups, 145
Sun Microsystems Java. See Java (Web browser programming language)
supervisor passwords, for viewing screened-out content, 77, 80
surfing. See browsing
survey forms
  creating, 231
  reviewing survey results, 231
Switch Identities dialog box, 135
symbols, inserting in Web pages, 193

Synchronization Settings dialog box, 45
synchronizing Web pages, 40, 41, 44, 45
system performance, improving, 88–89

Tab key, moving from link to link, 17
Table Properties dialog box, 224
tables, 222–23
  deleting columns/rows in, 223
  inserting, 222
  inserting captions in, 223
  inserting columns/rows in, 223
  layout options, 222
  modifying, 224
  moving from cell to cell in, 222
  See also cells (in Web page tables)
tabs (in dialog boxes), 20
taskbar (Active Desktop)
  adding/removing toolbars to/from, 116
  adding the Address and Links Bars to, 71
  doubling the height, 71
telephone calls. See calls
telephony (on the Internet), 161
templates, creating forms from, 230
temporary Internet files, 88
  increasing hard disk space for, 89
  viewing, 89
testing
  FrontPage Server Extensions, 247

hyperlinks, 199
text
  boldfacing, 210
  changing fonts, 86, 211
  copying, 31, 57, 60, 196
  cutting, 19, 196–97
  deleting, 192
  editing, 192, 193
  entering, 192
  finding, 31, 228–29
  formatting, 210–211
  indenting, 212
  italicizing, 210
  moving, 19, 196–97
  printing, 18
  redoing edits, 193
  replacing, 192, 193
  resizing fonts, 18, 86, 211
  saving, 68
  selecting, 193
  specifying colors, 86, 87, 210, 211, 219
  underlining, 210
  undoing edits, 193
text boxes
  in dialog boxes, 20
  inserting in Web page forms, 232
Text Color button (Format toolbar, FrontPage Express window), 189
text edits, undoing/redoing, 193
text files
  converting to Web pages, 207
  inserting in Web pages, 193
text styles, paragraph styles, 213
Text tool (Whiteboard), 175
"The page cannot be displayed" error message, 50
"The page cannot be found" error message, 50

"The request to the host has taken longer than expected" error message, 50
threads (of news messages), 143, 147
time controls (ActiveX), 234
Timestamp WebBot
inserting in Web pages, 227
modifying, 227
Tip of the Day, 27, 47
window (Outlook Express start page), 118
title bar (FrontPage Express window), 204
title bar (Internet Explorer window), 11
hiding, 18
toolbar buttons
chat tools, 183
displaying text labels on, 75
Format toolbar (FrontPage Express window), 189
Forms toolbar (FrontPage Express window), 189
getting help on, 189
removing, 75
repositioning, 75
shrinking, 75
Standard toolbar (Internet Explorer window), 11, 18, 19
Standard toolbar (FrontPage Express window), 188
toolbars
adding to the status bar, 75
customizing, 75
Format toolbar (FrontPage Express window), 187, 188
Forms toolbar (FrontPage Express window), 187, 188

listing, 74
making room for, 17
Outlook Express toolbar (News window), 142
Outlook Express toolbar (Outlook Express window), 119
Quick Launch toolbar (taskbar), 10, 116
showing/hiding, 19, 74, 116
Standard toolbar (FrontPage Express window), 187, 188
See also Links bar (Internet Explorer window); Standard toolbar (Internet Explorer window); toolbar buttons
tools
Whiteboard drawing tools, 175
See also toolbar buttons; toolbars
training, Internet Explorer Tour, 26, 27
tutorial, Internet Explorer Tour, 26, 27

"Unauthorized User" error message, 50
Underline button (Format toolbar, FrontPage Express window), 189
underlining
links, 87
text, 210
Undo button (Standard toolbar, FrontPage Express window), 188

Undo button (Standard toolbar, Internet Explorer window), 19
undoing actions, 19, 193
Unfilled Ellipse tool (Whiteboard), 175
Unfilled Rectangle tool (Whiteboard), 175
uniform resource locators. See URLs
unsubscribing from newsgroups, 145
Up button (Standard toolbar, Internet Explorer window), 19
updating
contact information, 120
Internet Explorer, 258
the Internet Explorer Suite, 239, 258
Office Web pages, 64, 65
Web pages, 44, 89
URLs (uniform resource locators), 13
user information. See personal information

vendor site addresses, 95
video
broadcasting, 110, 111
changing properties, 108
displaying statistics, 109
playing, 98, 106–107, 110–11
previewing, 171
streaming, 98, 110–11
turning off, 171
Web site addresses, 107
video clips
displaying Show Controls, 217

inserting in Web pages, 217
modifying the play, 217
playing over and over, 217
Video dialog box, 217
Video tab (Internet Options dialog box), 170
viewers, 94, 98–99
finding, 95
installing, 96–97
viewing
favorites, 35, 36, 37, 40–41
the Favorites list, 36
files, 37
the History list, 38
newsgroup messages, 142
newsgroups, 145
PDF documents, 99
PowerPoint animations, 235
screened-out content, 77, 80
temporary Internet files, 89
unread messages, 146
Web pages in Internet Explorer, 208
See also previewing
views, switching, 19
Views button (Standard toolbar, Internet Explorer window), 19
Virtual Reality Modeling Language (VRML), 112
virus checking software, updating, 51
viruses, avoiding, 51
volume, adjusting speaker/microphone volume, 171
VRML (Virtual Reality Modeling Language), 112
VRML animations, playing, 112
VRML viewer, downloading, 112
VRML Web site addresses, 112

Wallet (Microsoft), 81
    adding addresses to, 82
    adding payment methods to,
        82–83
    removing cards from, 83
    shopping with, 82–83
wallpaper (desktop patterns),
    creating, 59
watermark images, 219
Web
    browsing, 12–13, 207
    connecting to, 8–9
    directory services, 136
    finding information on, 18,
        29–48
    playing sounds and videos
        from, 98, 106, 110–11
    reading information offline,
        40–41, 152–53
    shopping on, 76–77, 82–83
    tutorial, 26, 27
    See also Web pages; Web sites
Web backgrounds. *See* back-
    ground images
Web browsers
    extensible, 94
    programming language
        (Java), 100, 101
Web buttons, Standard toolbar
    (Internet Explorer
    window), 18
Web discussions, 249
    deleting discussion remarks,
        252
    editing individual discussion
        remarks, 253
    entering discussion text, 251
    expanding/collapsing
        discussion remarks,
        251
    filtering discussion remarks,
        253

joining, 252–53
opening, 250
printing discussion remarks,
    251
refreshing discussion
    remarks, 253
starting and closing, 251
Web Document tab, Web site
    properties dialog boxs, 44
Web editors, starting, 18
Web file management, OSE and,
    248
Web items, adding to the Active
    Desktop, 24
Web Notification feature, 249
Web page elements, inserting,
    216
Web pages
    adding language character
        sets for, 84, 85
    attaching to mail messages,
        123
    blank, 191
    browser pane, 11
    browsing, 12–13
    changing colors/fonts, 86,
        87, 210, 211
    converting text files to, 207
    copying background images
        from, 58, 59
    copying graphic images
        from, 60
    copying text from, 31, 57,
        60, 196
    creating, 185–208
    creating/editing hyperlinks
        to, 198, 199
    creating with templates and
        wizards, 190–91
    as desktop backgrounds, 25
    displaying with style sheets,
        62, 63
    downloading files from, 50,
        51, 52–53

enhancing, 209–37
finding, 18, 29, 32–33
finding information on, 31
footer print variable codes,
    67, 201
getting up-to-date informa-
    tion from, 30
header print variable codes,
    67, 201
home pages, 190
inserting elements in. *See*
    inserting
jumping to your start
    page, 18
listing previously viewed, 18
loading, 16
managing offline pages, 44
moving to previous/next, 18
name/address displays, 11
navigating, 16, 17, 18
opening, 13, 38, 206–7
opening recently opened,
    207
opening Word documents
    for editing as, 207
previewing for printing, 202
printing, 18, 202–3
publishing, 244–45
refreshing (reloading), 16,
    17, 18
renaming, 205
save file formats, 205
saving, 65, 68, 204–5
saving text on, 68
setting up for printing, 66,
    67, 201, 203
size, 203
status display, 11
stopping loading, 16, 18
synchronizing, 40, 41, 44, 45
updating, 44, 89
using the Internet Explorer
    logo in, 243

viewing in Internet Explorer,
    208
visitor confirmation forms,
    231
See also favorites; hyperlinks
    (on Web pages);
    languages of Web
    pages; Microsoft Web
    site; Office Web pages
Web Publishing Wizard, 239,
    244–245
Web screen savers. *See* channel
    screen savers
Web servers, 245
    publishing Web pages to,
        244–45
    setting up, 246–47
Web site addresses
    Acrobat PDF sites, 99
    Java applet ratings, 236
    RealAudio sites, 99
    software collection sites, 95
    sound sites, 107
    vendor sites, 95
    video sites, 107
Web site properties dialog
    boxs, 44
Web sites
    accessing, 12, 18, 23, 72, 73
    ActiveX information site,
        illustrated, 101
    adding favorites to the
        Favorites list, 34
    adding to/removing from
        the Restricted Sites
        zone, 79
    browsing, 12–13
    downloading files from. *See*
        downloading Web site
        files
    download sites, 52
    file repository sites, 51
    finding, 18, 29, 32–33, 38

Web sites, *continued*
    gaming, 113
    inserting graphic images in
        Web pages from, 194
    interactive controls
        (ActiveX), 101, 102
    Java information site,
        illustrated, 100
    links to, 11, 73, 142
    rating, 80
    SBN Workshop site, 240
    security indicator, 79
    technical support sites,
        240–41
    ToolTips for, 33
    See also favorites; Microsoft
        Web site; Web pages;
        Web site addresses
Web Subscription feature, 249

Web tab (Display Properties
    dialog box), 22
WebBot Include Component
    Properties dialog box, 226
WebBots, 226–29
    deleting, 227
    form handlers, 233
    Form Page Wizard and, 230
    Include WebBot, 226
    interactive, 228–29
    Search WebBot, 228–229
    Timestamp WebBot, 227
WebBot Search Component
    Properties dialog box,
    228, 229
WebBot Timestamp Component
    Properties dialog box, 227
whispering (to individuals),
    during meetings, 172, 183
Whiteboard (NetMeeting), 165,
    174–75

    drawing tools, 175
    erasing elements on, 175
    exiting, 174
    locking, 175
    multiple pages, 174
    pointing to objects on, 175
    starting, 174
Window Layout Properties
    dialog box, 155
Windows Active Desktop. *See*
    Active Desktop
Windows Explorer, 248
    downloading files from FTP
        sites, 55
Windows Media Player. *See*
    Media Player (Windows)
wizards
    Audio Tuning Wizard, 163,
        170
    Personal Home Page Wizard,
        190

    See also Connection Wizard;
        Internet Connection
        Wizard
Word (Microsoft), macro virus
    checking, 51
Word documents, opening for
    editing as Web pages, 207
Word List To Search Field, 228
words, finding on Web
    pages, 31
working offline, 40–41, 152–53
World Wide Web. See Web; and
    specific Web topics
writing. *See* composing

Yahoo (Internet directory), 30

Douglas Allen is the Executive Director of Information Services at Johnson County Community College in Overland Park, Kansas. He has over 20 years experience in the Information Services industry in positions as diverse as computer programmer, hardware repair technician, and networking consultant. Doug has authored several courses and books on a variety of personal computer technologies, including Windows 95, Microsoft Word, Internet Explorer, and HTML/Web Publishing. Doug has a degree in music education from the University of Nebraska, Lincoln.

Author's Acknowledgments

I would like to thank my lovely, hardworking wife, Debbie and my two children, Nathan and Christopher for their support during this creative effort. I hope you all liked the trip to New York. I also need to thank Jane Pedicini, the editor who took my words and pictures and turned them into actual instructions that regular folks can understand. Thanks finally to David Beskeen and Steve Johnson at Perspection—the cooks who took my ingredients and made the masterpiece for you to consume.

The manuscript for this book was prepared and submitted to Microsoft Press in electronic form. Text files were prepared using Microsoft Word 97 for Windows 95. Pages were composed in PageMaker for Windows, with text in Stone Sans and display type in Stone Serif. Composed pages were delivered to the printer as electronic files.

Cover Design
Tim Girvin Design

Graphic Layout
David Beskeen

Compositors
Gary Bellig
Tracy Teyler

Proofreader
Jane Pedicini

Indexer
Michael Brackney
Savage Indexing Service

Stay in the
running
for maximum
productivity.

These are *the* answer books for business users of Microsoft® Office 2000. They are packed with everything from quick, clear instructions for new users to comprehensive answers for power users—the authoritative reference to keep by your computer and use every day. THE RUNNING SERIES—learning solutions made by Microsoft.

- RUNNING MICROSOFT EXCEL 2000
- RUNNING MICROSOFT OFFICE 2000 PREMIUM
- RUNNING MICROSOFT OFFICE 2000 PROFESSIONAL
- RUNNING MICROSOFT OFFICE 2000 SMALL BUSINESS EDITION
- RUNNING MICROSOFT WORD 2000
- RUNNING MICROSOFT POWERPOINT® 2000
- RUNNING MICROSOFT ACCESS 2000
- RUNNING MICROSOFT INTERNET EXPLORER 5.0
- RUNNING MICROSOFT FRONTPAGE®
- RUNNING MICROSOFT OUTLOOK® 2000

Microsoft®

mspress.microsoft.com

Register Today!

Return this
*Microsoft® Internet Explorer 5
At a Glance*
registration card today

Microsoft®Press

mspress.microsoft.com

OWNER REGISTRATION CARD

1-57231-964-X

Microsoft® Internet Explorer 5
At a Glance

_____   _____   _____
FIRST NAME   MIDDLE INITIAL   LAST NAME

_____
INSTITUTION OR COMPANY NAME

_____
ADDRESS

_____

_____   _____   _____
CITY   STATE   ZIP

                                                        (   )
_____   _____
E-MAIL ADDRESS   PHONE NUMBER

U.S. and Canada addresses only. Fill in information above and mail postage-free.
Please mail only the bottom half of this page.

For information about Microsoft Press®
products, visit our Web site at
mspress.microsoft.com

Microsoft®*Press*

BUSINESS REPLY MAIL
FIRST-CLASS MAIL   PERMIT NO. 108   REDMOND WA

POSTAGE WILL BE PAID BY ADDRESSEE

MICROSOFT PRESS
PO BOX 97017
REDMOND, WA 98073-9830

NO POSTAGE
NECESSARY
IF MAILED
IN THE
UNITED STATES